SPIRITUALITY
of the
BEATITUDES

SPIRITUALITY
of the
BEATITUDES

MATTHEW'S CHALLENGE FOR
FIRST WORLD CHRISTIANS

MICHAEL CROSBY, O.F.M. Cap.

ORBIS BOOKS
Maryknoll, New York 10545

Ninth Printing, November 1989

The Catholic Foreign Mission Society of America (Maryknoll) recruits and trains people for overseas missionary service. Through Orbis Books Maryknoll aims to foster the international dialogue that is essential to mission. The books published, however, reflect the opinions of their authors and are not meant to represent the official position of the society.

Nihil Obstat:

Rev. Francis Dombrowski, O.F.M. Cap., S.T.L.
Provincial Censor of Books
October 8, 1980

Very Rev. Ronald Smith, O.F.M. Cap.
Provincial Minister
Midwest Capuchin Province of St. Joseph
October 8, 1980

Most Rev. Richard J. Sklba, S.S.L., S.T.D.
Auxiliary Bishop of Milwaukee, Censor Librorum
October 16, 1980

Published with ecclesiastical approval:
Most Rev. Rembert G. Weakland, O.S.B.
Archbishop of Milwaukee
October 16, 1980

Ecclesiastical approval is a declaration that a book or pamphlet is considered to be free from doctrinal or moral error. It is not implied that those who have granted the ecclesiastical approval agree with the contents, opinions, or statements expressed.

Library of Congress Cataloging in Publication Data

Crosby, Michael, 1940-
   Spirituality of the Beatitudes.

   Includes bibliographical references and index.
   1. Beatitudes. I. Title.
BT382.C73   226'.9306   80-24755
ISBN 0-88344-465-8 (pbk.)

Contents

v

CHAPTER TEN
BLESSED ARE THOSE PERSECUTED FOR JUSTICE' SAKE; THE REIGN OF
    GOD IS THEIRS   199

PREFACE

This book builds on the biblical spirituality for First World Christians first outlined in my *Thy Will Be Done: Praying the Our Father as Subversive Activity*. Themes treated sketchily here, especially the Hebrew Scriptures, the North American political economy, and the nature of conversion, are treated more adequately in the earlier book. At the same time, this book can serve to flesh-out the rough outline presented in *Thy Will Be Done*. They should be treated as companion books.

I have tried to avoid using sexist words in the text; yet some may have slipped through. Despite this effort, this book may unconsciously reinforce sexist concepts or thought patterns. Where this may be the case, I beg the reader's pardon. Where quotations from other sources, including The New American Bible, contain sexist words, I have not altered the texts.

This book was written at various times and places between June 1979 and July 1980. I owe a debt of gratitude to all those who gave clearance to be included in these pages. I also am deeply indebted to all who offered assistance—from our Capuchins at Mount Calvary, Wisconsin, who housed me as I worked on the original manuscript, to the constant support offered by my Capuchin confreres in this Midwest Province and at St. John's, New York. The comments made by Rev. Peter Mann and Gerry Twomey of the Diocesan Television Center at Uniondale, L.I., New York, were very constructive. The indexing by Kevin McLane and Sr. Aimee Marie Spahn, O.S.F., was most helpful. I am also most indebted to Rev. Donald Senior, C.P., for his helpful suggestions and critique.

In a special way I am thankful to my co-workers at the Justice and Peace Center in Milwaukee. It has been our prayerful effort at the Center to help in the process of integrating religious experience and social concern. Our daily sharings have helped clarify my thoughts. While all staff members were involved in one way or another in the "Beatitudes Project," I'm particularly thankful to Virginia Schauble and Sisters Regina Williams and Carol Thresher for the painstaking critique they offered throughout.

I have learned much from and enjoyed being with so many dedicated people at the Justice and Peace Center in Milwaukee, as well as those involved in the corporate responsibility movement—those connected to the National Catholic Coalition for Responsible Investment and the Interfaith Center on Corporate Responsibility in New York. In appreciation, I dedicate this book to all of them, past and present, who have shared their lives and dreams of justice with me.

ix

CHAPTER ONE

The Relevance of Matthew's Gospel

The Context of Matthew's Gospel

When I began to research Matthew's beatitudes and their relevance for today, I had a mixture of motives. In turning to Matthew's eight beatitudes rather than Luke's four, I had no stronger motivation than to get eight chapters for this book. My pragmatism, however, evolved into an exciting journey of faith.

The more I investigated Matthew the more I discovered that the author of the First Gospel speaks to us First World Christians. His good news was written to address concerns similar to ours.

Who was this Matthew? What was his message? How does it present a biblical spirituality for us, especially for those who have questions about God's existence and the (mis)use of authority in church structures and society? Does Matthew's Gospel have anything to say about our responsibility toward those poor, (often) non-white, and marginated neighbors (domestic and foreign) whom we are to love *as* ourselves (22:39). Does this second half of the greatest commandment have political and economic requirements as well as individual and communal demands?

If exegetes agree on anything about Matthew, it's that the First Gospel's author is not the tax collector we meet in the "Gospel according to Matthew" (9:9f.; 10:3). In fact, the final author (or redactor) of "Matthew" (whose real name will probably never be known) was writing a good fifty years after Jesus' meal at the tax collector's house. He may have used an earlier Aramaic version of the Gospel attributed to the tax collector, St. Matthew. Yet, whoever the author, Matthew as we know him was steeped in rabbinic knowledge and Jewish ways. He was also quite at home in the Greek-speaking world, since the Gospel in the form we have today was written in that language.

Matthew recognized the need to offer a new redaction of the teachings and

1

beliefs held sacred in his community's history (13:51–52). He hoped to offer a spirituality for his contemporaries that would address his world of the eighties and nineties in the way Jesus revealed God's plan for all generations in the thirties. Thus, what Matthew wrote was not to be so much a biography or gospel about Jesus. Rather he tried to offer an ecclesiology, a way of living for his church, that would be faithful to Jesus' way of life. This way of living would become Matthew's spirituality. It would be applicable to every age desiring to pattern its life on the good news that Jesus proclaimed (28:20).

As I studied Matthew and what he was trying to say to his community, I discovered that Matthew was really addressing me, my community and family, and my membership in the church. If I were to let that good news become part of my life and of my society I would have to let his Gospel become part of my journey into the experience of faith.

Many scholars tend to say Matthew wrote his Gospel so that the community-in-transition could deal with questions that were affecting their faith. Where could the presence of God be found in the community's experience? How were authority and leadership to be exercised? How could the community move from a closed, nationalistic sect into an open, universalistic community with a message of hope for the whole world?

When Matthew brought together the various sources, writings, and traditions that became his Gospel as we know it today, he was trying to bring hope to his community, which had lost perspective about its identity and purpose. Matthew tried to help his church re-experience faith in its original nature and mission through a rearticulation of the life of its founder.

Since Jesus' death/resurrection fifty years before, the church had experienced difficult changes both in its understanding of correct teaching, or what it professed (orthodoxy), as well as correct behavior, or what it practiced (orthopraxy). To offset the disillusionment experienced by many members of the community, Matthew attempted to offer a new vision of Jesus that would equip the community to enter the future.

Understanding what the Scriptures mean is called hermeneutics. Hermeneutics is the ongoing interpretation of the word of God geared for new world-realities. Matthew's community experienced upheaval and change in its understanding of religious experience, of the nature of the church and its authority, and of the credibility of Christ's presence in the church in various cultures. A new hermeneutic was needed. Traditional interpretations no longer offered meaning to sustain faith.

In his *Christology beyond Dogma: Matthew's Christ in Process Hermeneutics,* Russell Pregeant notes that for a community experiencing such transition, be it Matthew's of the eighties or nineties or ours nineteen hundred years later, hermeneutics should accomplish two goals: (1) by reflecting on the past, current problems can be addressed (2) in order to show how authority can be taken over these difficulties so that we might create an alternative, hope-filled future. Since this is never a once-and-for-all procedure, a good hermeneutic will always be in process.

According to Pregeant, "a hermeneutical method that reveals the text's relationship to its own present and past, but ignores its thrust toward the future, violates that text's very nature to the extent that it implies that the true meaning of the work is thereby exhausted."[1] He makes it clear that any community experiencing loss of identity and purpose and unable to reflect on its past cannot create a viable future. Applying this insight to our reality, if we are unable to return to the word of God and find within this word some underlying principles that can empower us with perspective for the future, then we can no longer profess to be people who practice the Gospel of Jesus Christ. A Gospel unwilling to respond to the world in which it is proclaimed is not Matthew's Gospel.

I often have the feeling that many of us have come to the unexpressed conclusion that the Gospel is quite impractical for our society, even as we profess that we are "following the Gospel." I sense we too often divorce the Gospel from the burning issues of our day. Thus, when we try to understand the Gospels, we do so in academic isolation. We make our examination a discipline divorced from the search to bring faith-direction to our questions.

Unless contemporary interpreters share the existential questions to which the message of Matthew was addressed, their interpretation will remain wanting and lifeless. According to Pregeant, "these existential questions belong to human existence per se. This must be so if they are intelligible to all interpreters willing to question their own lives."[2]

The Problems Facing Matthew's Community-in-Transition and Contemporary Life

What were the existential questions belonging "to human existence per se" that Matthew addressed? Where can they be found in our contemporary experience? What paradigms, or basic visions and approaches to life, did he offer his community?

Matthew's community experienced religious upheaval, conflicts of authority and interpretation of law, as well as cultural clashes. Nineteen hundred years later, the same problems touch the experience of our church. To discover how we can address these problems in the 1980s and 1990s, we can return to the Matthean community for our direction.

Matthew's world was highly influenced by the apocalyptic tradition. Apocalyptic literature is crisis-oriented. It aims to offer perspective, hope, and release to people experiencing transition and upheaval. While every generation experiences events that give rise to an apocalyptic response, the period between 200 B.C. and A.D. 135 (especially 165 B.C. –A.D. 70) was more than usually influenced by this cataclysmic approach.

After the resurrection/pentecost event, an apocalyptic theme that sustained the community was expressed in the theory of the *parousia*. The community believed Jesus would return to earth very soon; thus a truly alternative lifestyle was able to become normative for the church.

Almost half a century came and went. The return of Jesus seemed a long time in coming (24:42, 48; 25:5, 19). People tired of waiting for Christ to manifest his presence via a dramatic epiphany that would restore community life, transforming the very structures of political and economic oppression. Consequently some apostasized. Others refused to change their theories, dying in their hope. Still others developed *anomia,* a kind of listlessness and lawlessness. The majority probably did not know what to think or how to act. All they knew for sure was that God was not with them in the way they once thought and experienced.

Added to this confusion, the Temple's destruction in A.D. 70 raised further questions about religious experience. The Temple had been considered the place traditionally identified with God's presence. With its destruction, the community was forced to re-examine its former theories. Where was God? Was God dead? Or could it be that the former way of thinking about God was dead?

Sensitive to the people's growing anxiety and disillusionment, Matthew recalled Jesus' words: "Be on guard! Let no one mislead you. . . . Do not be alarmed!" (24:4,6). Matthew tried to say to the members of his community that Jesus' presence would not be limited to cataclysmic situations (24:6–11). His coming-to-be-with-them would never again be limited to an isolated location (24:23–24) such as the desert or even holy shrines (24:26). The old Temple and its religion had become uncaring of the world of poverty and oppression. Jesus-with-the-church would construct a new temple within which the blind and lame would come to be cured—a sign of God's true presence (21:12–14; cf. 11:4–6).

Instead of being kept in fear by searching for Jesus in empty places (28:5–6), Matthew asked his community to return to its biblical roots by re-examining its genealogy (1:1f.). Thus, Matthew imitated the format used by the author of the First Book of Chronicles.

Chronicles began with a genealogy to offer the Israelites a sense of rooted-ness and perspective as they experienced the trauma of the Exile. It was written to help Israel evolve from the limited concept of nationalism to the new experience of Judaism. By using a genealogy, Matthew also hoped to help his own community-in-transition gain a sense of rootedness and perspective. This would help it evolve from the limited concept of Judaism to the new experience of universalism.

In his genealogy, Matthew used an apocalyptic pattern (three periods of fourteen generations) to show that God's breaking into history would always preserve the rootedness of continuity. At the same time, however, he adapted the genealogy to show that God's entrance would also involve a reversal of many established theories and categories.

As a sign that God will now be found not primarily in any building or institution but in those doing God's will, Matthew included four women besides Mary in his genealogy. These "new" instruments of God's plan for the world were not only non-Jews; they were foreigners as well! Furthermore, according to Eduard Schweizer:

It is striking that the familiar matriarchs Sarah, Rebecca, and Leah are omitted, along with the other women mentioned in the Old Testament. Matthew singles out the minor women—Tamar, Rahab, Ruth, Bathsheba—those who were not celebrated, to reveal something of the strange righteousness of God, which does not choose what is great in the eyes of men. Even more striking is the mention of Rahab, although the Bible says nothing of her marriage. What do these four women have in common? It might be suggested that all of them, rightly or wrongly, were suspected of adultery (Gen. 38:14–18; Josh. 2:1; 2 Sam. 11:1–5; Ruth 3:7–15). . . . The four are meant to prefigure God's activity—to culminate in Jesus (28:19)—that will embrace not only the Jews but all gentiles as well.[3]

Within the first sentences of Matthew's good news for his community, the first reversal of God's reign is declared: God's reign cuts through sexual as well as nationalistic distinctions.

Following his unique genealogy, Matthew directed the community's previous apocalyptic expectation for a new age into a realization that the God who was with Jesus and the early disciples need not be sought "here" or "there" (24:23) but within the life of the community itself.

Matthew began by showing that God's power, the Holy Spirit, was alive in Jesus (1:18). With God's power in Jesus, God's plan for the whole world could be established through him. "She is to have a son and you are to name him Jesus because he will save his people from their sins" (1:21). In Jesus, sins of the community's brokenness, tensions, and dismembering would be forgiven, enabling every person the chance to enter personally into a new experience of God. "All this happened to fulfill what the Lord had said through the prophet: 'The virgin shall be with child and give birth to a son, and they shall call him Emmanuel.' " This name, Matthew quickly explains to a community questioning where God could be found, "means 'God is with us' " (1:22–23).

With God's choosing to be with the community in Jesus, hope entered the world. Beginning with this Emmanuel passage, Matthew stressed to his community that Jesus was God-with-them.

If the members of the community believed God was with them, they would evidence their belief by imitating in their lives the pattern of Jesus' life. The Gospel of Jesus had to become their good news to their world. But how would Matthew make the connection between God empowering Jesus as Emmanuel and God being with the community as its source of power?

In no less than three places (4:23; 9:35; 11:1,5), Jesus is portrayed as inaugurating the apocalyptic age in his teaching, preaching, and curing. All these are forms of God's power. For Matthew, Jesus' teaching was summarized in the Sermon on the Mount (5:1–7:29). Next he presented Jesus as the wonderworker (8:1–9:35). However, Matthew showed that Jesus realized that these forms of God's power had to be extended to others:

At the sight of the crowds, his heart was moved with pity. They were lying prostrate from exhaustion, like sheep without a shepherd. He said to his disciples: "The harvest is good but laborers are scarce. Beg the harvest master to send out laborers to gather his harvest" [9:36–38].

Now Matthew could show Jesus extending the power of the good news about Emmanuel to the many. Jesus summoned "his twelve disciples and gave them authority" to share in his healing (10:1,8) and preaching (10:7), withholding the power to share in his teaching ministry until his final departure (28:20).

At this final departure Matthew presents Jesus transferring his power not only to a few disciples, but to all who would ever be baptized. Echoing the dream of Daniel 7:9 and 10:5–6, which spoke of the way the new age would finally break into the world, he said: "Full authority has been given to me both in heaven and on earth" (28:18). The power of God-with-him, the power that made Jesus Emmanuel (1:23), which Jesus once shared with the few (10:1), would now be shared with the community for all time. "Go, therefore, and make disciples of all the nations. Baptize them in the name 'of the Father, and of the Son, and of the Holy Spirit' " (28:19).

To enter into a name means to experience a share in its effectiveness. With the power of God's name in us, we are now the ones empowered to extend, as church, the healing, the preaching, and the teaching of the risen Jesus (see 28:20). Never again will Matthew's community—nor our church—fear being alone. "And know that I am with you always, until the end of the world" (28:20)! The long-awaited *parousia* and temple of God's presence has been established; God is present in those who live under God's power and faithfully practice what is to be proclaimed to every nation: Jesus is Lord! God is with *us*!

The community for all time is to live under this new authority. Yet, because the church is human, God's authority will often be confused with that of humans. Such was the case of Matthew's community. Consequently Matthew tried to offer a new understanding of authority and law in his Gospel.

The existential problems about authority that faced Matthew's community must be placed in the context of the destruction of the Temple in A.D. 70. The Temple's destruction had a devastating effect on both Jews and Christians. The last whimper of dissent against Rome's suppression (which gave rise to the Jewish revolt of 66) was heard around 73. Simon's Zealot Party (see 10:4) had long since disappeared. So had the dominant influence of former powerful groups like the priests and Sadducees. Previously the people's religious experience had been linked to the Temple structure. With the building destroyed, religion itself was in chaos. A pressing need arose for a re-articulation of faith that would establish new forms of loyalty to religion.

Without the Temple and its priesthood, the local synagogue gained in prominence. It provided a needed sense of continuity and community. The center of the Jewish life was no longer able to revolve around the worship of Yahweh through Temple sacrifices. Now the force for community identity would have to be found in strict obedience to the law, the Torah. Furthermore, this unity would be determined by submission to the interpretation of the Torah by the rabbis and Pharisees.

By the early eighties the Christians had gradually separated from the synagogue because they could not submit to the interpretations of the Jewish leaders. Matthew adduced earlier abuses of authority at Jesus' time and in the synagogue to address contemporary abuses in authority that were taking place in his divided community.

Christians were suffering because leaders were making their authority felt (see 20:20–28). Some members argued that strict obedience to the law as defined by existing leaders would unify the community. Others appealed to the law of Christ's authority over any human interpretation. Matthew's task was to re-member a community divided because of false use of authority. Matthew tried to outline an approach to authority in the community that would justify its base in God's power and its expression in human language.

First, he interpreted Jesus' power symbolically through positioning Jesus on the mountain—with its evident Mosaic overtones of authority. Second, he presented Jesus in situations wherein his direct (dis)agreement with specific laws and their human interpretation revealed his identity and relationship with the original Lawgiver, the source of all authority. This is shown especially in Matthew's insertion of the six antithesis statements (5:17–48). By these "you have heard it said . . . but I say to you" declarations, Matthew shows Jesus' union with God who originally gave the law on the mountain.

Building on the experience of the community's experience of God being with it, Matthew used the theme of the mountain (4:8; 5:1; 14:23; 15:29; 17:1–9; 24:3–4; 28:16–20) to show that Jesus (and the church) is more than a new Moses (or Israel). Since the mountain symbolized God's presence, it served Matthew as a vehicle to show how authority could reunite a divided community. Disagreeing with the current interpretations of authority within existing structures (4:8f.), Matthew's Jesus would offer the community a new moral code in the beatitudes (5:1f.). The beatitudes would be a kind of summary of the Sermon on the Mount. Whoever would live under their ethic would be under this new authority. At the conclusion of the Sermon, Matthew showed that the authority that practices what it preaches is the beatitudinal authority that should legitimate all power and legislation. "Jesus finished this discourse and left the crowds spellbound at his teaching. The reason was that he taught with authority [*exousia*], and not like their scribes" (7:29).

Matthew 7:29 is the first of ten times that Matthew used the word *exousia*, or authority. The second is in reference to Jesus' cure of the paralytic (9:6). Besides Jesus' exercise of authority in teaching (7:29) and healing (9:6), Matthew linked Jesus' *exousia* with the restoration of community life. Over half of Matthew's use of *exousia* (six of the ten) can be found in Jesus' debate with the high priests and elders (21:23–27). Jesus' authority to do "these things" that upset the leaders seems to refer to both his teaching and his curative powers.

Such an expression of authority had brought him and the church into confrontation with religious "authorities," who relied on their office and its power rather than religious experience and faith. Yet, even as they would rely on identifying God with their interpretation, outsiders, like the foreign centurion (8:9), would accept Jesus' authority.

The first place Matthew explicitly showed the authority that Jesus shared with the community was in 9:8. Following the cure of the paralytic, Jesus showed that "the Son of Man has authority on earth to forgive sins" (9:6). Matthew shows Jesus doing the curing; yet the crowds "praised God for giving such authority to *men*" (9:8).[4]

According to James Reese,

> The comment of Matthew focuses attention not on the physical cure but on an ongoing expression of the authority of Jesus that was not limited to his earthly existence. . . . It portrays the wonder of the primitive community at sharing in the divine saving power of forgiving sin.
>
> It is true that Matthew does not explicitly state the transfer of authority until the final scene of his Gospel. Yet the organization and dynamism of his presentation tells readers that this transfer is upper-most in the intention of Matthew.[5]

Earlier Matthew's Jesus summoned his twelve disciples to give "them authority to expel unclean spirits and to cure sickness and disease of every kind" (10:1). Now, on the mountain where he promised to be with his disciples and in the world through them, all who are baptized share in the authoritive presence of God by the same power of *exousia* (28:16, 18). God is with us in power!

With *exousia* in us all nations will be assured of hearing the good news. In this light, we can consider the final tension that split the early Matthean community, and that is part of our own reality, namely, that of cultural adaptation.

In the genealogy Matthew showed that God's work would not be limited to one group. Next, in the visit of the wise men, Matthew portrayed Jesus rejected by his own people and accepted by outsiders. This reflected the very experience Matthew's community faced as it found itself separated from the synagogue, while more and more non-Jews entered. By having the wise men, the representatives of alien nations, submit their power to that of Jesus (2:1f.), Matthew showed that the very center of the Jewish world—all of Jerusalem (2:3)—would have to question its religious theories in light of Christ's presence (2:4f.; 21:10f.). The one coming to be with them would come from "a town called Nazareth" (2:23; 21:11) to reorder not only Jerusalem, but the whole world according to God's plan (27:54f.).

Before Matthew's community could accept the implications of the universalism inherent in Jesus' words (28:20), his co-religionists had to change the very ideology that had reinforced their social arrangements of exclusivism and particularism. Some in the community, reluctant to change, probably reinforced their racism and nationalism by appeals to separatistic-sounding statements made by Jesus before the resurrection. The appeal to a God or a Jesus who seems to support exclusivism of one race, sex, age, or nation over another will always be done by people who fear criticizing their mindsets or power in light of the demand to base everything on God's new order of justice.

The appeal to a past exclusivism was dividing Matthew's community; it was a scandal (18:5ff.). As more non-Jews sought baptism, bringing with them their own cultural patterns, new problems arose for Matthew's community. According to John Meier:

> Most of the Matthean critics agree that *transition* is a key concept in the study of Matthew. No matter whether we think of Matthew's church as already separated from the synagogue or as beginning the process of separation, no matter whether we think of Matthew as a Gentile Christian inheriting Jewish-Christian tradition or as a Hellenistic-Jewish Christian growing out of narrow Jewish-Christian past, Matthew's church is modeled by its experience of a shift in its Christian existence. A once strongly Jewish-Christian church is becoming increasingly Gentile in composition. This transition demands a reinterpretation of many of the venerable Jewish-Christian traditions that had been handed down in Matthew's church. Matthew wishes to affirm, not reject, his Christian past; but he knows that *his* situation is different and that consequently the tradition must be understood in a new light (cf. the possible self-portrait in Mt. 13:52; also 9:17).[6]

From 11:1 on, Matthew portrayed Jesus as teaching and preaching "in *their* towns" (signifying the separatism already experienced by the Matthean Christians). What was the way Matthew went about reinterpreting the core of Jesus' message to deal with this cultural upheaval?

First Matthew would stress those parts of Jesus' life that represented the existential milieu of his community. He would present Jesus both affected by, yet rising above, separatism.

Matthew shows that, before the resurrection, God's *exousia* was limited by cultural controls in Jesus' life as well as in his shared mission with the disciples. "Do not visit pagan territory and do not enter a Samaritan town," Matthew has Jesus cautioning his twelve disciples. "Go instead after the lost sheep of the house of Israel" (10:5-6).

While Matthew presented a Jesus whose approach to non-Jews reflected the exclusivism of the pre-resurrection community, he also portrayed Jesus able to transcend such prejudices. For instance, Matthew presents Jesus with an initial reaction of traditional disdain toward the Canaanite woman

(15:24–26); his attitude was shared by the community (15:23). He shows Jesus using a prejudical remark about her, disdainfully referring to her ethnic group. She was one of the dogs (15:26), a term used by Jews against Canaanites, not unlike similar terms used by various groups about each other today.

Yet, even before the resurrection, Matthew's Jesus was the model of someone who was never so locked into prejudices that he could not rise above the ideology of his culture. Even though Matthew showed that Jesus legislated community discipline with rules that reinforced existing prejudices (10:5–6), he also showed that Jesus was the first to break his own rules (8:7; 15:28)! Jesus was able to rise above the social sin of cultural alienation which was tearing Matthew's community apart. He was able to overcome his prejudice because of the woman's persistent faith (15:27–28). In this sense, the woman became an evangelizer to the one who was evangelizing: the Canaanite to the Jew, the woman to the man.

Matthew's way of dealing with the cross-culturation of his community has much to offer the white, male-dominated mainline churches of today. Often they find themselves struggling to break through these human categories to become one with those who have been traditionally excluded: non-whites and women. As Matthew asked in his day, so we must question today: What forms of wealth—power, possessions, and places of honor—must this rich, white, sexist church give up? What must it do to be saved vis-à-vis its solidarity with non-whites and women as well as the poor and oppressed wherever they may be? (see 19:16–30).

As the Christians found themselves more alienated from the synagogues or found themselves rejected by them, they gradually left Jerusalem and "their towns" (11:1). Many settled around Antioch, where many scholars place the origin of Matthew's Gospel.[7] According to G. D. Kilpatrick, Matthew's community was also located in an urban environment. He finds Matthew using the word "village" (*kome*) only four times; yet *polis* (used in 11:1), or city, occurs twenty-six times. Some of the settings appear to relate to contemporary conditions experienced by Matthew's community.[8] The difficulty of preaching the Gospel in urban settings, with wider opportunities for pluralism and diversion, seems to have been a problem almost from the beginning!

Another cultural similarity between Matthew's community and that of our own church relates to our commonly shared socio-economic status of growing affluence.

Matthew was keenly aware of the conflicts facing an increasingly secure community called, by a common baptism, to radical discipleship. Rather than skirt the issue, he even altered his sources to deal directly with the socio-economic obstacles that were adding to the dilemma of his community-in-transition. Jack Dean Kingsbury details some of these alterations:

> The Marcan Jesus commands the disciples in conjunction with their missionary journey to take with them no "copper coin," i.e., small

change (6:8), but the Matthean Jesus commands them to take no "gold, nor silver, nor copper coin" (10:9). The Lucan Jesus tells a parable about "minas" (19:11–27), but the Matthean Jesus tells a parable about "talents" (25:14–30), one of the latter being worth approximately fifty times as much as one of the former. The Lucan Jesus says in the words of the householder in the parable of the great supper: "Go out quickly to the streets and lanes of the city, and bring in the poor and maimed and blind and lame" (14:21); but the Matthean Jesus simply says in his version of these words: "Go therefore to the thoroughfares, and invite to the marriage feast as many as you find" (22:9). And in Mark (15:43) and Luke (23:50–51), Joseph of Arimathea is a member of the council who is looking for the kingdom of God, but in Matthew he is a "rich man . . . who also was a disciple of Jesus" (27:57). Finally, it is also quite in harmony with all of the preceding that Matthew should not have appropriated from Mark the latter's story of the poor widow's mite (Mark 12:41–44; Luke 21:1–4).[9]

Kingsbury also shows that Matthew's community seems to have been accustomed to dealing regularly with various sums and ranges of money. Matthew uses the terms "silver," "gold," and "talent" twenty-eight times, while Luke refers to them four times and Mark but once. It makes sense, then, Kingsbury concludes, "that Matthew should appropriate Mark's warning against riches in 13:22 (Mark 4:19) and sharpen the logion of Jesus at 19:23 so that the difficulty in entering the kingdom is predicated, not merely to 'those who have means' (Mark 10:23), but to the 'rich man.' "[10]

As the community moved from the financial insecurity characteristic of an agrarian culture to a degree of relative affluence, Matthew needed to offer a spirituality for a people who had "come into money." He also had to address the question, "How does an urban community live the Gospel?" Much more, "How does a considerably affluent urban community live the Gospel?" How do such a community's members, with growing power, possessions, and prestige, determine how much of these forms of wealth they truly need? How can this wealth be used for the benefit of those with whom Jesus had come to identify, namely, the poor and those whom society rejects? How would they maintain some sort of dignity and yet not abuse that dignity? How were they to share their growing resources to uphold every human being whom they were to love as their very selves (22:39)?

The Hermeneutic Circle: Biblical Spirituality and Personal Biography

Earlier we referred to Russell Pregeant's statement: "a hermeneutical method that reveals the text's relationship to its own present and past, but ignores its thrust toward the future, violates that text's very nature to the extent that it implies that the true meaning of the work is thereby exhausted."[11] The more I examined how Matthew tried to cope with the existential situation of his community by reflecting on the life of Jesus, the more I realized he was providing us with a new understanding of spirituality that can give direction to many of our contemporary questions.

The hermeneutic or method that has best enabled me to bring the Scriptures to bear upon the existential questions of my life and world—and which also faithfully reflects the approach Matthew seems to have used with his questioning community—is based on that model proffered by Juan Luis Segundo in his book *The Liberation of Theology*. Before sharing his model, it is important to describe the existential questions that brought me to discover how this hermeneutic was happening in my life.

I had come to that reading with at least ten years of trying to understand my world and God's word, especially my world as a Roman Catholic committed to living the Gospel as a follower of Francis of Assisi. My first assignment as a Capuchin Franciscan was to a parish in Milwaukee that was rapidly changing from German-Polish to black. St. Elizabeth's lost over 1,000 families in the first three years I was there, 1968–1971. These years were filled with hatred, anger, fear, and mistrust among the parish's members. Yet, these parishioners had heard God's word about universal love for years. I found myself asking: "Why is it that so many Catholics can hear about and profess love for one another, yet practice hate so deeply?"

Around this time I discovered that the problems at St. Elizabeth's were deeper than racial and religious. They were economic and political as well. I discovered a system had been created to benefit a few, through panic selling, red-lining, and the gradual economic depression of an entire district. I discovered our neighborhood rapidly becoming underdeveloped. It manifested all the signs of depression: outside ownership, high prices, deficit balance of payments, inflation. We had more money going out of the community than coming in; unemployment was rampant.

In 1973, I discovered that St. Elizabeth's was a microcosm of a bigger, global reality. My analysis came full-circle at a meeting in Dallas, where I listened to experts talk about the "Third World," a relatively new term for me.

This Third World was for the most part poor, non-white, and non-Western European. Furthermore, speaker after speaker was saying, the same economic depression I found on a micro-level at St. Elizabeth's could be found on a macro-level globally. They explained that multinational corporations and banks, along with elites in the governments of the developing nations, were significant influences in creating structures of dependency that furthered underdevelopment. The final straw for me was a speech delivered by Radmiro Tomic, former Chilean ambassador to the United States. He was then head of the Christian Democratic party of Chile.

Tomic explained that the Third World was being exploited from within by its elites and military forces. They worked in combination with political and economic forces from without. The ambassador said that, in such a situation, the poor have only one hope for relief—God. Yet, too often, it seemed God's church was part of the problem. Consequently, for these poor, the only sentence of the Scriptures that seemed to make sense and ring true was: "To the man who has, more will be given until he grows rich; the man who has not will lose what little he has" (Matt. 13:12; cf. 25:29).

Hearing Tomic, I vowed to myself that the poor would have a different God revealed to them by me, a citizen of the United States living within its institutions. But how was I going to re-discover this God who cared about the contemporary world?

The more I studied the Scriptures, the more I kept returning to the very beginning, the first part of Genesis. In the first chapter of Genesis I found God's plan for the world. It outlined the call for everyone to co-create with God a community of ordered life. Gradually I became convinced that, somehow, Genesis was written not so much to describe the past but to offer a goal for people of all time.

I soon became convinced that if God is God and if humans are made in the image of God, then, *whenever* people are in need of resources, that very need or lack represents a deviation from the divine plan. Consequently, I concluded, God has to intervene, in some way, to deliver the people from that *chaos*. But I could find no theologian or Scripture scholar saying this was the underlying theme of all of God's revelation.

My answer came when I was visiting Bill Cieslak, a Capuchin from our province who was studying at Berkeley. By the time we left the airport in San Francisco, Bill and I were arguing about my thesis: all people are made to image God and, therefore, should have the resources they need for life. "But no Scripture scholar will support that, Mike," Bill said.

"I don't care. That has to be God, if there is a God," I could only reply.

So we shared my hypothesis with Mike Guinan, a Franciscan Scripture scholar. Listening to me, Mike responded, "I've got just the article for you."

He introduced me to Walter Brueggemann's article describing the insights of the Priestly school, the authors of the first chapters of Genesis.[12] In the midst of the chaos of the Exile in the sixth century before Christ they remembered the chaos of the Exodus six hundred years earlier. They found in that experience of God's deliverance of the people the archetype of God's purposes for creation itself. Thus six hundred years after the Exodus, in the upheaval and darkness of the Exile, the Priestly writers described the beginning of the world not so much to express a historical fact but to articulate God's perpetual goal for creation. "In the beginning, when God created the heavens and the earth, the earth was formless wasteland, and darkness covered the abyss . . ." (Gen. 1:1), the Priestly scribe wrote to his community. The Hebrew word "abyss" used to describe the condition of the Exile, was *tohu wabohu*.

The creation theme describing God's plan for the abyss of the world of every generation experiencing transition, chaos, and meaninglessness would state simply that every person is made to image God. But to image God, every person needs to have access to life's basic resources. Thus, the Priestly school, I discovered, was not just speaking to its community-in-exile; it was addressing every people-in-transition, especially those seeking to understand what God wants to happen in their particular histories.

> God said: "Let us make man in our image, after our likeness. Let them have dominion over the fish of the sea, the birds of the air, and the cattle, and over all the wild animals and all the creatures that crawl on the ground."
>
> > God created man in his image;
> > in the divine image he created him;
> > male and female he created them.
>
> God blessed them, saying: "Be fertile and multiply; fill the earth and subdue it. Have dominion over the fish of the sea, the birds of the air, and all the living things that move on the earth" [Gen. 1:26–28].

With Genesis 1:26–28, the community could be given a new perspective in place of its former darkness. Where the experience of the Exile not only jarred the community's traditional understanding about God, but even found it calling God into question (see Ps. 137:1–4), so the remembrance of the Exodus would provide the community with a new vision applicable to its future. If God had once seen the community in need and showed care by delivering it from that abyss (Exod. 3:7–12), would not this same God want this to happen all the time?

I had rejected a traditional understanding of religion that effectively divorced professions about Gospel living from application to all levels of life in my world. I had moved from my initial questioning at St. Elizabeth's to become disillusioned with the traditional way of separating God's word from the struggles of humanity. With this discovery, I now was equipped with a biblical approach toward my world of the twentieth century.

With this background, we can return to my reading of Segundo's *The Liberation of Theology* one afternoon in 1978. I was struck by the following paragraph:

> In this chapter I shall present my four sample attempts at fashioning a hermeneutic circle. But first I think it would be wise for me to reiterate the two preconditions for such a circle. They are: (1) profound and enriching questions and suspicions about our real situation; (2) a new interpretation of the Bible that is equally profound and enriching. These two preconditions mean that there must in turn be four decisive factors in our circle. *Firstly* there is our way of experiencing reality, which leads us to ideological suspicion. *Secondly* there is the application of our ideological suspicion to the whole ideological superstructure in general and to theology in particular. *Thirdly* there comes a new way of experiencing theological reality that leads us to exegetical suspicion, that is, to the suspicion that the prevailing interpretation of the Bible has not taken important pieces of data into account. *Fourthly* we have

our new hermeneutic, that is, our new way of interpreting the foun-
tainhead of our faith (i.e., Scripture) with the new elements at our
disposal.[13]

At that point in my reading, I put the book down. I went across the hall to
Mark Ramion, showing him the passage. I said excitedly, "Look, I'm a
liberation theologian!" How did this happen?

The contradictions—economic, political, and religious—that I experienced at St. Elizabeth's had led me to a deeper analysis of my world and God's
word. I had begun to question seriously any theology that would not deal
concretely with the tearing apart of God's human community. Realizing that
uncritical acceptance of the status quo reflected a deep-seated ideology of
compliance by sinful silence, I returned to the scriptures. I had come to
conclude that Genesis 1:26–28 spoke about the image of God in each person
and the need to share the world's resources more equitably. To me Genesis
revealed God's underlying plan for the world. This plan had to touch every
part of society—individuals, groups, and structures themselves.

Not only was I reflecting on my *world* and God's *word* in this process style, I
was recognizing my need to live under the influence of this revealed word in
my world. I wanted theology (christology and ecclesiology) to become my
spirituality. My biography had to reflect biblical theology.

Good biblical hermeneutics should lead to gospel spirituality. Orthodoxy
should lead to orthopraxy, and vice-versa. Realizing this, I adapted Segundo's
"hermeneutic circle" into categories that made sense to me about my world
and God's word. I discovered that each of us, in our own ways, must go
through this hermeneutic circle if the Scriptures are to be translated in our
lives by our profession and practice:

WORLD   WORD

1. I have an experience that   4. This reveals to me a new
jars the worldview that has   understanding of God, who
previously guided my values   now is revealed as part of my
and behavior.   experience for my life and
                                  the world's.

2. This leads me to gradually   3. Rejecting this former
call into question the very   concept of God, I return to
ideology that once rein-   the Scriptures to search for
forced my understanding of   similar experiences others
the world, including God.   have had.

Because my questions led me back to re-examine the Scriptures, I came to
understand that Genesis 1:26–28 could become the basis for a whole new
kind of spirituality. Grounded in a personal experience of God walking with

me in the Garden of Life, this spirituality would enable me to witness to God's presence in me through my ministry.

Gradually I began to see more implications of spirituality for me—a white, male cleric from a relatively secure religious order. What specific responsibility was mine, my community's, and my institution's toward society? What role did we have in this complex world as we said we vowed to "live the Gospel of our Lord Jesus Christ living in obedience, without property, and in chastity?" At this point of my questioning Matthew offered me a guide.

As I researched the First Gospel I began to see that chapter 11 was critical for Matthew. In the previous chapters he laid the groundwork. He offered a new ethics in the Sermon on the Mount (5:1–7:29). He showed how Jesus' deeds would meet the needs of broken people (8:1–9:38). In 10:1–11:1, however, Matthew shows that these forms of Jesus' *exousia* were to be extended into the life of the community. I discovered that the life and ministries of the community of Jesus' time were to become those of any community living under *exousia* (28:18) and wisdom (see 28:20) until the end of the world.

The "works" that John had heard about while in prison (11:2) were not just Jesus' teaching and healing in the past. More importantly for Matthew, these works were those that the community was to perform. By placing questions and doubts in the disciples of John, Matthew seems to have made the Baptizer a type for the questions being raised by many in his community. According to Schweizer:

> Matthew . . . wants to make the point that the same authority to perform miracles is also given to the community. Jesus' response to the disciples of the Baptist is thus also the response of the community to adherents of the Baptist in the period of the evangelist. Jesus' authority can still be seen at work in the Christian community. It answers all doubting questions.[14]

As I interpreted John the Baptist's search for authentic spirituality, his doubts became an invitation for Matthew's questioning community to journey through the hermeneutic circle. This paralleled the way in which the community in the Exile had gone through its hermeneutic circle to Genesis 1:26–28 by recalling the Exodus.

I discovered that the questions of John (really the questions of Matthew's community) were my questions and those of many concerned friends. His doubts were our doubts. Just as I had begun at St. Elizabeth's with a clear impression of how people could be converted, so I too began to realize that the ideology that had guided me before was not bringing about change. In fact, as for John, it had too often been a source of frustration and trouble.

In prison, the once apocalyptic John experienced the jarring shock of incarceration. The hermeneutic circle began. He had been hearing about "the works Christ was performing" (11:1). Examining these works against his previous theology and its ideology, John gradually called into question his whole previous worldview and his former method of evangelization. Had he done the right thing or was it all in vain? He was now at step two of the hermeneutic circle. He sent disciples to ask Jesus: "Are you 'He who is to come' [add: " 'to be with us' "] or do we look for another" (11:3) to bring an answer to our doubts and alienation?

In reply, Jesus' response to John became Matthew's invitation to his community to re-read the scriptures about the messiah and to experience the third step of the hermeneutic circle. This re-examination might lead to a rediscovery of that authentic spirituality Jesus not only preached about but *brought* about: "Go back and report to John what you hear and see: the blind recover their sight, cripples walk, lepers are cured, the deaf hear, dead men are raised to life, and the poor have the good news preached to them" (11:4–5).

Immediately upon hearing these words, which outlined Jesus' understanding about his own spirituality, the community would recall Isaiah 61. It would understand that Matthew's Jesus was saying to all his disciples for all time that authentic spirituality will incarnate in history the promise about the coming presence of the Messiah predicted by Isaiah 61. The fourth step of the hermeneutic circle is the good news itself. It must always be fulfilled for communities-in-transition will always be faithful to the Isaian prophecy about the restoration of all community.

Matthew showed a John questioning his previous understanding of Jesus' "works." With the description of what Jesus was not only preaching about in the Sermon on the Mount (5:1–7:29) but practicing in ministry (8:1–9:38), Matthew's hermeneutic would come full circle. A new spirituality would be offered for all ages to come. And blessed would John be, as well as any others in the church of Matthew's time and until the end of the world who would not be scandalized. Biblical spirituality must be incarnated in every age on behalf of the rejected ones of society (11:6)!

In many ways, the pericope of John in prison is central to Matthew's gospel spirituality. To individuals and communities once quite sure about spirituality, Matthew showed there could be but one authentic spirituality. Authentic biblical spirituality fulfills in the personal and communal biographies of people the theology of revelation itself. Jesus' spirituality fulfilled Isaiah's revelatory theology about how God would be with the people. Now Matthew's theology about Jesus offered the church a spirituality for all ages and places. Within the church of our era, our spirituality is called to manifest Matthew's theology about Jesus. This is the only spirituality the world has a right to expect from us (11:3). Blessed will we be if this style of life, evidenced in our own conversion, also invites the world to conversion to restore God's original intent for creation.

In the alienation of the Exile, it is little wonder that the Priestly writers, as well as Second Isaiah (who was quoted most by Matthew), would return to the basic creation themes and wisdom motifs to offer hope to their divided communities. Recalling the great experience of the Exodus, where God saw the people in need, cared about them, and called them to freedom (Exod. 3:7), these writers came to describe God as the one always ready to deliver humans from conditions of need.

Picking up on this universal theme, Matthew would apply the same principle to his church-in-transition. Faithful to the wisdom of the Priestly writers and Second Isaiah, Matthew would bring his good news into the alienation and chaos of his community by starting his Gospel with the words *biblos geneseos,* the book of beginnings (1:1). By so doing, Matthew was faithful to Genesis as the archetype of wisdom's message about God's purpose for the world.

The Challenge of Structural Analysis for Biblical Spirituality

To be at the heart of the world with good news, we must understand our world. We need to analyze society in its entirety—the individual, the interpersonal, and the societal dimensions—if we are to go into "all the nations" (28:19). In a special way, because they have so much influence over the lives of people and groups, we must understand the institutions, "isms," and ideologies around us so that we might discover how to address them with the authority of the word within us.

The gathering of people and groups into institutions finds them, as well as the earth's resources, arranged in certain ways. These "isms" arrange people according to race, sex, age, and nation, as well as cleric-lay, powerful-powerless, gay-straight, etc. Resources are also arranged according to producer-consumer, military might, and technology. Each of these social and resource arrangements is legitimated through an ideology or worldview. Ideology is promoted through education and the communications media. The interrelationship of institutions, "isms," and ideology is what I call the infrastructure.[15]

It is much like seeing a monumental building such as the World Trade Center in New York or the CN Tower in Toronto. The untrained eye observes only the steel, cement, and glass. An architect sees beyond the surface appearance. An architect perceives the pressure areas and the stress points, which enable such buildings to remain standing. Similarly, spirituality and evangelization that limit their address to the first two dimensions of life—individual and interpersonal—remain surface or truncated.

In the past we have tended to limit our Gospel and spirituality to the first and second dimensions of life (individual and interpersonal). Even though Matthew could view the individual in terms of the whole generation (12:39–43), we have not taken sufficient cognizance of the impact of the infrastructure (with its institutionalization of people into social arrangements reinforced by ideologies). Spirituality based on the awareness of the infrastructure and the impact of social sin on people and groups goes largely ignored in our country and in other developed nations. Consequently we have been unable to promote seriously the cosmic change demanded by the Gospel.

LEVELS OF OUR WORLD
|
INDIVIDUAL
|
INTERPERSONAL
|
INFRASTRUCTURAL

INSTITUTIONS	ISMS	IDEOLOGY
Economic	(Re: *Dignity of Persons*)	Communications
	Sexism	Media
Political	Racism	—Language
	Ageism	—Symbols
Religious	Elitism	
	Clericalism	Education
Other	Nationalism	—Formative
	Other	—Continuing
	(Re: *Sharing of Resources*)	
	Technologism	
	Consumerism	
	Militarism	
	Economic Imperialism	
	Other	

Meeting in Rome in 1971, the Roman Catholic Synod of Bishops came to realize that God's word had failed to address the infrastructure that so affected both individuals and groups. The bishops came from all parts of the globe. They brought with them experiences of poverty and wealth, famine and luxury, malnutrition and throw-away societies, and racial and national conflicts. Their analysis of these realities convinced them of the need for a revitalized gospel message.

They urged:

Scrutinizing the "signs of the times" and seeking to detect the meaning of emerging history, while at the same time sharing the aspirations and questions of all those who want to build a more human world, we have listened to the Word of God that we might be converted to the fulfilling of the divine plan for the salvation of the world.[16]

The bishops concluded:

Even though it is not for us to elaborate a very profound analysis of the situation of the world, we have nevertheless been able to perceive the serious injustices which are building around the world of men a network of domination, oppression and abuses which stifle freedom and which keep the greater part of humanity from sharing in the building up and enjoyment of a more just and more fraternal world.[17]

The underlying theme of God's plan for the world found in Genesis showed that all people are to image God by having access to the earth's resources. However, if the analysis of the bishops is correct—that people's freedom was being stifled and the greater part of humanity was not sharing in the earth's resources—then our world stands in direct opposition to God's plan for creation. As long as people are not free they cannot image God as fully as they should. As long as the goods of the earth are not shared with equity, people cannot easily increase, multiply, fill the earth and subdue it or enter into a relationship of care with the goods of the earth. This is a condition of social sin. This "network of domination" is the infrastructure of institutions and "isms". It includes the ideology that must feel the impact of a call to conversion if God's plan for the earth will be realized.

We are part of society's institutions. We share in its social arrangements. We are touched by its ideology. Many of us are the beneficiaries of the injustices that are part of this network. Not to develop a model of evangelization that brings Matthew's gospel spirituality to bear upon this part of the world is to deny the very commission given us at baptism (28:19). This is especially important for many of us in the First World who benefit from the infrastructure. In this sense we are challenged to conversion in the same way as was Matthew's rich young man. Our spirituality and hermeneutics must be grounded in solidarity with the poor (19:21).

The Circle of Care and Matthew's Message

The more we examine the individual, interpersonal, and infrastructural levels in the world, the more we sense growing alienation and dismemberment within it. What does God's word have to say about this abysmal condition of chaos and darkness?

Returning to the Priestly writer (as well as the writer of Exodus 3 before and Matthew after), and using a diagram adapted from Richard Byrne,[18] we see that the Priestly scribe was describing God's circle of care.

"In the beginning" (a symbol for "whenever") God *saw* chaos and darkness, God *cared* about it. Chaos was a deviation from God's own nature, from God's word. Therefore God delivered that emptiness from this condition by *calling* it into meaning. Creating *human life* so that all people might image the divine nature, God constituted men and women with the ability to *respond* by *caring* about everything in creation in a way that would advance God's plan for the world.

Fidelity to that plan would result in God *seeing* the divine image in the goodness of their deeds. Thus *God*, who made all things good to image the divine reality, would be recognized in these deeds of care. The writer showed that the circle of care is essential for human living on earth. Entering the circle of care is the way God is revealed in our experience and the way we express that revelation.

In his gospel spirituality, Matthew offered his community a way to enter the same circle of care found in Genesis 1 and Exodus 3, the archetypes for all religious experience. Two sections in the First Gospel make this clear.

The first half of Matthew's circle of care is found in the Sermon on the Mount. God *sees* all that we need (6:32). Because God *cares* for us more than any earthly parent (7:9–10), God gives "good things to anyone who asks" (7:11; cf. 6:33). These good things represent all the resources of the earth, which God always sees as good. Above all, these good things are found in *exousia,* God's own power. *Called* by God, we are empowered to bring the circle of care to perfection by extending God's care to others in need (25:31–40). Under this power, as the Last Judgment scene demonstrates, we are to complete the second half of the circle of care. We *respond* to others in need with a life of *care.* In this way we will be *seen* by God. We will hear the words: "Come. You have my Father's blessing! Inherit the kingdom prepared for you from the creation of the world" (25:34). Faithful to God's eternal plan for the world, we receive God's blessing. We have faithfully imaged the beatitudinal spirituality of Matthew's Jesus.

Matthew's Gospel offered a beatitudinal theology about life in the present creation, which was faithful to traditional wisdom spirituality (Prov. 3:10; 8:35; 9:6; Sir. 4:12). Since wisdom literature always deals with order in life, the promotion of integrated, peaceful life must be seen as central to Matthew's task of bringing meaning to his divided community.

In the key eleventh chapter, Matthew offered his community a portrait of Jesus as incarnate wisdom. Those who came to him would learn from him the authority and wisdom (13:54) he received from the one he called Father (11:27f.; cf. 7:21). From this wisdom perspective, Matthew's Gospel stressed two incontrovertible facts about the goal of all life and how all life must be promoted: (1) every person, made in God's image, is very good; and (2) reflecting the image of God demands that every person share in God's blessing by having access to the earth's resources and the ultimate resource, God.

Matthew's Gospel affirmed the dignity of each person as God's image. Matthew also articulated the need to cherish each person's unique image in various ways throughout the Gospel (18:1f.). Each person is precious (12:12). Matthew added the levitical prescription to the first and greatest commandment (22:37), making it (22:39) the foundation of his spirituality (22:40).

Matthew offered his community a Jesus who imaged God's justice in the world by healing every obstacle to personal dignity. Donald Senior has written:

Christology not only gave Matthew's church historical perspective, but even more fundamentally, gave it a sound vision of who God is. One's image of God might seem a bit remote from the pressing concerns of social justice, but for the Gospels—and Matthew in particular—one's understanding of God is the ultimate source of Christian responsibility in the world. This thesis too, is rooted in the kingdom of God motif. The Lord's saving actions on behalf of the poor, the defenseless, the oppressed, hone Israel's awareness of its communal responsibility.

Matthew's portrayal of Jesus' energetic Kingdom ministry sculpts the Gospel's image of God. Jesus' relentless acts of healing, or reconciliation, of confronting evil are the works of the Father (cf. 3:15; 12:15–21). Jesus fulfills the Scriptures—fulfills God's commands—by lifting the burden of pain and oppression from God's people. Thus the God of Jesus is a saving, liberating God.[19]

Essential to the world-order of this liberating God is the affirmation of the value and importance of each person: ". . . it is no part of your heavenly Father's plan that a single one of these little ones shall ever come to grief" (18:14). To place any obstacle in the way of these little ones was to reject Jesus, the image of God who was to be welcomed, or "seen," in the image of the most seemingly insignificant member of society (18:5–6; 10:40–42). What society might reject is considered of greatest significance by God (18:1; 12:12). The theological assumption, essential to the Genesis message of the Priestly school, undergirded Matthew's understanding of the person-as-viewed by Jesus. "Whoever welcomes one such child [disciple] for my sake welcomes me" (18:5). Each person should be accepted as the *alter ego,* the image of Jesus, upon whom God's favor rests (see 18:10–14).

If this spirituality is to be applied to our lives, it must touch all levels: the individual, interpersonal, and infrastructural. Each person is sacred. Communities and structures should exist, not to dominate people, but to affirm their dignity. The ninety-nine exist to re-member anyone who has lost identity in the community (18:12).

The fact that each person, as God's image, must be affirmed as very good brings us to Matthew's second principle about life: reflecting God's image demands that each person share in God's blessedness by having access to the earth's resources (see Sir. 39:16–22). This includes God as ultimate resource.

In the Exile, being denied access to resources reflected the curse of being kept in need. This curse was to be replaced by God's blessing for each person made to image that God in whom there is no need. "Be fertile and multiply; fill the earth and subdue it. Have dominion over all [resources]" (Gen. 1:28).

Doing good deeds toward others (22:39) is the way of reinforcing God's image in others. In fact, doing good by sharing resources with those in need enables a person to become like the only one who is good (19:16f.) and reflect in the closest way possible the very perfection of God (19:21; cf. 5:48). Actively cooperating with God's plan for the world, the way of perfection demands that the needs of each person must be met. According to von Rad, this "includes everything that a man, in his isolation, might need: wealth and honor (Prov. 8:18, 21), guidance and security in life (Prov. 1:33ff.; 2:9ff.; 4:6; 6:2; 7:4f.), knowledge of God and rest for the soul (Prov. 2:5; Sir. 6:28; 51:27)."[20]

When we respond to others in need by doing good toward them, God's blessing comes upon us. Since God is only recognized in such images of the divine goodness, doing good in this way enables us to be seen by God as images of the divine nature. Within this perspective we can best understand the classic Last Judgment scene of Matthew. The blessing of salvation for fidelity to God's plan is linked to care for those in need (25:31–46). By doing good to others God blesses us as good, as God-like. By imaging God who does good, by doing good ourselves, we are called by God to a deeper experience of the blessing of divine life. The second half of the circle of care, the normative dimension, leads back into the first half, the constitutive dimension. This stress of Matthew throughout his Gospel reflects the best in authentic wisdom spirituality. As von Rad notes:

> A good or evil act affect[s] the author of that act himself. Only recently have we had a clearer idea of the so-called act-consequence relationship, for Israel, too, shared the widely-spread concept of an effective power inherent both in good and in evil and subject to specific laws. She was convinced that by every evil deed or every good deed a momentum was released which sooner or later also had an effect on the author of the deed. To a great extent, therefore, it lay within his own power whether he exposed himself to the effects of disaster or blessing.[21]

To develop a spirituality of doing good and receiving God's blessing demands that we bring our moral concerns to all levels of life. It means imitating the life of Jesus by incarnating in our spiritualities Matthew 11:1f., just as Jesus imitated the life of Second Isaiah by making Isaiah 61 the center of his spirituality.

Matthew was unique among the writers of the New Testament in linking the beatitudes proclaimed by Jesus with Isaiah 61. Those who lived by the ethic of the beatitudes, Matthew was saying, would be blessed by God, seen by God, and have the Spirit of God upon them (see Isa. 61:1). Whoever follows these instructions for correct behavior, by good-doing, will be personally constituted with a further share in the goodness of God's blessed presence.

Matthew's portrait of Jesus shows this spirituality fulfilled primarily in the person of Jesus. With Jesus' power in us (28:18) this spirituality can be fulfilled in each of us. If we fail to live under the ethic of the beatitudes in our present world, we will not easily experience their promise.

Every person, group, or institution proclaiming such a spirituality in its practice and profession can expect the world's rejection. But this very negation can become an affirmation of the effective power of God's reign and its blessing in our lives (see 5:10–12). Furthermore, the experience of this blessing need not be anticipated in some future end time beyond our experience. "The New Testament beatitudes are not just imitations of the future or consolations in relation to it," Friedrich Hauck declares in his explanation of *makarios* (blessing) in the *Theological Dictionary of the New Testament*. "They see the present in the light of the future."[22]

Sharing in the life of the gods made one part of the *makarioi*, or blessed one. To live the beatitudes is to be seen by God as reflecting the divine image. To be recognized as the divine image is to receive the divine blessing of *exousia*.

Society may judge such a lifestyle to be foolish and scandalous. It may even persecute those who take the beatitudes seriously in a scandalous society, "marked by the grave sin of social injustice."[23] Yet, Matthew makes it quite clear (11:28), to the believer who has experienced the mystery of God's care and plan for the world, that the beatitudes offer a way of wisdom productive of God's everlasting favor.

CHAPTER TWO

Whose Is the Reign of God?

What God's Reign Is Not

Many spiritual directors recommend reading the last part of the collected works of St. John of the Cross before the first part. They feel the beginning books can be best understood in light of the final section. Similarly, once we understand the last part of the first beatitude, it is much easier to approach questions raised about those who are poor in spirit.

This chapter will first show what it does not mean to be under the reign of God. After defining what it means for a person, community, and institution to live under God's reign, the chapter will describe the central project of the society in which we live. It will explain how its thrust is diametrically opposed to the central project of God's reign as expressed in the parables. It will also show that God's reign and that of the powers and principalities find their central dynamics in serious tension. Consequently, we must choose which central dynamic will become the basis for our lifestyle. Living under the influence of one central project puts us at odds with the primary thrust of the other.

For Matthew, the reign of God is not a matter of once-and-for-all membership. Making the equivalent of the nine First Fridays does not assure acceptance into God's presence. Salvation is never a certain reward. "Mark what I say," self-assured members of the community were warned. "Many will come from the east and the west and will find a place at the banquet in the kingdom of God with Abraham, Isaac, and Jacob, while the natural heirs of the kingdom will be driven out into the dark. Wailing will be heard there, and the grinding of teeth" (8:11–12).

Weeping and gnashing of teeth refer to the apocalyptic breakthrough of God's reign into concrete historical situations (13:42,50; 22:13; 24:51; 25:30), criticizing those realities in light of the wisdom of God's word. While traditional exegesis presented the "natural heirs of the kingdom" as the Jews, recent scholarship has extended this passage to include those in the church. In a special way it referred to the leaders, who seemed to think they were beyond criticism because of their position in the church. The fact that one is a Jew does not mean that one is automatically part of God's reign, Matthew's Jesus declares. Equally, membership in the church does not assure a place in the reign of God, even for a leader.

Matthew articulates this theme in various places. Nowhere does he address it as strongly as in the parable of the tenants. He portrays a Jesus who makes it clear that the very one rejected by the structure, probably in the name of God (21:31), would be the first to enter it (21:42). "For this reason, I tell you, the kingdom of God will be taken away from you and given to a nation that will yield a rich harvest" (21:43).

The word "nation," or *ethnos*, used here and elsewhere by Matthew (see 28:19) does not refer primarily to a nation in the sense of the United States, Canada, Israel, or Nicaragua. It refers to any people in whom God's reign or plan will be fulfilled. The nation yielding a rich harvest refers to all persons, groups, or institutions whose spirituality reflects their experience of that reign which, in turn, they make present in the world (see 9:37–38; 13:4–30, 36–42). The rich harvest bears fruit in wisdom's deeds (11:2). It is foolishness to think that once-and-for-all membership qualifies any persons to claim that they are always under the authority of this reign.

Matthew's approach to the reign of God has serious consequences for any theories that equate present or future union with God with membership in any institution. First of all, Matthew makes clear, God's reigning presence cannot be equated with the church. People in the church or the Jewish community are not, by that fact, automatic heirs. Even though baptism and circumcision signify entrance into the community, remaining a full member of the community requires more. Matthew says that all kinds of people not considered part of the community (8:11; cf. 2:1f) will come within God's reign if they submit to the gospel. Oftentimes they will be members without realizing it (25:38,44).

A few years ago, Alan McCoy, OFM, president of the Conference of Major Superiors of Religious Men, displayed a visual representation of what the reign of God is not. He drew three interlocking circles, labelling them "world," "church," and "kingdom." Such a visual aid makes it clear for our church what Matthew was saying to his community: some in the world who are not official members in the church will be part of God's reign. In the same way, not everyone in the official church, including even those who make a great protestation of their faith (7:21), will share in God's final reign. Only those who perform wisdom's deeds of goodness will be recognized by the good God as those with spiritualities reflecting the divine goodness.

The next things Matthew's Jesus disassociates from a simplistic identification with the reign of God are rules and regulations, if they are viewed as ends in themselves:

The scribes and the Pharisees have succeeded Moses as teachers; therefore, do everything and observe everything they tell you. But do not follow their example. Their words are bold but their deeds are few. They bind up heavy loads, hard to carry, to lay on other men's shoulders, while they themselves will not lift a finger to budge them [23:2–4].

What a contrast Jesus shows! This approach to law becomes a foolish yoke of slavery compared to the yoke of God's total plan, which reflects wisdom's way (11:29f.; 23:34ff.).

These leaders may have stressed observance to God's law as a way of achieving community identity after the fall of Jerusalem. The law would help keep people faithful to Yahweh. In the process of articulating this goal, the leaders' zeal had become restrictive. They were enslaving and binding the community to observe their own subjective interpretations of the law. These "laws" controlled others as they protected the leaders in power. As almost all of chapter twenty-three makes clear, Jesus saves his worst condemnation for those in authority who control others through such legislation. While such interpretations definitely protect human power, positions, and prestige, they may have little to do with the true will of God.

God's reign is not simply a matter of rules and regulations, much less is it anything that reinforces the position of human legislators. "I tell you," Matthew's Jesus warned, especially those in leadership, "unless your holiness surpasses that of the scribes and Pharisees you shall not enter the kingdom of God" (5:20).

In our institutional church, leadership positions have created a new elitist class. Through centuries of councils and catechisms, dogmas and decrees, norms and traditions, the power of the presbyterate can easily identify itself with its source. God's will has often become equated with the will of humans who make the rules. When I was in college, people in charge of the infrastructure that affected my life were part of my Capuchin religious institution. They were socially arranged apart from us. We were students; they were priests. They were the "elites." Having power over us, they could use ideology, or a way of thinking, sociologically speaking, to reinforce their positions of authority by the simple appeal to God's will. Yet, in many concrete situations, such a response could come more from their positions of authority than from authority arising through discernment.

During my senior year in college in Indiana, I repeatedly asked to visit my father, who was slowly dying of heart disease. My well-meaning superiors told me: "It is God's will that you stay here. You can do more good for your father by obeying than in doing what you think is right." At the same time, my Capuchin brother, Dan, was allowed to go home each month from our theologate in Wisconsin. God had a change of will at the Illinois border!

In such situations, authority is often buttressed by the subjective belief that it truly articulates what God wants. Yet to these same situations (which thankfully have disappeared in our province!) Matthew's Jesus says: "Why do you for your part act contrary to the commandment of God for the sake of your 'tradition'? . . . God has said, 'Honor your father and your mother' " (15:3–4).

Many times ideology can be used to protect unjust social arrangements. If God can be made an idol to reinforce those ideologies that legitimize certain actions, so much the better! I am becoming convinced that this is the only way to understand the well-deserved critique of the Scriptures made by those atheists who reject a biblical god who sanctions death, even genocide. *Insight* magazine, a section of the Sunday *Milwaukee Journal* carried a letter to its editor from such an atheist. It stated:

> Later this year our foundation [Freedom from Religion Foundation, Inc.] will be publishing a book called *The Born Again Skeptic's Guide to the Bible*. One chapter of this book is a simple, but chilling, list of the murders committed by, ordered by, or approved by God. This list comes to 10 pages.
>
> It starts with God's killing of the entire population of Earth at the time of Noah, except for eight persons. It continues through the killing by God of every inhabitant of Sodom and Gomorrah and of the surrounding plain, except for Lot's family, which fled. All the firstborn of Egypt, all the hosts of pharaoh, those 3,000 Israelites massacred by the Levite tribe at the command of God for worshiping the golden calf, the Canaanites at Hormah utterly destroyed by the Lord, the Ammonites decimated by the Lord, the Horims slain by God—the list goes on and on.
>
> How, we ask, can any kind and civilized person, whether Christian or Jew, choose to worship a God who is a mass murderer?[1]

An institution can often manufacture a god to reinforce its social arrangements—be they sexism or racism, consumerism or militarism, or whatever "ism"—through its control of ideology. It can maintain its "kingdoms" and its social arrangments without submitting them to the fuller way of wisdom that promotes life and the sharing of resources as God's gift for everyone. For instance, the current discussion about the legitimation of violence seems to have arisen only as the Northern church faced violent reactions to structures of *institutionalized* violence of which it had traditionally been a part. Physical violence, however, cannot be criticized separately from its roots in institutionalized violence.

Defenses and fear often arise when these institutional arrangements and their ideologies are threatened. This subtle control must be faced especially in times of ideological and behavioral transition when an appeal to traditional orthodoxy is used to keep us from orthopraxy. I witnessed an example of this fear at a provincial meeting in 1974.

Our men met at that time to consider ways to better apply the gospel to our world. We committed ourselves to a process of conscientization, which has subsequently helped us promote justice on all levels—individual, interpersonal, and infrastructural. Since we did not know very much about the conscientization process, we decided that an educational process involving all our leaders would be a step in the right direction.

One of the people asked to speak to us was Sister Francis Borgia Rothleuber, then president of the Leadership Conference of Women Religious. She spoke about sexism. She showed how we Capuchins, as well as the church as a whole, were discriminating against women in leadership, liturgy, and even in our very language. When she finished, one of the men was livid.

"What's the matter?" a couple of us asked him.

"It's her talk," he responded. "It's just not true. This idea that God is male/female is just totally untheological. She's just wrong. God *is* male."

"You've got to be kidding!" we said, almost in unison.

"Never! God is male. He is Father; he is Son. That's simple revelation," he countered.

"But," I said, "if God is just Father and Son without being equally Mother and Daughter, there is discrimination in God and that's incompleteness. And God can't be incomplete."

Why was this priest so angry? Was it really because he was that convinced God was male? Or was it because God *had to be male?* Would it be the only way this male cleric could maintain his elite position in this sexist institution? Centuries of ideological reinforcement supported his network of beliefs. Yet, if he had analyzed the way dogmas about God's sexual identity had evolved to become ideology, he would have found that the only persons who had the power to make the declaration at such places as Chalcedon and Nicea were males!

In their effort to articulate the community's historical experience of God, the Council "Fathers" were limited to a culturally and historically conditioned understanding of God. Reflecting within a worldview that did not even consider women to be equal, God had to be seen as male. Maleness was the essence of power, possession, and prestige. Maleness was the peak of perfection understandable at that time. Today, however, when we admit that God's perfection goes beyond sexuality, limiting the full divine reality of God to that human articulation demands that this social sin must be challenged. We must first address the ideology that is reinforced by language and symbols. Language always limits. To use it to help understand reality is one thing; to limit God to its historical delineations is another.

During his short pontificate in 1978, Pope John Paul I said that God is "more" mother than father.[2] Our angry priest would probably not agree with the pope's judgment. What disturbed him was not limiting God to one or the other sex (a human condition, Jesus makes clear in Matthew, which does not adequately reflect the reign of God [19:12, 22, 30]). He was threatened at the point of his male security. He needed this sexist theology to reinforce his position as a male cleric in the church. If God is not limited by sex, then priesthood might not be defined by sex either. If he could see the contradictions in his "orthodoxy," he might develop a new orthopraxy by facing up to the contradiction there is in not having women priests in the institutional Catholic church.

I am sure this priest prayed daily for God's reign (which will have no such distinctions) to come on earth as it is in heaven (5:10). But by refusing to extend priesthood beyond the members of his own group, he is ignoring the contradictions in his church that prevent the coming of this reign.

Distinctions and discrimination may reinforce certain power relationships. Matthew contends, however, that they have little to do with God's true reign.

Finally, the reign of God is not a matter of great religious experience—unless it leads to concern for others beyond the community. Matthew was writing at a time when the wandering charismatics were beginning to wane in numbers and influence; their ability to mislead well-meaning seekers, however, was something he wanted to address. While others had gradually changed their apocalyptic ideology to conform with the eschatological theology of God-with-us-now, some were still expecting a cataclysmic *parousia*. Their expectations were fanned by the false messiahs and false prophets who appeared, performing signs and wonders. This added to their confusion (24:24). Addressing their anxieties, Matthew's Jesus says:

> Be on guard! Let no one mislead you. Many will come attempting to impersonate me. "I am the Messiah!" they will claim, and they will deceive many. You will hear of wars and rumors of wars. Do not be alarmed. Such things are bound to happen, but that is not yet the end. . . . Many will falter then, betraying and hating one another. False prophets will rise in great numbers to mislead many [24:4–6, 10–11].

Matthew addressed this problem of the false prophets in his last discourse. Their influence was also addressed as part of the Sermon on the Mount. The first and last discourse indicate the influence of the wandering charismatics on the community's understanding of spirituality. "None of those who cry out, 'Lord, Lord,' " Jesus says of such people who limit God to their own interpretations, "will enter the kingdom of God but only the one who does the will of my Father in heaven" (7:21). "When that day comes," (and it will come in the 1980s and 1990s whenever charismatic activity does not extend to others who are in need):

> Many will plead with me, "Lord, Lord, have we not prophesied in your name? Have we not exorcised demons by its power? Did we not do many miracles in your name as well?" Then I will declare to them solemnly, "I never knew you. Out of my sight, you evildoers!" [7:22–23].

This "day comes" whenever someone can be heard enthusiastically saying, "Wow, last night at our prayer group we had three prophecies and the power of affirmation by the gathering showed God was with us in a mighty way!" That "day comes" whenever someone stresses deliverance from demonic possession within an individual without wanting to address the demonic possession of the powers and principalities in violent institutions that structurally deny life and, therefore, God. This "day comes" for many people who seek the miracle of personal and interpersonal healing of pains, memories, and relationships without realizing that there is another kind of healing of structures and temples that must take place if the rejected ones of society are to experience God's presence with them (21:14).

Prophecies, exorcisms, and miracles signify the reign of God breaking into the world (12:28). Yet these must be accompanied by a deeper sign: the witness of our lives committed to those in need. Without this witness, we can expect to hear: "I never knew you. Out of my sight, you evildoers!" (7:23). Here and in other places in Matthew, there is no question about the authenticity of the prophecies, the exorcisms, or the miracles done in the name of Jesus. What is rejected is a spirituality that stresses charismatic activity to the exclusion of that ethical obedience which identifies us with the poor and oppressed. This uniting of charismatic activities with ethical obedience to wisdom's way, Matthew implied, earmarks a wholistic approach to authentic spirituality (11:3ff.).

Paradoxically, the other time when people who consider themselves loyal disciples are rejected can be found in the Last Judgment. Toward the end of the Sermon on the Mount, Matthew portrays Jesus rejecting those who do not extend God's reign to those in need. At the conclusion of all his discourses (26:1) Matthew also articulates a spirituality of prayer and ministry, of charismatic activity and ethical obedience, which would enable the members of the church to be recognized as the images of Jesus.

Redefining God's Reign

If once-and-for-all membership, legalistic observances that are ideologically based, and even great religious experiences do not describe the reign of God, how does Matthew describe it? The good news of God's reign that must be proclaimed by words and deeds within all the nations (24:14) is quite simple. It demands that we deeply experience God's presence within us that we might be converted continually to God's authority. In this experience, we understand how God's plan can be extended throughout the world by our good deeds. For Matthew, to come under this reign is to live in wisdom and under its teaching. According to Walter Brueggemann:

> The theology of the wisdom teachers which we have tried to exposit is consistent with the major thrust of Jesus' teaching. The Kingdom of God is, he proclaimed, a realm of wholeness, freedom, responsibility, and security where men can be the men God intends them to be. Indeed, to affirm that we do live in that kind of world is a close approximation of the world in which the wise said we lived. Jesus'

teaching, particularly in Matthew, has remarkable confidence in man's capacity to be free, safe, whole and responsible. He affirms that men are responsible for the future they choose (cf. Matt. 25:31–46). He celebrates man as one who is especially precious and loved (Matt. 6:25–33). His teaching has the same buoyancy, confidence, and openness as that which characterizes wisdom teaching at its best.[3]

What is wisdom's way which enables us to become persons, communities, and institutions under God's reign? Building on what has already been said about Matthew's theology of wisdom, the process of coming under the reign of God involves a total reformation of life. God's reign demands that we submit to the authority of its central purpose. From and in that authority, we then work to make it present in our society, with a willingness to suffer the consequences this might entail.

This process begins with a total reformation, a reversal of anything that is an obstacle to the good news of God's reign. This reversal is *metanoia*, conversion. Both the spirituality of John (3:2) and Jesus (4:17) begin with a platform that demands reformation for everyone hearing the good news. "Reform your lives, the reign of God is at hand." To enable this power to be at work in our lives today also demands a *metanoia*. It necessitates a reversal of all values and behavior.

The "kingdom of heaven" and "God's reign" are euphemistic ways of referring to the dynamic of the relationship we have with God, which enables us to accomplish what God wills. The will of God, the name of God, the dynamic of God, the presence of God essentially mean the same thing: the reign. To be part of that reign means to enter a process of continual evangelization, the dynamic of continually experiencing conversion. A person living in that reign accepts the fact that faith can never be presumed. There is always a need to deepen that personal experience of and relationship with God which unceasingly invites us to continual evangelization. Becoming a person under that power will continually entail a process of becoming more and more one who shares in the perfection of God.

The authority and reign of God's saving presence, for Matthew, was present in Jesus' person and deeds. One of the signs of God's messianic presence breaking into history was to be the forgiveness of sins. The name given to Mary's son established his identity as this saving authority of God, inaugurating God's reign of salvation: "She is to have a son and you are to name him Jesus because he will save his people from their sins" (1:21). Because the name indicates the person's totality (identity and actions), so in the person of Jesus, sin is forgiven. Jesus takes away the sin. He forgives it. He has authority over sin, a power given God alone (9:6; 21:23–27).

In times past, God had once seen the needs of the people, cared about them, and announced their deliverance from all forms of oppression, including sin (Exod. 3:7–8). Israel's deliverance revealed that the liberation of people was a sign of God's presence (Exod. 3:12). This freedom was indicative of the authority of the very name Yahweh, which represented the fulness of liberation (Exod. 3:13–14). Realizing the central importance of this historical fact in the religious experience of his hearers, Matthew saw in Jesus' authority the continuation of this good news for the world. All this happened to fulfill what the Lord has said through the prophet:

> "The virgin shall be with child and give birth to a son, and they shall call him Emmanuel," a name which means "God is with us." (1:22–23).

Matthew makes it clear that the definitive reign of God was not just God working *through* Jesus. He *was* God's authoritative presence with the people. In Jesus, God inaugurated a new dimension of the divine presence throughout history (1:1–17). In his person Jesus was the manifestation of what it means to be a person under God's rule. In three ways he showed by his deeds his submission to this authority and its resulting power over him and over creation: teaching (acting), preaching, and healing the people of every kind of disease and illness (4:23).

In various ways, the Jews had come to expect God's reign to break into their history in such a manner that a radical reordering of all structures of society and its institutions would take place. While Jesus' deeds evidenced this reordering, the Jews and members of the early community were so controlled by their previously conceived ideologies about the messiah and the coming of God's reign that they were quite unable to recognize it in their midst when the signs surrounded them (16:1–4).

Both his contemporaries and Jesus had the same goal; the means of achieving this goal were different. Jesus showed the need to change ideologies about those means if the authority of the reign of God were to break into their lives.

Since God's plan was essentially related to the inclusion of those very people ideologically excluded by society, the means Jesus used to accomplish this—his nonviolent norms, which were part of his teaching, his invitation to conversion through his preaching, and his restoration to health of those who were broken in themselves and society—brought him into conflict with the authority figures of his era (21:15f.). This same rejection still happens when nonviolent measures are taken to reorder patterns of society which deny the dignity of whole groups of people and leave them systemically without resources. Reacting in nonviolence to this structural violence will find many who are the beneficiaries of the structural injustice which leads to violence saying: "I agree with your ends, but not your means."

I realized the "that man is you" dimension of this approach during the late sixties and early seventies when I found myself among the many people who questioned the nonviolent marches James Groppi was leading for open housing in Milwaukee. He and many in the community had come to realize that this was the only way to bring about institutional change. They were forced to march. Yet I found myself saying "I agree with their goals, but I don't agree with their means." Further social analysis convinced me that there were no other means available to change an intransigent institution. I realized that the means used by the infrastructure in the name of "community order" and "security" were perpetuating a form of institutionalized violence. This deeper violence was the real obstruction to the reordering of society. Yet the established order proclaimed its goal to be the same as that of the people who found themselves outside the mainstream of society!

Concerned with the earth's need to experience God's good deeds in every person, Jesus "continued his tour of all the towns and villages." He used his authority to manifest this new reign of God by his deeds. Thus he "taught in their synagogues, he proclaimed the good news of God's reign and he cured every sickness and disease" (9:35).

Since there were so many people who longed to experience the authoritative presence of that new way, Jesus could not limit the manifestation of that authority to his own ministry. God had seen the affliction of the people and delivered them through that authoritative presence which was shared with Moses and the elders. Now seeing that affliction in new forms, Matthew presents Jesus extending that care of God through his disciples.

> At the sight of the crowds, his heart was moved with pity. They were lying prostrate from exhaustion, like sheep without a shepherd. He said to his disciples: "The harvest is good but laborers are scarce. Beg the harvest master to send out laborers to gather his harvest" [9:36–38].

Jesus was aware of the need to multiply his efforts. He also knew that his use of authority and means of bringing about the reign of God on earth would result in the "authority" of the "kingdom" coming to bear upon him through persecution. Consequently, Jesus called together his disciples (4:18–22) ". . . and gave them authority to expel unclean spirits and to cure sickness and disease of every kind" (10:1). Finally, with the full authority of the resurrection, he extended this authority to us. Now our mission is to bring about God's reign in those areas of society entrusted to us (28:16–20).

One of the longest passages of the mission discourse involves the theme of persecution. Evidently, Matthew elaborated on this theme because of those internal and external divisions and rejections that reflected the existential experience of the community. In 10:11–42, and especially in 10:16–39, Matthew outlines the consequences of this spirituality for his community's members. Jesus' words identify their society's own acceptance or rejection of their authority with Jesus' own experience (10:24–25, 40–42). Perhaps the reason for such a stress was the fact that commitment to live under the authority of God's rule was bringing many in the community more and more into conflict with the authority of society's powerful people.

Authority in the World's Rule and God's Reign

To understand how this first beatitude can be concretized in our own experience today, we must investigate the authority or central project of our society. Such an examination will help determine where our society does or does not reflect God's authority. We must live under either God's authority or society's (6:24), willing to accept the rewards of the authority we choose as well as rejections of the opposite authority. One power or authority excludes the other (see 6:24).

How is authority or power itself exercised? Power, biblically defined, means reform of mind and behavior (3:2; 4:17; 28:20). It is the ability to influence change. Traditionally, power's operation or effectiveness has been exercised through education, coercion, or persuasion. People are led to see (either rightly or wrongly) that something is good for them to be or do; this is education. They can be forced (legally or illegally) to do something that results in rewards or sanctions; this is coercion. Finally, they can be inspired (overtly or covertly) to accept a way of life; this is persuasion. Power can be granted by some to others. It can be taken by some from others. It can be nonviolent or manipulative, liberating or exploitative. Its control can be founded in truth as well as in the distortion of truth.

How is authority exercised in the United States? According to Charles Lindblom, Sterling Professor of Economics and Political Science at Yale:

> One can use each of such diverse controls as indoctrination, legal and illegal threat of deprivation, offer or benefit, and persuasion, including deceit, to control another person either directly or by the indirect route of inducing him to grant authority to the controller, that is, to give permission, to accept a rule of obedience. Every specific control can be *used either as a method of direct control or as a method for establishing a rule of obedience (authority) which, once established, itself suffices for control as long as it stands.* And existing authority can assign new authority.[4]

The political economy exercises its control through the media, education, and various forms of pressure. Specifically it uses a form of persuasion that leads people to believe they are free, but which effectively brings them under its power. Such persuasion, according to Lindblom,

> . . . is a ubiquitous form of social control and is of special importance in the analysis of politico-economic systems on three counts. In the form of ideological instruction and propaganda, persuasion is a major method of elite control of the masses, much more so in communist systems than in liberal democratic ones. In the form of commercial advertising, it is a major instrument of corporate control of masses of

consumers in market societies. In the form of mutual persuasion in "free" societies—that is in the form of "free competition of ideas"—it is fundamental to liberal democracy.[5]

Advertising is a way of persuading the masses to submit to the goals of elites. The elites are no longer limited only to individuals. They are found among oligopolistic forces which alone have the financial resources to have access to the minds of the masses.[6]

The rise of this corporate class has created a phenomenon not envisioned by Adam Smith. People no longer directly sell their labor or other resources for what they want to buy. Now, selling and buying finds people entering labor and other factor markets to sell their work and resources for money. With this money they can enter a second set of markets— the consumer market—to sell that money in exchange for goods and services.

In both the labor and consumer markets, people face another market of huge proportions—the business market. Representing itself in the form of large financial and industrial corporations, business presides over the whole market system. Within this third set of markets, the business enterprises buy and sell with each other, often to the exclusion of smaller buyers and sellers, even as they tell these same people through multi-million dollar advertising barrages that "we do it all for you"! Meanwhile, among these emerging giants, Adam Smith's invisible hand shows itself in the form of joint ventures, trusts, mergers, and holding companies. Managers seek to regulate production among themselves as they have already regulated it within each of their companies.

In addition, no longer is the process limited to one or another nation. The pattern is global, with multinational corporations in capitalistic countries relating to similar enterprises from centrally planned economies in a way that benefits both to the detriment of the poor and helpless nations of the Third World and the majority of their citizens. As a 1979 front-page article in *The Wall Street Journal* noted: "In many nations beset by widespread poverty, investment and trade by multinationals has done little to create jobs. There is even evidence that foreign investment, along with unenlightened government policies, has done just the opposite: make jobs disappear." In the case of Indonesia, the article continued: "All of this has brought benefits. A few Indonesians have gotten very rich. Multinationals got a 56% return on investment in 1977. . . . But the poorest Indonesians aren't any better off than they were a decade ago. Some are worse off."[7] "To the man" (individual, group, or nation) "who has, more will be given until he grows rich; the man who has not, will lose what little he has" (13:12). Often too, multinational corporations make alliances with elites in developing nations who are closely allied with the military, if not the military itself. In a more recent front-page article on Indonesia, *The Wall Street Journal* noted:

The military elite, along with its bureaucratic and business associates, gets many of the choice concessions, contracts and licenses. Projects opposed by the country's development experts are often approved anyway, and, at least partly as a result, the gap between the rich and poor is widening. . . . Richard Robison, an Australian academic who first documented the military's complex connections two years ago, sees the pattern repeated in many of the military-dominated countries of Asia and Latin America. "The spread of capitalism," he says, "hasn't been accompanied by the emergence of liberal democratic bourgeois states."[8]

Having the power to control communications effectively, the inner logic of these huge multinational institutions affects life and even national security here and abroad. They must work to bring as many people as possible under their influence. Personal values give way to public values; public values are geared to the one goal of the market.

The ethical consequences of this reality are mind-boggling, for most multinationals are headquartered in First World nations. As Gregory Baum has written:

The production and distribution of goods in our society follow the laws of the market. It is wholly illusory to think that Christian values can be inserted into this process. Of course, the market system has been modified, but the major pressure on it comes from monopolies and the coordination of various types of production in the same giant corporations. These corporations often control the market and determine the price they demand for their goods. The free market becomes an illusion here. Already in 1931, Pope Pius XI wrote the startling sentence: "Free enterprise has committed suicide; economic dictatorship has taken its place." The free enterprise system is still praised by the chambers of commerce in our society, but in fact the market is largely under the control of the giant corporations, and they, following the law of increasing profit, make decisions regarding the production and consumption of goods in accordance with their own rational interests. We now have a market that is largely controlled, but the logic of this control remains profit and competition, even though on a higher organizational level. The public values remain the same.[9]

In addition, the corporation is able to control effectively, or have authority, over governments. Thus, when an industry becomes oligopolistic (three or four companies with 50 percent of an industry's market share), the government itself must submit to its power, as both Britain and the United States learned when dealing with Chrysler. Furthermore, the corporation is able to get support from the people by effectively controlling the dissemination of ideas and products through its influence on the media. As a result, according to Lindblom:

> It is possible that the rise of the corporation has offset or more than offset the decline of class as an instrument of indoctrination. That the corporation is a powerful instrument for indoctrination we have documented earlier. That it has risen to prominence in society as class lines have muted is clear enough. That it creates a new core of wealth and power for a newly constructed upper class, as well as an overpowering loud voice, is also reasonably clear. The executive of the large corporation is, on many counts, the contemporary counter-part to the landed gentry of an earlier era, his voice amplified by the technology of mass communication. A single corporate voice on television, it has been estimated, can reach more minds in one evening than were reached from all the platforms of all the world's meetings in the course of several centuries preceding broadcasting. More than class, the major specific institutional barrier to fuller democracy may therefore be the autonomy of the private corporation.[10]

The authority thus exercised by the corporation enables it to buy and sell the very lives and destinies of whole societies of people. With very few other institutions able to pay $250,000 to produce a single commercial and upwards of $500,000 for a single 60-second airing, only certain corporations can survive. By spending twice as much as its competitors in advertising dollars per barrel for its newly acquired Miller Brewing Company, and by writing off its losses through tax breaks, Phillip Morris was able to increase Miller's market share from 4 percent in 1972 to 25 percent in 1980. It could spend over a quarter of a billion dollars in 1980 for advertising, a large part of which was Miller's. Meanwhile, one independent brewery after another failed—due in large part to their inability to approach the consumer through the media. During this time the same approach enabled the brewery industry as a whole to become more and more oligopolistic. The number of breweries dropped from around 100 to about 40, with the top five having over 70 percent of the market, a 100 percent increase since 1965.

The Conflict between Two Authorities over Their Central Projects

With large sums of money enabling access to the media only for the rich, the corporation is able to promote its specific institutional ends through the manipulation of peoples' fears, anxieties, guilt, and need for security. It replaces a personalistic-self, serving others, with a commodity-self, served by the production of consumer goods. This, then, represents an authority that can educate, coerce, and persuade the society to give its life to attain this "kingdom." It represents the central project of our nation.

According to James P. Gannon, formerly of *The Wall Street Journal* and

now editor of the Des Moines *Register,* this authority over peoples' lives
solidifies the central project of the political economy:

> And what is the central project? Well, if a lunar tribe sent a spaceship
> down to the earth to find out what those Americans are up to, (Colum-
> bia University's Amital W. Etzioni) explained, the moonmen would
> return home to report that the central project of the U.S. society seems
> to be the production of resources during working hours and the con-
> sumption and destruction of them in leisure time.
>
> In other words, we Americans work hard so that we can play hard:
> earning more to spend more, driving ourselves so we can drive our cars,
> producing and consuming in an ever-intensifying cycle that keeps
> gobbling up a growing portion of the earth's limited resources.
>
> It wasn't always thus, the professor reminds us. Other societies had
> other central projects. Ancient Sparta made war its central project.
> Some medieval societies ordered their activities around the cultivation
> of the arts and learning. In the golden age of Greece, politics was the
> central project.
>
> What's different now is that the central project involves the masses,
> whereas in the past perhaps 2 percent of the society was directly
> involved in the central pursuit while the masses subsisted as serfs. Now,
> we are all out there producing and consuming hard every day, execu-
> tives and steelworkers alike, doing the proper American thing of filling
> our production quotas and sales goals so that we can fill our gas tanks,
> vacation homes and two-car garages.
>
> History has never known another central project so demanding of
> energy resources. "The main question for the future," says the
> Columbia professor, "is whether we will go on with the production-
> consumption project."[11]

This central project of the American society is found in the market
economy which seeks new markets and "finds" them in the people, who then
can be "sold" by "buying into" that production-consumer project. Paradoxically this was already unconsciously realized by Jesus in Matthew's Sermon
on the Mount. Seeking to bring his hearers under his authority rather than
society's, Jesus said:

> Stop worrying, then, over questions like, "What are we to eat, or what
> are we to drink, or what are we to wear?" The unbelievers are always
> running after these things. Your heavenly Father knows all that you
> need. Seek first his kingship over you, his way of holiness, and all these
> things will be given you besides (6:31–33).

We have already seen that the authority of the political economy has its
influence over people through a process of the market wherein the steps of

seeking and finding, selling and buying take place. These same processes Jesus outlines as steps for becoming a person under the authority of God's rule.

According to Dominic Crossan, the parables of Jesus describe the dynamic of the reign of God. The process of entering this reign, or submitting to its authority, can be summarized in the seeking-finding-selling-buying steps of Matthew 13:44–46:[12]

> The reign of God is like a buried treasure which a man found in a field. He hid it again, and rejoicing at his find went and sold all he had and bought that field. Or again the kingdom of heaven is like a merchant's search for fine pearls. When he found one really valuable pearl, he went back and put up for sale all that he had and bought it.

Not understanding the central projects of this particular world and Matthew's particular world, biblical spirituality will remain otherworldly as well as unbiblical. Matthew offers a theology about life that affirms the dignity of each person as an image of God in a world that proclaims that the dignity of each person is imaged in commodities. If we remain unaware of this contradiction, our spirituality will never recognize the need to examine those structures that perpetuate such inauthentic human existence. Yet, with so many of us among those who now are "always running after these things" (6:32), spirituality (as John and Jesus showed) must first direct its efforts at the false ideology of consumerism. In the challenge, a change of persuasion might bring about new loyalty on behalf of God's reign (3:2; 4:17).

Consumerism has become the new authority infecting every element of our individual and group lives. It has become the underlying base, the network that touches each individual, family, and community. As the central project of this infrastructure, it is reinforced by an ideology through the persuasion of mass media advertising in such a way that individuals and families are valued only in light of the central project. A few years ago I shared my concern with Henry Duncombe, then an international vice president and chief economist for General Motors. The gist of the conversation was as follows:

> "When I go to meetings in New York," I said, "I often stay at one of our Eastern Province's parishes on the lower east side of Manhattan. As I walk there from the Delancey Street subway stop, six blocks away, I get the feeling that the thousands of people in that neighborhood don't really matter to our corporate world, especially a corporation like General Motors. Is this the case?" I asked.
>
> "Well, Mike," he responded, "I hate to say it, but this is the only way it can be. We can't be concerned about them because they are outside our market projections."

"Well, then, Henry," I could only say, "this is where our plans for society and yours will always differ. Every person is equally significant in God's eyes."

When people are reduced to market projections, they become commodified. They are part of quotas to be met and objects to be sold as an ad by the *San Jose Mercury/News* unwittingly made clear in that "bible" of the advertising market, *Advertising Age*: "Fifty miles out of San Francisco, people have more to spend than anywhere else in California." Then, in inch-and-one-half letters, it boldly urged: "BUY THEM."[13]

Today, in a manner never dreamed of by Matthew, people exist to keep the central project alive. Chairs of Economics in our Catholic colleges and Praise the Lord Clubs to the contrary, this is not the way Adam Smith originally envisioned our economic system. The whole purpose, or central project, of the economic institution and of production, he said, was to satisfy the needs of the consumer. The economy existed for the sake of the people. However, as this economic system became more concentrated, it also became a political economy. More and more, with the growing concentration of wealth in the form of power, possessions, and the ability to affect legislation that reinforces that position and ideology, we no longer can legitimate our political economy by saying production satisfies the needs of the consumer. Now the consumer exists to satisfy the needs of the producer.

A new authority exists wherein people can be bought and sold in the global market place. The producer becomes the consumer; the instrument of control becomes the media, especially television. As the United States Catholic Conference's Administrative Board stated in 1975:

What American commercial television is all about is not primarily either information or entertainment, either news or culture. . . . Its primary objective is to create a meeting place for consumers and advertisers. American television is essentially concerned with the sale of consumers to advertisers.[14]

Those now consumed are the people. The identity of the masses is no longer linked to wisdom's way of life wherein people are affirmed as images of God. Now they are controlled by the Madison Avenue image of the commodified self. They became resources, or market shares, to be exploited.

One might ask, "What has this got to do with the authority of the reign of God?" Simply stated: the central project of our nation, as articulated by *The Wall Street Journal*, is presenting us with a clear structural analysis of the society in which we are to witness to a biblically based spirituality. We have been told to go into the whole world (20:19) proclaiming the authority of the central project of the gospel. If our spirituality witnesses to the authority of God's reign in our lives, it has to address the false ideologies of the central project of our society or it represents infidelity to its very commission. I once had an occasion to address the creators and disseminators of this ideology when I was asked to speak before a section of the American Marketing Association. I chose this forum to discuss the awesome power its members possessed to create perceptions about life and to create needs in people. I wanted to show that such authority bears concomitant responsibility to make sure people are not misled regarding ideas, goods, or services. So I began by addressing the phenomenon of corporate image advertising or idea advertising. Having successfully sued in court to remain "individual entities" (as our Constitution determines, thus making Exxon Corporation equal to you, the reader!), corporations were spending millions of dollars promoting their worldview so others might be influenced by their authoritative argumentation. With such power they could say the energy problem is not really so or, if it is so, then it can only be tackled in such and such a way. And why should we believe? Simply because of corporate care: "We want you to know."

When an institution has the financial resources to discuss the social arrangements of our nation through the power of the media, it can influence individuals and groups to start thinking a certain way. Meanwhile, others of opposing persuasions lack similar resources to get their views across to the public. Their only resort will be to use other means, such as press conferences, letters to editors, demonstrations, etc. And, while the former method effectively gets its way even at the expense of the nation as a whole, as was witnessed by actions of many energy companies in 1979,[15] those who are left with only alternative means are considered to be against the "system"!

Protected by such a public ideology, a company like Mobil can spend millions of dollars in idea advertising. I used Mobil as a case study for the American Marketing Association members because at that time it was the largest spender of corporate dollars for this form of mass media marketing: $12 million a year. The goal of such advertising, in the words of Mobil's media expert, is: "We want others to see Mobil as we do."[16] If individuals and groups targeted by Mobil could remain under the influence of Mobil, they would see the world as Mobil wants. Meanwhile, they could be blinded to the gospel approach (cf. 13:15). They would thus continue in their ways, living by the dogmas of the media experts, the blind led by the blind (cf. 15:14).

Whoever has money enough to make dogmatic pronouncements in *The Wall Street Journal*, *The New York Times*, and the Sunday rotogravure sections, also has the power to define reality and to create it. You can mold society's social arrangements according to your own ideologies, I concluded.

Next I addressed the power of advertisers to reinforce the central project of consumerism through product advertisement. As I used Mobil to showcase the negative effect of idea advertising in our market economy, I used Nestlé and the American infant formula oligopoly of Abbott, Bristol Myers, and American Home Products to highlight some negative effects of product advertising. Their advertising was used to reinforce the social arrangement of consumerism in the Third World by the sale of infant formula. It had to seek and find ways to control the peoples' perceptions so that, having "sold" them on the need, their product would be purchased. Market share was at stake. Thus, even at the height of the infant formula controversy (1978), Keith V. Monk, the manager of Nestlé's Advertising and Sales Promotion Service, would give a talk at *Advertising Ages*'s "EurAm3" in Paris, entitled: "Battle for the Consumer's Mind and Pocketbook."

As markets stagnated in North America and Western Europe partially due to declining birthrates and increased breastfeeding, the infant formula companies began the process of seeking and finding new markets. As global companies, the world could become the market; thus they discovered a new source of sales in the Third World. Usually making contracts with the elites in these developing nations, an infrastructure was created: the global corporations persuaded the masses to purchase a new consumer item through various forms of ideology. These included free samples, mass media, and encouragement from medical personnel. The only problem was that—except for the small percentage of those with sick babies and those who could not breastfeed—those who were "sold" on this new product neither needed it nor could afford to buy it.

For instance, I visited Managua, Nicaragua, in November 1977, and purchased a can of infant formula from each of the U.S. companies represented there. The price averaged 15–20 cordobas or, roughly, $2.50. Two cans a week would demand an outlay of $5.00. If you multiply this by the number of weeks before a baby is weaned, the figure approximates $150—the median yearly income per person in Nicaragua at that time!

After explaining this, a dialog began between the AMA members and myself:

"Such an example shows that you are not responding to the needs of individuals and groups," I said. "You are creating those needs." "And," I continued, "that's the problem I have with your part in our market economy. In order for you to survive people have to be sold on products which, in some cases, can have a devastating effect on their whole lives."

"Well," someone said, "that's just an isolated example."

"In no way," I countered. "It's really just one example of the underlying dynamic used by the market in this country, and the rest of the world."

"That's not true," they insisted. "We do not create needs or false needs. The people are too smart. Sooner or later the market will find any such useless items disappearing."

As the meeting degenerated into claims and counterclaims, I said, "Okay, let's not argue; just let me explain what I'm trying to say."

At that I told these young executives about a shopping trip I took with my brother Pat and my nephew Craig. Craig was then in kindergarten, which is about second-shelf, eye-level in the supermarket. We were in the supermarket's cereal section. Here, good audience analysis would tell you, Craig

Crosby, Pat (and Carol) Crosby, and the cereal oligopoly came together for a spontaneous meeting in the aisle. As we walked, Craig spotted the sugar-coated cereals, pointed to one, and said, "Daddy, buy me that."

What guided Craig's choice?

The advertisers knew, for they are paid to understand what motivates such a little mind and how to touch it. Craig was influenced by the ideology of advertising. It was saying something like: "My Daddy loves me. My Daddy wants good things for me. I know 'Lucky Crisps' are good for me, so Daddy will want to get them for me because he loves me."

Pat, however, didn't realize the power of those other forces trying to take authority not only over Craig's mind, but over both their behaviors. So he nonchalantly responded, "No, Craig, that isn't good for you."

What now faced Craig was not so much that his Daddy would not buy him the cereal; his *Daddy did not love him* anymore. And Pat would be the first to wonder why his logical response would elicit tears or a pout from Craig.

At that point, I said: "Pat, look what's going on here." Then, taking Craig by the hand, we went down that aisle. We stopped at the stations inviting consumer loyalty from four-and-five-year-olds. We noted all the products at the eye level of youngsters. "Look," I said as I pointed to one after the other; "Pat, those cereal companies don't give a damn about Craig or you. They're even willing to use Craig against you. And don't think it's limited just to their cereal advertisement!"

Hearing this example, those who were the controllers of the ideologies through the media—the advertising authorities—no longer were defending their occupations; they had become the Pat and Carol Crosby's. Where earlier their hostility could have been cut with a knife, it dissipated as they reflected on their own supermarket journeys. They, too, had to shop in the local supermarket oligopolies who served other oligopolies (from soap and snacks to lamp bulbs and laundry detergent) in the name of consumer choice. They and their children were also part of that network. It controlled them, its creators and defenders. The gods of their hands had enslaved them as well.

When resources become an end in themselves, when the goods of the earth take control over the people of the earth, images of God have become slaves of idols. This is idolatry.

In face of the institutions that seduce us to serve the god of the brand name, idolatry must be resisted under the name of another authority. Once under this saving authority of Jesus' name, we enter the process of making God's reign the central dynamic of our lives as individuals, communities, and institutions.

Entering God's Reign by the Way of Perfection

Matthew articulated the process of living under the authority of God's reign through the literary form of the parables. He portrayed Jesus offering the parables to those willing to be freed from the infrastructure's ideologies, which closed the people's eyes and ears and made their hearts sluggish (13:15). This process of turning our lives over to the power of God and coming under its life-giving influence involves the dynamic of seeking and finding the reign of God's presence, selling or reversing whatever creates an obstacle or stumbling block to that presence, and buying into a beatitudinal way of living that signifies our acceptance of this new authority.

This process of entering God's reign will never be possible without going through each of the following steps. The process begins with seeking and finding, experiencing the living God in such a powerful way that God's authority is desired above all. But like the mustard seed (13:31–32) and the leaven (13:33), we cannot control its presence in our lives. We merely submit to its hidden and powerful dynamic. Such growth in wanting to seek God's reign takes time. It demands the soil of reflection and the ingredients of purity of heart.

Once discovered, the reign of God demands a reversal of any thinking or acting that does not reflect God's purposes. This reign of God's purpose is always identified with the dignity of each person made in God's image, and the need for all people to share in the goods of this earth. However, we live in a society whose behavior—if not its stated values—reinforces exactly the opposite. Where once we may have been part of a society with certain attitudes toward almsgiving (6:1–4), prayer and fasting (6:5–18), or even authority itself (20:20–28), living under the ethic of God's reign calls for conversion and reversal.

As his community grappled with the contradictions of living gospel spirituality in an increasingly affluent and urbanized situation, Matthew was saying, in effect: "God's reign and submission to its authority demands for all its disciples not just a commitment of words, but a willingness to bear a cost through behavioral and relational change." The issue then, as now, is: which central project will exercise its authority over us? As Pope John Paul II (then Karol Cardinal Wojtyla) said when he visited the United States in 1976:

> We are now standing in the face of the greatest historical confrontation humanity has gone through. I do not think that wide circles of the American society or wide circles of the Christian community realize this fully. We are now facing the final confrontation between the Church and the anti-Church, of the Gospel versus the anti-Gospel. This confrontation lies within the plans of divine Providence.[17]

Matthew was not willing to mitigate the demands of true biblical spirituality to win his contemporaries' favor. Insisting that spirituality must address his society's changed, more affluent situation, he alone, of all the synoptic writers, used the word *teleios*, or perfection. *Teleios* relates to the completion or the reaching of a goal. *Teleios* was the goal of the spiritual life, which reflected the breaking into history of a new age and style of life. Those who wholeheartedly entered the process of abandonment—totally obedient and completely dedicated to God—would be perfected *(teleioi)*.

The first two of the three times Matthew used *teleios* can be found at the end of the antithesis statements, which challenged a purely legalistic approach to spirituality (5:21–45). Inviting his hearers to develop a spirituality that would set them apart from society (5:46–47), he presents Jesus issuing a new command that involves cost: "In a word, you must be made perfect *(teleioi)* as your heavenly Father is perfect *(teleios)*" (5:48).

In the past, retreat directors and spiritual writers let us off the hook of costly discipleship by telling us, "We can't be as perfect as our heavenly Father is perfect; that isn't what the passage means." However, contemporary exegesis indicates that Jesus was not asking the impossible when he issued this evangelical command. It also shows that this passage does not allow us to think that we can enter some sort of once-and-for-all state of perfection setting us apart from our society. Matthew shows that our share in the perfection of God is both possibility and process.

First of all, it is possible to be made perfect in the way that God is perfect. God's plan for perfection revealed that everyone is an image of God able to share in the earth's resources. Hebrews also says that Jesus was perfected through his submission to God's plan, becoming the power of eternal salvation to those who identify with his pattern of submission (Heb. 9:8–9). So, whoever lives under this authority of God's reign is also "made perfect" in the way Jesus revealed perfection to be manifest. Becoming perfect as God is perfect is impossible on our own. Sharing in the *exousia*—in the authority of God's Spirit who makes all things possible—enables Jesus' words to become a realizable goal.

Secondly, Matthew showed that the word *teleios* reflects that process by which we can become people living in God's reign. Within such a dynamic we are able to reflect, as closely as possible, God's presence, reign, and perfection within an affluent society. Jesus addresses the young man with many possessions: "If you seek perfection *(teleios)*, go, sell your possessions, and give to the poor. You will then have treasure in heaven. Afterward come back and follow me" (19:21). As such, the young man becomes representative of any person, group, or institution honestly wanting to live discipleship in any nation of wealth.

Just as the central project of our nation consists in seeking and finding, selling and buying, and just as the parables showed that the central project of God's reign consists in seeking and finding, selling and buying, so Jesus directly challenges the dynamic of society's reign with his own way of perfection. This too consists of seeking and finding, selling and buying!

Trying to live under the reign of perfection is at the core of the message of the Gospel. According to Donald Senior:

Israel was called to be "holy as your God is holy" (Lev. 19:2). The Christian community, and the individuals who make it up, stand under the same call (5:48). For Matthew (again in concert with all of the New Testament), that call to align one's life with God—to be "holy"—is illustrated in the person and mission of Jesus. Jesus not only reveals God (11:27) but in that very act reveals the true nature of the human person. Here again, the Kingdom motif is at work. To accept the rule of God means conversion to authentic and responsible human existence. The Matthean Jesus consistently links announcement of the Kingdom to the call for conversion of life: one must repent (4:17), one must sell all to purchase the Kingdom's pearl (13:45), one must let go of other treasures to buy the field in which the treasure of the Kingdom is buried (13:44), the dead must be abandoned for the way of life (8:22), entangling riches must be given away to free one for the way of discipleship (19:21).[18]

The possibility and process of perfection are realizable through the experience of God's presence within us which enables us to seek and find, sell and buy.

The only additional comment Matthew's Jesus makes to the young man (a symbol of the church as it grew in affluence) was the phrase about giving possessions to the poor.

Possessions, the wealth we have in the form of power, property, and prestige, are to be used to reverse those conditions of poverty in the world that most contradict the breaking in of the reign of God. This contradiction denies God's image in the poor who lack resources. However, once this reversal takes place in converted hearts and converted communities, which have found the joy of living under a new authority, an automatic experience of God's reigning presence is revealed. "You will *then* have treasure in heaven" (19:21). Having treasure in heaven is predicated on making the good news of that reign come first to the poor in the way Jesus made it present to them.

Aware that societal controls keep this essential requirement of authentic spirituality from occurring in our lives, Matthew's Jesus lets us know that he, too, realizes the problem we face. "I assure you, only with difficulty will a rich man [group or nation] enter into the kingdom of God" (19:23). To convert to God's reign is difficult indeed.

We live in a society in which people can easily convert from a gas range to a microwave oven. They have sought and found a new mode of living. We are willing to sell many things so that we can buy into new forms of eating, recreating, living, driving, etc., because we have found them to be more meaningful or valuable. Each one of these actions reflects an economic conversion, which puts us under the authority of the central project of our society. We seek and find something new: a product, a house, a job, we sell what we have so we can buy it. This dynamic of selling and buying represents the central project of the gospel as well. The good news about this reign of God demands an equal conversion. Why is this conversion so much more difficult? To me, it can only be realized when we find God's power to be more significant than society's. Until we *experience* the face of God, becoming contemplatives and radically rooted in faith, keeping our eyes fixed on God and experiencing God's *exousia*, we will be unable to sell anything; we simply will have not yet found true life and wisdom.

Failing to live in *exousia*, we have tried to develop a spirituality that somehow does not invite us to give up anything of our individual, interpersonal, or infrastructural power, possessions, and prestige to the poor, even as we continue to "go to church" and say "Lord, Lord" (see 7:22).

This spirituality, which talks much about the word of God but does not incarnate it in the concrete world, was illustrated for me in late 1979 in a talk given by a young Jesuit priest from India. As long as he articulated a spirituality making Jesus his personal savior, he was strongly affirmed by the audience. But whenever he spoke of God's demands on us vis-à-vis the poor (11:2ff.), there was dead silence.

The silence with which a previously enthusiastic crowd in Yankee Stadium greeted Pope John Paul II's words in late 1979 points to the same. In the United States, we are not accustomed to applying the Scriptures to all levels of life, especially the structural arrangements. Yet this must be done, as the Pope indicated: "Within the framework of your national institutions . . . you will also want to seek out the structural reasons which foster and cause the different forms of poverty in the world and in your own country."[19]

With great difficulty will the church in the United States enter the reign of God. We seem unable to give anything of our power, possessions, and prestige to those most in need. So we are not yet a people under God's reign. We do not yet have enough leaders in the church who, from the depth of their faith experience, can speak with authority and invite others to this costly commitment of discipleship. We have not yet sold very much. Those of us in leadership seem too much in need of power, possessions, and society's prestige. But into this very situation, into our communities and families, into our individual lives, Jesus' invitation again can offer us a new kind of security: "Your heavenly Father knows all that you need. Seek first his kingship over you, his way of holiness, and all these things will be given you besides. Enough, then, of worrying about tomorrow. Let tomorrow take care of itself. Today has troubles enough of its own" (6:32–34).

CHAPTER THREE

Blessed Are the Poor in Spirit

What Poor in Spirit Is Not

Matthew's beatitudes were first fulfilled in the life of Jesus. Matthew's theology or Gospel of Jesus was to be translated into the lived witness or spirituality of the church. Consequently, to understand what it means to be poor in spirit in the church, we must first examine Matthew's articulation of how Jesus fulfilled and preached poverty of spirit.

For the author of the First Gospel, poverty in spirit is not based on a dualistic approach to human beings. Present poverty is not sanctioned in light of a future reward. Such a poor-now/rich-later approach is rejected by Matthew, especially in light of his extensive discussion of the final judgment (25:31–46). Here any future share in heaven is equated precisely with our ongoing effort to alleviate various forms of poverty.

In no way does this beatitude reinforce a concept that says it is God's will that there be poverty. On the contrary, poverty is a sign that God's plan is not being fulfilled. Therefore, if the reign of God is to have any impact on the world today, it has to be constituted of people striving to reflect God's perfection. It needs to be comprised of those who try to reverse the conditions of poverty.

The reign of God is composed of people who "sell" their power, possessions, and prestige in such a manner that they enable conditions of powerlessness, poverty, and depression in others to be alleviated. Whoever lives within God's reign is undoing pain and suffering through preaching, healing, and teaching, with the person, group, or institution inviting others to join in this process as well. Such a norm or ethic represents the style of that resurrection-person who, under the authority of God, is committed to accomplishing the divine plan for the world. We are to create on earth a world which reflects the reign of God in heaven (cf. 6:10).

Next, this beatitude does not say you can be unconcerned about external

49

riches as long as you have some sort of "inner poverty." Nowhere can such a rationalization be found in Matthew's Gospel. The rich young man who sought perfection (19:21), went away sad; he was unable to be converted from his lifestyle. By not sharing his resources with the poor, he remained under the control of the main obstacle (6:24) to that perfection demanded of disciples (5:48). The rich young man typifies everyone with wealth who refuses to be converted.

Noting the young man's inability to change his lifestyle, Matthew applied Jesus' saying to all those who refuse to share their wealth with those in need: "I assure you, only with difficulty will a rich man enter into the kingdom of God. I repeat what I said: it is easier for a camel to pass through a needle's eye than for a rich man to enter into the kingdom of God" (19:23–24).

As a youth, I remember preachers saying that Jesus did not really mean what these words say. I was told that many ancient walled cities had a narrow defensive gate called "Needle's Eye." Camels could pass through only in single file. Jesus did not refer to anything all that difficult about wealth. Since it was a bit cumbersome for camels to get through the Needle's Eye, his words were more an admonition to be careful.

In the first place, the Needle's Eye was not built until the Crusades—if ever. Secondly, the early community *did* seem to be having a problem justifying its attempts to live under the ethic of the Gospel. It was becoming more wealthy, if not exactly rich. It realized there were poor in its society. It recognized a conflict. Those in the community who were becoming affluent realized they were to love their neighbor as themselves (22:39). "How," they must have asked themselves, "can we evidence the gospel when we live this way?"

We must ask the same question. How are we to submit to Jesus' authoritative statement that links our very spirituality (as it did with his [11:2–5]) to the poor having good news preached to them? Such a question takes on urgency when we realize this preaching by profession as well as practice can come to the poor only if it comes through us. Jesus' disciples were not willing to use rationalizations that justified abundance while the poor around them remained in need: "When the disciples heard this they were completely overwhelmed," and questioned, " 'Then who can be saved?' " (19:25).

In response, Matthew's Jesus did not offer an opiate, a religiosity that reinforced the lifestyle his contemporaries were running after (see 6:32). Rather, he faced head-on the basic human and psychological fact about the difficulty of having wealth.

Responding to the disciples' complete shock at his declaration about the difficulty of submitting their wealth to this reign of God (19:25), Matthew shows that Jesus makes it clear that he is not asking the impossible:

I give you my solemn word, in the new age when the Son of Man takes his seat upon a throne befitting his glory, you who have followed me shall likewise take your places on twelve thrones to judge the twelve

tribes of Israel. Moreover, everyone who has given up home, brothers
or sisters, father or mother, wife or children or property for my sake
will receive many times as much and inherit everlasting life [19:28–29].

As in the Last Judgment scene, Matthew again connects the themes of the
throne of God, the Son of Man, the reversal that reorders the life of the poor,
and God's dynamic reign, with the theme of the blessedness of everlasting life
(25:31–46). All these themes have overtones of wisdom literature, which
always relates to ordered life in society. Such an ordered life refers to a just
and righteous relationship with God, neighbor, and this world.

When Jesus speaks about "the new age," the Wisdom Teacher is saying, in
effect: "It is necessary to have the goods of the earth, in all their basic
forms—material, emotional, psychological, psychical, relational, etc. Yet if
you hoard them for yourself and have more than enough, you just do not
reflect the style of life I have received from my God who is evidenced in my
spirituality and communicated to you (see 11:25–30). If you use power,
possessions, and prestige for your own building up rather than directing it
toward others, you do not manifest the traditional wisdom person of the
Scriptures. Your base values and behavior counter the very purpose of
creation. You do not represent a person under the authority of everlasting
life: instead your life is dictated by the ideology of Pennsylvania Avenue,
Wall Street, and Madison Avenue. You are not a person of God's reign. You
cannot be blessed. You are not poor in spirit in imitation of me."

Jesus' challenge of discipleship can be realized only by deepening our
personal relationship with the living God. Then we say with Peter, "Here we
have put everything aside to follow you" (19:27). Following Jesus, based on a
personal experience of his presence with us, demands imitating his example.

Leaving all things for the sake of experiencing God's presence reorders
one's attitude toward everything. It results in a blessing. Since the time of
Seneca, worldly wisdom has said there are but two ways you can make
persons happy: you add to their possessions or you subtract from their
desires. We either strive for more and more or we reorder our covetousness
based on new priorities: "Remember," Jesus warned, "where your treasure is,
there your heart is also" (6:21).

Faithful to Jesus' insight, Martin Luther commented that whatever is most
important in people's lives will be their god. In a society equating God's
blessing with personal wealth, there can never be a reordering of life without
a deeper experience of the living God. "No man can serve two masters. He
will either hate one and love the other or be attentive to one and despise the
other. You cannot give yourself to God and money" (6:24).

"Giving yourself" *(douleuein),* for Matthew, involves liturgical overtones.
"Giving yourself," for Matthew, refers to a servant who is committed to a
god. Nobody, Matthew is saying, easily gives up his or her worship, be it true
worship or idolatrous worship. It is not easy to be a wealthy disciple of Jesus.

Another reason we reject a dualistic approach to understanding "poor in spirit" is that the Hebrew did not make such distinctions. Matthew's Gospel, though finally redacted in Greek, was too linked to Hebrew thought-processes to distinguish between body and spirit. Hebrews viewed the person in totality. Only later, under a more sophisticated Greek philosophy, were distinctions between body and soul, body and spirit introduced. From this Hebrew influence, Matthew does not say you can be poor in body and rich in spirit. (He does not deny it either.) Neither does he say you can be rich externally as long as you are poor in spirit. Matthew presents at the core of his spirituality a God who lacks nothing. Every person has been made to image this divine nature. Thus, to lack anything essential to life denies that image of God. Poverty simply is not good. It is ungodly.

Matthew's interpretation of what it means to be poor in spirit cannot be seen as a kind of watered-down version of Luke's more radical rendition: "Blest are you poor; the reign of God is yours" (Luke 6:20). However (as I discovered while writing this book) such is the common assumption of many. One time, for instance, I was talking to someone very involved in liberation theology and social justice. I happened to mention I was developing a spirituality for First World Christians, using Matthew's beatitudes. "Why Matthew's beatitudes?" I was challenged; "Luke is much more concrete because he just says, 'Blessed are the poor.' When Matthew talks about being poor in spirit, it shows he's already begun to sell out to his situation."

Matthew does not canonize the poor or poverty as ends in themselves. Neither are the rich or riches blessed. For Matthew, blessedness, or sharing in God's life, comes only when God's image is recognized in our good deeds. The resulting blessing enables us to share more deeply in God's own power or reality.

Both Matthew and Luke based their Gospels on Mark as well as on an early document called "Q." The differences in their final redactions from Q would be to develop the nuances in God's word for their particular communities. Differences would result from stresses they wanted to make to address their peculiar situations. Since Matthew's community (unlike Luke's) was not that poor, and because he did not view poverty as a value except when it was accepted to reorder society in a way that would reflect the kingdom, Matthew would say, "Blessed are the poor *in spirit.*" According to Eduard Schweizer:

> In Matthew, the change . . . and the assimilation to Isaiah 61:2 go back to the community. . . . The expansion of "poor" to "poor in spirit" is also a later gloss; according to Matthew 11:5, the words of which go back to Isaiah 61:1, Jesus preaches his good news simply to the poor without further qualification. . . .
>
> By his amendment of the phrase Matthew has made a most significant change—his version points out the danger of thinking that poverty is an honor. Poverty is not a virtue; it should no more be boasted about by the poor than despised (and upheld) by the rich.[1]

This brings us to the final thing "poor in spirit" does not mean. It is not a sanctioning of poverty as a condition. Neither is it an idealized state of life to be valued. Poverty never glorifies those who suffer its misery. Yet today we get saturated with simplistic clichés (often coming from those who have not directly experienced poverty and the poor): "Isn't that beautiful—the uncluttered life of the poor!"

In one of his first speeches on his way to Puebla in 1979, Pope John Paul II reportedly said something to the effect that the poor should be very happy because of the simple joys their poverty would enable them to experience. The news accounts noted the hisses from the people in the church that greeted his words. In the final document, representing the "official" statements coming from Puebla, no such words can be found!

There is nothing beautiful about poverty. It is miserable. We automatically resist and reject poverty whenever we experience it. In itself, poverty denies the goodness of God. God's goodness has always been revealed precisely in the elimination of those conditions that reflect poverty and need (Exod. 3:7–8). God's goodness has been revealed as identifying with the very ones rejected as outcasts by society, even when (un)conscious ideological sanctions from religion reinforce such rejection.

In some earlier parts of Scripture, poverty was viewed as the responsibility of the person who was poor. This attitude cannot be found in Matthew's Gospel. Jesus never judged how the poor and the outcasts, the prostitutes and the tax collectors, the lepers and the sinners, got that way—nor even why they remained that way (unless he addressed the structures which contributed to that condition [see 21:12–16]). He ministered directly to them because of their need. This unsettled the people who so easily could judge why the poor were poor. Jesus' attitude created consternation in the rich elite, who felt they had a right to reject the poor from their neighborhoods and communities, and even those places identified with God's presence (8:4).

Whether at the house of Simon the leper (26:6) or Matthew the tax collector (9:10), Jesus related to the very people society rejected. His affirmation made them at home in his presence. Yet, all too often, then as today, these very ones with whom Jesus sought to be identified are rejected. They are rejected not only from the mainstream of society but even from ecclesiastical institutions and arrangements (21:14).

One of the few exceptions to this attitude is St. Benedict the Moor (the Black) Community in Milwaukee where my province ministers to street people, gays, those suffering from addictions, and those denied access to mental institutions. Here, especially during the weekly liturgy (and even at an annual weekend picnic for the parish) all classes come together around the common table.

Unfortunately there are too few "Benedicts" in the American Catholic church where people can come together in a daily meal open to all. There are too few places where a weekly liturgy acts to strengthen a shared commitment to alleviate the conditions of oppression on the streets, in the jails, and in the government.

Matthew never promoted poverty as a value in itself, despite our use of passages from Matthew that seem to indicate he or Jesus did so. Poverty for Matthew's Jesus (and as people like those at St. Benedict's know all too well) is misery. The plight of the poor demands that we no longer make it a value, else we might remain controlled by an ideology that denies responsibility to touch that reality with the healing presence of God.

Another Scriptural passage often used to justify poverty is: "A scribe approached him [Jesus] and said, 'Teacher, wherever you go I will come after you.' Jesus said to him, 'The foxes have lairs, the birds in the sky have nests, but the Son of Man has nowhere to lay his head' " (8:19–20). Traditional conferences on poverty have invariably pointed to this text to legitimize poverty, both voluntarily and involuntarily endured. Jesus chose it, therefore poverty must be a value.

If this interpretation, with so many individual, interpersonal, and infrastructural ramifications, is to be accepted, it should be reinforced by the general thrust of Matthew's spirituality. Yet such a reinforcement about Jesus and poverty cannot be found. At no time during his earthly life does Matthew describe Jesus with nowhere to sleep. On the contrary, Jesus' instruction to the first disciples assumed there would always be a place to sleep: "Look for a worthy person in every town or village you come to and stay with him until you leave" (10:11). Neither can we find any time when Jesus went hungry, thirsty, or where he or his disciples lacked any resources. He even had the resource of being with friends and of taking time for himself to commune with God. The fact that you do not have housing, food, leisure time, health, a means of support, conditions for prayer, are all signs of poverty. None of these privations can be found in Matthew's description of Jesus' public life nor did Matthew expect such privations to be present in his own community (25:31–46).[2]

Jesus was not truly poor according to his society's norms. However, he was willing to put up with temporary inconveniences, of not always having the same house to sleep and eat in, of often being dependent on others for food—all for the sake of preaching about the reign of God. Thus 8:20, which so often has been used to canonize poverty, really refers to a lifestyle connected with preaching the gospel. Fidelity to that goal of following Jesus and preaching the gospel demands that we be willing to put up with temporary inconveniences. This is also the way to understand 10:9–10.

Even the inconvenience of being born in a stable, which is part of Luke's way of describing Jesus' birth (Luke 2:7), cannot be found in Matthew. In fact, one would get the impression from Matthew's infancy narrative that Jesus was born in a house that had nothing to do with poverty. The Greek word he used for the place where Jesus was discovered by the wise men is also used by Matthew to refer to the dwelling of the centurion (8:6), Simon the leper (26:6), and even the Temple itself (21:13). It would seem from this silence about the economics surrounding Jesus' birth that Matthew has no special reason to portray Jesus as being in need either as a child, during his active life, or even at death.

When he was crucified at Jerusalem, Jesus was away from his family's home where it might be expected they had a burial place. If any message can be received from Joseph's giving of his tomb to Jesus, it would seem that this true disciple of Jesus, in his wealth, becomes a sign of a true disciple who shares his resources (25:57–60).

At this point you may be saying, "Aha! But you are not dealing with the other place where Jesus even seems to tolerate poverty as an economic condition—the anointing at Bethany."

While Jesus was in Bethany at the house of Simon the leper, a woman carrying a jar of costly perfume came up to him at table and began to pour it on his head. When the disciples saw this they grew indignant, protesting: "What is the point of such extravagance? This could have been sold for a good price and the money given to the poor." Jesus became aware of this and said to them: "Why do you criticize the woman? It is a good deed she has done for me. The poor you will always have with you but you will not always have me" [26:6–11].

Probably more than any text in Scripture, "The poor you will always have with you" (26:11) has been used to justify poverty. It has also justified neutrality by so-called religions in face of the personal, interpersonal, and infrastructural stumbling blocks that often reinforce this situation to the benefit of the wealthy. As Jesus' own words indicate, the point of the pericope has nothing to do with the poor at all. Its purpose is meant, he said, to honor a person who shared her resources with another: "I assure you, wherever the good news is proclaimed throughout the world, what she did will be spoken of as her memorial" (26:13).

In this reference to the poor, however, Jesus is not placing a value on the fact of poverty any more than when he commented on the weather (which we always have with us also [16:2])! He is simply saying, "You do not always have me" (see 9:15).

Jesus realized he was soon to die. In light of the traditional burial preparation (26:12), his silence seems to justify the expense. His words do not say here or anywhere else that the reality of the poor with us does not necessitate a response.

Jesus never refused to share his resources with those in need even when he might have tried to avoid them (14:13). On the contrary, he directly linked the legitimation of his spirituality with the way he ministered to the poor. This ministry evidenced God's reign in him and God's concern toward them (11:3–5).

With the same *exousia* in us which motivated Jesus to minister to the poor, the disciples for all time are to do the works Jesus did (11:2). The poor's presence in the disciples' midst demands an ongoing reciprocal responsibility to bring good news to them in imitation of Jesus. Consequently, interpreting "the poor you will always have with you" (26:11) in the context of Jesus' whole ministry, we are justified in concluding that—after speaking about the perpetual presence of the poor (26:6–12)—Jesus could have said: "I assure you, wherever the good news is proclaimed throughout the world, its first recipients will be the poor who will recognize in the disciples of Jesus those who share in my *exousia* by calling for a reversal of ideas and institutions which will restore the poor to wholeness!" To interpret 26:11 in any other way (especially to legitimize non-involvement on behalf of the poor) is to manipulate the text so that it becomes an ideological reinforcement of the social arrangements of injustice that keep the poor in misery.

Poverty in Spirit, the *Anawim,* and Abandonment

From what we have considered thus far, poverty is a curse and a scandal if it remains unrelated to a way of bringing about the plan of God and submitting the whole world to this new authority. Poverty can be sanctioned only if it is freely embraced as a way to promote that reign of God more concretely in our world. Otherwise it contradicts the blessedness and goodness of God; it is a curse that violates God's plan. It signifies that the reign of God has not yet fully arrived. To experience that reign more fully, to experience its authority and power, it is necessary to reorder our possessions on behalf of the poor (19:21). Jesus offers no other way to experience the treasure of heaven except solidarity with the poor (see 19:29). Give to the poor; then you will have treasure in heaven.

We will never have the courage to reorder our personal, communal, and collective lives on behalf of the poor unless we have first sought heaven's treasures (13:44–46). We will not be able to part with those things that give us security, those things that the unbelievers of the world are running after, until we have discovered the reign of God's presence (6:32–33), which is found in religious experience. We are poor in spirit when we seek God in ever deepening moments of contemplation and mystical experience. Experiencing God as Father, Son, and Spirit in prayer, we are disposed to reorder our lives, sell what we do not need, and give to those who do not have what we formerly thought to be so important.

Consequently we reflect in our lifestyle the power of God that has taken authority over us. Totally absorbed in the power, the presence of God as Mother, Daughter, and Holy Spirit (which is contemplation), we are brought into a new reality. We begin expressing that power on behalf of the poor in a way that separates us from society.

Earlier, Peter had been able to proclaim Jesus as "Son of the living God" (16:16). He made his faith-testimony from an experience offered him by God (16:17). So deep was this experience that he sold everything as demanded by Jesus. From the strength of this and other experiences (see 4:20), he would be deepened in faith. In confidence he would be able to say: "Here we have put everything aside to follow you" (19:27).

Discipleship implies putting everything aside; but it also means gaining much more (19:29). Given this paradox, it becomes important that we ask, "What are these 'everythings' that we must put aside if Peter's words are to become ours?"

By description, poverty means the lack of access to resources. It means to be in need. From such an understanding of poverty, we see why poverty violates God's plan and nature. Jesus received everything from God (11:27). He received not only the mysteries of 11:25, but every resource possessed by the creator. If God had held one thing back, Jesus could not have been fully the image of God. Everything, every good thing, was given to Jesus as one sharing fully in God's life. Only in this way did he become the image of God's plan. Experiencing a share in that fullness of revelation (16:17) given Jesus and his disciples (11:25), Peter would be able to share in that perfection by selling everything just as the Creator handed over all to Jesus (11:27).

To be in need contradicts God's nature, since God is never in need. There is no *teleios* or perfection if God is in need. If everyone is to "be made perfect as your heavenly Father is perfect" (5:48), we can never justify any condition of true need in society. The good deeds we do enable us to manifest the plan of God and to enter more fully in its dynamic power. Sharing in this power is predicated on responding to the basic needs of people.

The "everything" of Matthew refers to all resources. To be in need of any resource (material, physical, temporal, emotional, relational, spatial, psychical, etc.) indicates a lack that violates God's plan. "Everything" includes such human needs as the need to be affirmed and forgiven, to be understood, healed, and given hope. However, in a special way, the whole context of Matthew identifies material need, or poverty vis-à-vis wealth, as the need that must be especially addressed. In our society, those material needs that represent the fundamental resources (without which people's dignity cannot be realized) are primarily water, energy, food, clothing, livelihood, health care, safe environment, leisure, shelter, and mobility.

In the United States of America, by the later 1950s and early 1960s, these basic human needs were generally achieved for the white male part of society. With the above fundamental needs being met for some, what would a market economy do in light of the fact that it was dependent on growth vis-à-vis the dominant class that controls the wealth of the land? It would promote an ideology that redefined previously accepted luxuries as basic human needs. These new needs would insure security. If such old "excesses" could be defined as new "needs," rights would be predicated on luxuries, as rights had once been attached to needs.

A right to newly articulated "needs" would be justified on the individual, interpersonal, and infrastructural levels. Appealing to these rights, it would not matter that much if these newly acquired needs denied other individuals, groups, and nations their basic necessities. It would not matter that our luxuries would be the needs of those we call our brothers and sisters. Reinforced by such an ideology, we would be able to go to war to protect our "rights" against those we professed to love as ourselves (22:39).

The contradictions in this attitude are evident in two articles in the same issue of the *Milwaukee Sentinel*. The banner headline announced: "US Hints at Military Role in the Mideast" (if the United States were not supplied with 30 percent of the world's energy resources). The second article discussed former Secretary of the Treasury W. Michael Blumenthal's warning to China's leaders to refrain from violating the territorial rights of the Vietnamese people by military intervention![3] Our ideology about sovereignty of other nations does not apply when we "need" to keep living at a certain level.

It is very difficult for people, much less an institution, to apply to themselves their theories for others. Since the conversion this demands seems so difficult, we adapt God's word to rationalize our lifestyle, rather than criticize our lifestyle on the basis of God's word. Yet, as long as we justify our behavior, we will never recognize a need for conversion. As long as the theories are good for women outside the church but not inside, for China but not the United States, then Matthew's Jesus says to us:

> . . . Your verdict on others will be the verdict passed on you. The measure with which you measure will be used to measure you. Why look at the speck in your brother's eye, when you miss the plank in your own? How can you say to your brother, "Let me take that speck out of your eye," while all the time that plank remains in your own? You hypocrite! Remove the plank from your own eye first; then you will see clearly to take the speck from your brother's eye [7:1–5].

To recognize the plank in our own lifestyle, we have to reconsider what our "needs" truly are.

My religious superior in college would always respond to my requests: "Do you really need it?" In those days, I and others used to make light of his response. Yet today, I realize his question reflected true wisdom. I find myself asking it. Raising such a question will enable a new ethic to touch every dimension of life. This norm will help bring about wisdom's goal: the reordering of all creation according to God's plan.

Wisdom teaches a theology about life that affirms the dignity of each person as God's image and emphasizes each person's right to share as fully as possible in the resources of the earth for each person. Therefore wisdom's expression in the commandment to love (all) others as one's self (7:12; 22:39), calls for a new ethical principle. This norm must be applied equally on every level of our society. This norm requires that we and everyone else have, in the words of Denis Goulet, "enough in order to be more."[4]

Everyone has a right to enough of the earth's resources in order to more fully image God. But since we are all interconnected, whenever any person, group, or nation has more than enough, it not only denies basic resources to others, it becomes less human! If the goal of creation is to offer just enough in order to be more, to have more than enough is to be less human. If we are less than human we are less than God's image. Living in a society dominated by an ethic that proclaims "the more the merrier" demands a radical detachment. Only then will we be living under the authority of God's reign.

This consideration now brings us to determine finally who Jesus proclaimed blessed with God's abundant life for being poor in spirit.

Matthew was highly influenced by certain texts from the Hebrew Scriptures. The author of the First Gospel saw these fulfilled in the life of Jesus. Central to many of these passages were servant themes from Second and Third Isaiah as well as ones from the first eleven chapters of Isaiah (which were written in light of the Exile). Herein the theme of identifying the one anointed with God's authority as the poor servant filled with the spirit becomes dominant (see Isa. 6:7f.; 11:2f.; 42:1f.; 49:3f.; 53:4f.; 61:1f.). Although Matthew refers directly to Jesus as servant, or *pais,* only once (12:18), the above Isaian references show that Matthew presents Jesus as preeminently God's servant who is poor in spirit.

Under the authority of God, Jesus became radically poor in that spirit, like a servant or slave. Totally given over to God, Jesus desired above all to accomplish what had been revealed to him by this God (26:39,42,44). His life would become true worship because of this commitment.

As we saw earlier, the beatitudes of Matthew, the ethic they proclaim, and their lifestyle represented in Jesus' own biography, are all founded upon Isaiah 61. In a special way the opening verses of 61 indicate what the first half of this beatitude describes about the poor in spirit:

> The spirit of the Lord God is upon me,
> because the Lord has anointed me;
> He has sent me to bring glad tidings to the lowly,
> to heal the brokenhearted,
> To proclaim liberty to the captives
> and release to the prisoners,
> To announce a year of favor from the Lord
> and a day of vindication by our God . . . [Isa. 61:1–2].

The sixty-first chapter of Isaiah, like many other passages written in this post-exilic book, outlined the characteristics of a social group who were radically committed to God within an alien culture. These were called the *anawim.* The *anawim* were a group of people who had their own experience of what we have called the hermeneutic circle. They had become alienated from the infrastructure of their society. The result was a growing sense of separation from a religion whose ideology seemed to reinforce the infrastructure.

The *anawim* gathered themselves in basic communities. They saw themselves as a faithful remnant within a wider culture of infidelity. They sol-

idified their identity and supported each other through a kind of conscientization wherein they reflected on their world and recognized its enslavements. Realizing that these enslavements violated God's plan of freedom,
they dedicated themselves to a kind of a communal action-reflection. They
began to live and act in a manner that separated them from those infrastructures. They led a lifestyle seeking ongoing conversion.

The process for a new style of life representative of the *anawim* spirituality,
which Matthew envisioned for his community, is best summarized in the first
beatitude. "How blest are the poor in spirit, the reign of God is theirs" (5:3).
This dynamic represents for us a way of living the gospel in the face of those
real obstacles presented by our wealth.

In fidelity to Isaiah 61 and the way of the *anawim,* Matthew detailed the
spirituality of a person, community, or institution that is poor in spirit. In a
particular way, he elaborated on this spirituality in the fifteen verses (19–34)
found in the Sermon on the Mount (chapter six). Matthew 6:19–34 consists
of wisdom sayings presented by the Teacher of Wisdom. These specified a
new way of spirituality that had been outlined earlier for his disciples (5:1–
2ff.).

Addressing his contemporaries' temptation to forms of consumerism,
Matthew presents Jesus showing its ultimate futility (6:19). Jesus invites his
followers to experience a deeper dynamic, which could be the basis of their
life (6:20–21). Aware that the world of the senses reflects inner attitudes
(6:20–21), Jesus declares that the world's preoccupation with wealth (6:24) is
diametrically opposed to the development of an inner attitude of submissive
openness to the active power of God's presence in one's life and world
(6:25–34).

It seems evident that Matthew was trying to face the concrete problem that
challenged his increasingly affluent community: the temptation to find security in consumer goods. "Do not lay up for yourselves an earthly treasure.
Moths and rust corrode; thieves break in and steal (6:19)." Such sayings
reinforced a traditional wisdom ethic that flowed from an understanding of
creation itself (see Exod. 16:20; James 5:1–3).

Every person is created to reflect a commitment to the plan God originally
envisioned for the world. This commitment grows from a religious experience and evidences itself in a new, simple lifestyle. "Make it your practice
instead to store up heavenly treasure, which neither moths nor rust corrode
nor thieves break in and steal" (6:20). The final part of the first wisdom saying
of this section is based on the traditional way of reversal and contrast. It flows
from the assumption that wealth assumes an authority over people. Consequently they become so preoccupied in seeking to amass power, possessions, and prestige that they no longer can experience God in the depth of
their being. "Remember, where your treasure is, there your heart is also"
(6:21).

Realizing the impact that society's infrastructure makes on each person,
Matthew next shows that the seeking of treasure for one's self means separa-

tion from the good God. The external evidence of such a consumeristic lifestyle, marked by a sensate approach to life, reflects a darkness, an emptiness within. "If your eyes are good, your body will be filled with light; if your eyes are bad, your body will be in darkness" (6:22–23). The use of the adjectives good and bad, related to the words light and darkness, recalls Genesis themes regarding the correct order for creation. These words are faithful to good anthropology, which is the base for spirituality; "badness" refers to a lack of generosity or miserliness (see 20:15). This kind of selfishness flows from misplaced values which need purifying.

Without such single-mindedness, every person easily will become liable to be sold into slavery by the market economy which demands no less loyalty than God. "No man can serve two masters. He will either hate one and love the other or be attentive to one and despise the other. You cannot give yourself to God and money" (6:24). "Giving yourself" *(douleuein)* involves both a style of life and liturgical expression that is connected to total submission to another, like slaves to their owners.

In the final analysis, Matthew is inviting his community to choose its gods. In contrast to the gods of the present age who play on fears and insecurities, Jesus invites his hearers to discover the faithful God of our memories and imagination. If God is God, and if this world is God's and we are part of this world, does it not follow that God will be with us as God? Will not God affirm life in us by sharing all resources we may need?

Inviting his hearers to recall the past generosity of this God remembered from Deuteronomy, Matthew makes it clear that then, as well as now, "Your heavenly Father knows all that you need" (6:32). *Then* realizing their need, God chose a people from all creation (Deut. 7:6). Affirming them as God's own (Deut. 7:7), God shared all resources with them (Deut. 7:8). *Now* God is presented as a God of care, affirming the importance of each person (6:26f.; 10:29–31), made to image God (7:11), always willing to provide them with whatever resources are needed (6:30).

Appealing to this covenantal God, Matthew invited his church to deepen its faith (6:30) rather than be controlled by the struggles, anxieties, and preoccupations of a consumer mentality (6:31–32). To be poor in spirit means we no longer reflect the unbelief of society as it urges its members to run after the commodity self (6:32). "Seek first his kingship over you, his way of holiness, and all these things will be given you besides" (6:33).

The underlying attitude demanded for such spirituality, if it is to survive in society, is trust. God must be trusted as a "heavenly Father [who] knows all that we need" (6:32), who does not want us to remain controlled by our needs. As loving parent, this God only asks that we request what we need (7:7–11) in a spirit of dependence matched by a spirit of confidence. If our daily life reflects commitment to fulfill this parent's plan, our needs will be met. "Enough, then, of worrying about tomorrow. Let tomorrow take care of itself. Today has troubles enough of its own" (6:34).

The simple request by Matthew's Jesus for our trust that his God will be as faithful to us as to Jesus himself (10:40; 16:19) underscores a central requirement for being poor in spirit: abandonment to divine providence. With our life affirmed (6:25), why can we not trust that God will take care of our needs? God wants us to trust that our cries will be heard and our needs will be met. God merely asks us to give over ourselves, our communities, and institutions to this divine providence.

When I was in the novitiate, one of the books that influenced me strongly and helped mold my spirituality at that time was de Causade's *Abandonment to Divine Providence.* This eighteenth-century classic helped me feel affirmed at a point in my life when I most needed it. I discovered that history was like a book, with each person in history constituting a letter or a word, a period or a semicolon. How great, I thought, that we all have a role in history. God did care for me (10:30); so why was I not more trusting that God would remain such a God?

At that time, my understanding of abandonment seemed limited to a passive waiting on God to meet my needs (which were so psychologically strong that I cannot remember caring too much about the material needs of others).

Although it cannot be found specifically in de Causade, I was influenced by a religious ideology regarding abandonment that expressed itself in this passivity. We just sit back and let God do it all. God "out there" will intervene if God wants. Is it not pride and contrary to perfection to think that we can do anything? I did not fully realize then that the God who loved me also wanted to use me for an overall plan for the world. I did think that history was being written by God *through* my life and that I was to be inexorably linked to every other person.

Authentic abandonment or poverty in spirit realizes that God is not "out there." God is "with us," inviting us to work actively as co-creators, totally dedicating our lives to accomplish the divine plan in that part of history entrusted to us by the span of our life (6:27). This invitation requests merely the giving of ourselves (6:24). We are to be totally at the service of our Maker who has inaugurated the plan. We are to submit to its ethic in our life and proclaim it to our world. This kind of abandonment finds us freely choosing to live under the authority of this power of God within us to accomplish God's purposes in our society. In this way we become poor in spirit, anointed with God's favor. We can bring good news to the poor of our world.

Realizing our own needs and our powerlessness, we can respond in God's power to care about other powerless brothers and sisters whom we see in need. As God has seen us in need and not left us helpless, so we too exist, by our nature, to respond in care to those we see in need.

Analyzing Social Structures and Cultural Addictions

Such abandonment is neither passive nor romantic. It is both a commitment to radical discipleship and a realization that this discipleship must be exercised in the face of a very powerful infrastructure that penetrates all aspects of our world. This form of abandonment, in fact, is the only realistic approach to take when we understand, with the 1971 Synod of Bishops, the implications of this infrastructure's power. Abandonment becomes a *sine qua non* for authentic gospel response—since the infrastructure is part of that whole world into which we are to bring the good news (28:19). If we fail to touch this part of the world, which affects more individuals and groups than any other, we can hardly say we have developed an attitude of abandonment to bring about God's will! At the Synod, the bishops said of this infrastructure:

> Even though it is not for us to elaborate a very profound analysis of the situation of the world, we have nevertheless been able to perceive the serious injustices which are building around the world of men a network of domination, oppression and abuses which stifle freedom and which keep the greater part of humanity from sharing in the building up and enjoyment of a more just and more fraternal world.[5]

Some might react to such an analysis of our world with an appeal to an old understanding of abandonment that passively states, "If God wants to do something about it, he will." However, the bishops make it clear that this very problem demands a new kind of abandonment which recognizes both our powerlessness as well as our responsibility to work as co-creators with God to affect this infrastructure, this network. The bishops show that our global reality of sin demands a form of active resistance against any network, any infrastructure that denies the image of God in people and keeps the majority of people on our earth from sharing in the resources:

> In the face of the present-day situation of the world, marked as it is by the grave sin of injustice, we recognize both our responsibility and our inability to overcome it by our own strength. Such a situation urges us to listen with a humble and open heart to the word of God, as he shows us new paths toward action in the cause of justice in the world.[6]

This sentence provides us with the springboard and new agenda for contemporary groups of the *anawim,* of the poor in spirit, desiring to affect the whole world with the gospel (28:20).

The bishops declare that our world is equated, or marked, with the grave sin of injustice. The network of domination, oppression, and abuses within institutions and social arrangements (along with their ideologies) denies freedom and human rights for the majority. Meanwhile the minority—the "haves"—benefit, while keeping the greater part of the world from sharing in the resources. With armaments to protect its interests, the minority continues to exploit those same resources. What the bishops refer to as injustice, wisdom literature calls disorder, *tohu wabohu.* Psychologists call it insanity. Such a reality simply is not according to God's order for creation.

If the new ethic proposed by Jesus can be summarized as having enough-to-be-more, any infrastructure that reinforces the disorder with an ideology of more-than-enough demands a new form of resistance to bring about a new kind of order. With the Spirit, or *exousia,* of that new order within us by baptism, we are those who are to respond in that power to create new paths toward action that will promote justice in the world (see 3:15; 21:32). Yet, with the bishops, "we recognize both our responsibility and our inability to overcome it by our own strength."[7]

Why would the bishops seem to be throwing in the towel with one hand, yet with the other be striking their breasts indicating that they must do something? Probably because their very analysis showed how huge, all-pervasive, and controlling this infrastructure truly can be. It has almost limitless authority over everything. In the face of our society's infrastructures, the bishops realized that our culture contains within it values and attitudes so deeply ingrained that we experience a powerlessness to do anything about them.

The response to such a realization is further aggravated when we realize that our church institution—its social arrangements, and even its theology—reinforces this infrastructure too often. If it does not do so directly, then it too often inadvertently does so by its silence. Facing this, we can do one of two things: be controlled by this network's authority and then despair, or admit its power and influence as addictive. On the question of dependency, we can learn from others who have faced personal addictions such as alcohol, narcotics, food, and gambling. Learning from them will provide us with a model to deal with our newly recognized cultural addictions within the infrastructure.

The cultural addictions controlling us are myriad: racism, sexism, ageism, elitism, clericalism, nationalism. These addictions deny God's image in groups of people precisely because they are not part of the group in power, with authority to define reality through the ideology they control. The cultural addictions also control us through the ways the earth's resources are exploited by our nation through its consumerism, technologism, and militarism. These dynamics of the infrastructure, or "network of domination, oppression, and abuses which stifle freedom" (human-"isms"), are a deep part of our culture, prohibiting a more equal sharing of resources (resource-"isms").[8] As part of the very fabric of our nation, we suffer from a cultural addiction which we have not personally created, but for which we are now told by the bishops we are responsible.

Creating Communities to Challenge Cultural Addictions: The Twelve Steps to Sanity in an Insane Society

Many people get depressed when they consider this huge global reality and the very significant part the United States plays in its negative dynamics. As a result, I have been seeking to develop a model to help people who, as Christians, want to do something about it.

In *Thy Will Be Done,* I began by outlining the way God seems to operate in oppressive situations in our world.[9] In response to the infrastructure, with its prevailing institutions, social arrangements (isms), and ideology, there is an alternative:

LEVELS OF OUR WORLD
|
INDIVIDUAL
|
INTERPERSONAL
|
INFRASTRUCTURAL

INSTITUTIONS	ISMS	IDEOLOGY
Economic	(Re: *Dignity of Persons*)	Communications
	Sexism	Media
Political	Racism	—Language
	Ageism	—Symbols
Religious	Elitism	
	Clericalism	Education
Other	Nationalism	—Formative
	Other	—Continuing
	(Re: *Sharing of Resources*)	
	Technologism	
	Consumerism	
	Militarism	
	Economic Imperialism	
	Other	

COMMUNITY	CONSCIENTIZATION	CONVERSION
The Gathering	*Read Reality*	Intellectual
	Enslavements	
The Gifts		Moral
	Empowerments	
	To Write History	Religious
	God's Image in All	
	Sharing Resources	

INFRASTRUCTURAL
|
INTERPERSONAL
|
INDIVIDUAL
|
EXPERIENCING THE WORD

God seems to gather people, with their unique gifts, into *community*. Within this community they begin to read the reality of these alienations and addictions. They begin to realize how they can take authority over them with the power of God's word within themselves. This *conscientization* process leads to an ongoing *conversion* that is intellectual, moral, and religious. This conversion admits that the analysis we have given thus far is basically correct, that this negative part of the infrastructure violates God's norms for the world. If we try to reorder this situation we can be assured God will be with us. Yet while I have been told that this model has been helping reflection groups and formation groups I still sensed that it was not providing basic communities with sufficient tools to deal with all the cultural addictions.

In early 1978, it occurred to me that I might be able to apply Alcoholics Anonymous's twelve steps to *cultural* addictions. Possibly the steps could be used in communities of conscientization to help the conversion process of people imprisoned by cultural addictions.

It has always been the role of wisdom figures, who found serious disorders in their societies, to begin gathering disciples around them. Probably they did so for support in face of impending persecution as well as to assure continuance of their message. There is significance in gathering regularly with people having similar problems. The twelve steps of dealing with addictions can become the agenda for communities of conscientization who seek conversion from their cultural addictions. Thus, whenever the community gathers with its gifts, it can operate from a model of reflection and mutual sharing, guided by the twelve steps, to deal with its enslavements. Addressing these newly recognized addictions through the power "of God as we understood him" through Matthew helps us to realize we now have tools to facilitate a conversion process that can be applicable to the whole infrastructure in our country.

Each basic community can develop as does every AA group the way the twelve steps might be discussed and implemented. In the following pages I will quickly walk through each of the twelve steps. A brief reflection will show how these steps might be used. Whether the group be a weekly or a monthly group, Review of Life gathering, Marriage Encounter Retorno, prayer group, Ultreya, adult discussion group, or Tuesday morning coffee klatsch, these steps can be used in communities of conscientization to deepen the conversion of each of their members.

1. We admitted we were powerless over our cultural addictions and that our lives had become unmanageable.

As they looked at the world, the bishops realized they were impotent in the face of the infrastructure's authority over life. This infrastructure touched the life of every person and group. Its negative elements perpetuated in the world the grave sin of disorder. These disordered social arrangements, now global (expressed in all the various "isms"), were dividing women and men, whites and non-whites, young and old, cleric and lay, North and South, rich and poor. These "isms" made global life unmanageable. The bishops recognized the need to be healed from these ruptures within the community.

For instance, considering the cultural addiction of racism, which of us who are white wants to hate people of other races and live in fear of them? Yet we do. This fear seems to control us. Or which of us who are male really seeks to be part of the pain that women experience in our male-dominated church? Yet the hurting of women continues. What family wants to feel it is inferior, that it has to be competing for more and more? What can parents really do when they seem to continually hear from their children: "I want." "I need." "Why not?" "Everyone else does?"

If such concerned people would be able to come together and find their unity in their very powerlessness over these addictions, they might be able to discuss how these have affected them and their relationships and contributed to disorder.

Once we can admit that our lives are unmanageable, that our lifestyle contributes to ruptures in the human family, we have come to an intellectual conversion. We can admit, "Yes, this is what is happening in our nation and world." Then we can apply to these addictions the universal norm of Genesis and the beatitudes. We can move to the next stage of moral conversion. We can say: "No, I realize this isn't the way the God of the beatitudes wants us to live." Now we are ready for the final stage of conversion: a religious conversion.

2. We came to believe that a power greater than ourselves could restore us to sanity.

Persons or groups are ready for a religious conversion when they admit that those forces and powers that once dominated their values and behaviors can no longer be justified as normal.

After dealing for years with people's brokenness and insanity, Sigmund Freud realized that their problems were influenced by a deeper disorder arising from society itself. He recognized the need for therapy, a form of healing and conversion, that would take power over that brokenness in the world. His student Carl Jung discovered that some of these attitudes arise from what he called the collective unconscious. He called them archetypes. They are deeply ingrained in whole groups of people and communicated through parents, relationships, and cultural patterns. When we realize that these attitudes and symbols of alienation are part of the very ideology of the sex, race, or group into which we are born, we conclude that there is a need for a dynamic or power that is stronger than these obstacles.

Jung said that most of our human problems are religious at their core. Remembering this, we again realize that good spirituality addresses basic anthropological alienations. The more we are healed of human brokenness, the more we become like Christ. Since we live in a church that is equally experiencing these divisions, we discover, with Matthew's Gospel, that we can experience a new power greater than our brokenness. This power can free us through a new kind of "christotherapy."[10] Christ's beatitudes for church and world offer a therapy leading to wholeness and peace.

3. We made a decision to turn our will and our lives over to the care of God as we understood him.

God showed care for the Israelites by saying, "I have witnessed the affliction of my people in Egypt and have heard their cry of complaint against their slave drivers, so I know well what they are suffering" (Exod. 3:7–8). "Therefore I will free them from their oppression," says the God of care. Matthew presents Jesus as the one who cares. Jesus took all infirmities, all addictions, upon himself (8:17) even to the point of turning his will over to God as he understood God (26:36–46). These addictions would be nailed to his cross; they would be put to death for the life of the world.

Understanding God's care through Jesus' care, we discover a new power that can free us from all brokenness. This new power touches the emptiness and longings of our heart. "Come to me, all you who are weary and find life burdensome, and I will refresh you. Take my yoke upon your shoulders and learn from me, for I am gentle and humble of heart. Your souls will find rest, for my yoke is easy and my burden light" (11:28–30).

Submitting our life to God and the divine plan, we understand God as a provident parent who cares for us. Coming together in our basic community, we realize this God cares for each of us in our uniqueness (7:11). In this experience of God's care we can care for each other. Experiencing God removing our burdens, we can help remove them from each other. We can celebrate this faith of ours by sharing it with each other.

When I observed their meetings as a student, I was always deeply edified at the way alcoholics could share their faith in "God-as-they-understood-him." Now I have become equally impressed at the way people are beginning to share their efforts to be free of their cultural addictions. And they are doing this in the context of shared faith and prayer. Faith-sharing in groups will encourage us to respond further to the call to abandon ourselves, to become poor in spirit, to desire to turn our wills and lives over to God's provident care. It will help us model our lives after the one who offers us a way to be free from our cultural addictions by honestly being open to others' needs (see 8:1–14, 15:21–28). So we will grow in understanding this God in Christ as the one who calls us to believe we too are to live for others in need (see 11:2ff.). We can share that conviction with others who share that same faith.

4. We made a searching and fearless moral inventory of ourselves.

A moral inventory based on the norms Matthew presents in the beatitudes is quite a challenge. The fourth step is always a major part of dealing with addictions. Yet, if we desire to be persons under the authority of God, the search must be made. As long as we are controlled by the authority of the infrastructures, we will not want to face the implications of either our attitudes or our lifestyle.

Reinforced by an ideology that plays on our fears and tensions through the advertising media, an experience of God's presence can invite us to become free. Like Peter, we can seek liberation from those anxieties. At such critical times, we need to say with assurance: " 'Lord, if it is really you, tell me to come to you across the water.' 'Come!' he said. So Peter got out of the boat and began to walk on the water. . . " (14:28–29). The more we move toward the experience of the living Jesus, with our God-parent, and their Spirit within us, the more that experience will free us from fear and its controls.

Fear controls people, groups, even whole nations. Fear of the one who has hurt me in the past keeps me from growth. Fear of women keeps priests from working with them to make parishes more powerful in God's love. Fear of the city affects working patterns and living patterns that separate the races. Matthew shows that submitting to the power of Jesus in our midst enables us to rise above these fears and take control over them (28:8–9).

Matthew's words for our church-in-transition necessitate a moral inventory that applies God's ethical order on all levels of the world. Previously we may have limited ourselves to individual and interpersonal applications of morality; now we must join together in groups and fearlessly create new forms of bonding and coalitions. These will promote the ethic of the beatitudes within the various elements of the infrastructure itself. Naturally this will result in applying our ethical stances through concrete actions such as lobbying, shareholding actions, boycotts, bringing our values to bear on energy, military decisions, unemployment, the tax structure, etc.

5. *We admitted to God, ourselves, and another human being the exact nature of our wrongs.*

In dealing with addictions, the admission of the brokenness is essential for healing. Thus, this fifth step is very significant for our effort to develop a new kind of spirituality which mourns over our wrongdoing. We need to admit that our lifestyle, our pattern of thinking and acting, on all levels of society, has contributed to a grave wrong: a denial of freedom and individual rights for millions and the creation and perpetuation of systems that keep denying resources to them. And lest we be accused of self-hatred or excessive national breast-beating it is important that we reflect on our national character from the perspective of contemplation, or from God's viewpoint.

Paradoxically, denial is part of the *exact* nature of our wrongs. We must admit, Pope John Paul II said when he visited our nation in 1979, the structural barriers to God's plan that are part of the fabric of our country.[11] Until we are ready to bring morality to bear upon the levels of the infrastructure as we do on the individual and interpersonal levels, we will never be willing to admit our wrongdoing and our complicity in the wrongdoing of our nation, as in Iran and Nicaragua. Unwillingness to admit our involvement submits us even more under the control of these cultural addictions from which we pray for deliverance.

Sharing in the group helps us deal with guilt in a constructive way. We are guilty only if we refuse to recognize the exact nature of the wrong and/or fail to do anything about it. The exact nature of the wrong is within the infrastructure, so the sin is in the structure. Guilt will be incurred only when we fail to be as free as we possibly can from its force in our lives and those of others.

6. *We were entirely ready to have God remove all these defects of character.*

If only we could move from an ideology that proclaims "In God we trust," to ask this God to heal our country from its internal and international defects and divisions! There is a defect in the national character when we reflect a corporate personality, like David toward Uriah, that justifies the exploitation of even the little others have (see 2 Sam. 12:1–12) through taxation, trade and tariff laws, commodity controls, forced joblessness, as well as destruction of the land itself with chemicals and nuclear material. The exact nature of our wrongs has created that global situation outside our nation and that poverty condition within our nation whereby "to the man who has, more will be given until he grows rich; the man who has not, will lose what little he has" (13:12).

Rather than protesting our religiosity by putting words about God on the face of our coins, we need to mourn for our nation's sins and invite it to conversion. We need to remind our nation, with the psalmist, that there is an ethic under which it will be judged other than its ideology of consumerism, which is reinforced by the character of militarism (see Ps. 33:8–22). Today Chorazin and Bethsaida (11:21) are Toronto and New York. Jerusalem (23:37) is Washington and Ottawa.

The God who looks at the earth sees not just our nation, but the globe. If our nation has more than enough, God views this as a national character defect. We need to ask this God, in a spirit of repentance, for the grace of conversion. (As a footnote, wouldn't this attitude be beautiful to bring into the Penance Service and the Reconciliation Rite of our Liturgy?)

7. *We humbly asked him to remove our shortcomings.*

Humility or meekness is simply spiritual realism. Spiritual realism tells us that the God who has invited us to be perfect creates the possibility of perfection for us. Consequently God will remove whatever shortcomings and obstacles will keep that perfection from being more manifest in our world.

We rarely seem to *ask* God for help in dealing with our failings and needs. We may recognize our failings and admit that they are not promoting God's plan for the world. Yet, even as we confess that we are part of the problem and feel powerless to do anything about it, we fail to be so poor in spirit that we ask God to remove our shortcomings, which contribute to the problem. Just look at the absence of such an attitude in our regular Prayer of the Faithful during liturgy! While we ask God to do something about the nebulous "poor" we rarely ask God to remove those conditions within our personal and societal lives that contribute to the creation of the poverty we pray will be removed!

We should expect God to reorder those pains of poverty into healing. It should be equally expected that this may mean reordering those conditions that contribute to these various forms of suffering. "Ask, and you will receive. Seek, and you will find. Knock, and it will be opened to you. For the one who asks, receives. The one who seeks, finds. The one who knocks, enters" (7:7–8).

What "we need to humbly ask for" more than anything is the gift of wisdom (Prov. 11:2; 16:16; Eccles. 7:25; Wisd. 6:20; 7:7; 9:4). In fact, as we face the addiction of seeking power, possessions, and prestige, asking for wisdom enables us to bring correct perspective to all of life. This is especially important for leaders to realize during times of transition (see 2 Chron. 1:10–12).

As in seeking God's reign, those who seek wisdom obtain "all these things besides" (6:33). This kind of wisdom enables us to realize what shortcomings we can honestly change with God's power in us, which ones are beyond the immediate power within us and our groups, and which ones still need to be resourced. In this way we will not suffer unnecessary burnout or despair at the slowness of social change. With any addict, we can humbly ask: "God give us the courage to change the things we can; the serenity to accept the things we cannot change, and the wisdom to know the difference!"

8. *We made a list of all persons we had harmed and resolved to make amends to them all.*

The list of people adversely affected by our nation begins with Native Americans and continues today to the millions of brothers and sisters at home and in Third World nations. How? Through the dictators we support, through the practices of our transnational corporations, our technologies, and our military training programs of assistance, which can counter efforts to change such systems. The list goes on and on as it addresses institutions, isms, and ideologies. This list can be drawn from a regular reading of past history as well as current events.

The needs and brokenness of our lives, our families, and our world, supply the agenda that brings us together. Realizing our role in creating and perpetuating ageism, anti-Semitism, racism, and so forth finds us more willing to make amends by changing our part in these social arrangements and inviting others who may also be part of these "isms" to change.

9. *We made direct amends to such people whenever possible, except when to have done so would have injured them or others.*

Once we recognize the nature of our prejudices and alienations, we also face the need to do something about the situations they reinforce. In 1969, after listing the historical examples of harm sustained by minorities, James Forman demanded that the churches make reparation to American blacks for the exploitation they suffered. Often this exploitation was justified in the name of the Scriptures. Sustained by an ideology that found God reinforcing the political economy, God could not be concerned about structures of enslavement. Slaves were to obey their masters (21:34–36; Eph. 6:5; Tit. 2:9).

The amends we need is the effort to change those structural reinforcements and their ideologies. This will result in a reordering of society that promotes the dignity of God in each person by a fuller sharing of resources.

In the sixties and seventies much injury was added by the efforts of well-meaning people to those persons who were hurt in the past. Often, false hopes were created in the poor without sufficient social analysis. Consequently insufficient analysis seduced both the poor and well-meaning Christians into working for social change aimed at getting the poor into existing institutions or at creating parallel institutions. Often, however, this merely brought more people into the same kind of system without working to change its underlying assumptions.

This often has been done in the way Catholic schools were opened or changed to meet the needs of racial minorities. Much effort was made to enable children from poverty areas to compete equally with their more affluent white peers. However, assumptions about consumerism and competition in society and education geared to "make it" often went unaddressed.

Within the Catholic Church, as many women have begun to make clear, it would be injuring the cause of women's ordination to work to get women ordained without also challenging the clerical concepts of power that dominate the church.

10. We continued to take personal inventory and, when we were wrong, promptly admitted it.

In the past decade, while trying to implement what the God of Genesis plans for the world of my nation, church, family, and personal life, I have learned that things do not change overnight. We can never expect to have the full reign of God on earth. Yet becoming poor in spirit demands that we always be involved in those processes whereby we can more fully bring this dynamic of God's presence to earth in all its dimensions.

This includes ongoing action/reflection, taking inventory of our personal, communal, and corporate lives in light of the gospel. It involves an equal willingness to change our behavior when it violates the norms of the beatitudes. Fidelity to this process will be the best hope of any social change. The more we grow in contemplative reflection and understand from this religious experience what God's will for us and for the world might be, the more promptly we will be ready and willing to change our lifestyle when personal and communal discernment indicates we are again being controlled by our culture's addictions.

11. We sought through prayer and meditation to improve our conscious contact with God as we understand him, praying only for knowledge of his will for us and the power to carry it out.

The only way we will be freed from our cultural addictions, particularly in face of the false security coming from forms of materialism and consumerism, will be by experiencing that power, the *exousia,* of God in us through prayer.

Daily improving our "conscious contact with God" will help us understand God more experientially. God will become a loving presence who understands our insecurities and anxieties and how our unbelieving society influences us to run after such things (6:32). With this daily contact with the loving God, we will be more open to hear God inviting us to be free of these addictions—not forever but one day at a time. "Your heavenly Father knows all that you need. Seek first his kingship over you, his way of holiness, and all these things will be given you besides. Enough, then, of worrying about tomorrow. Let tomorrow take care of itself. Today has troubles enough of its own" (6:32–34).

One of the serious problems we face in dealing with our cultural addictions is our worry and fear about the future. Often the anxiety is reinforced through the insurance industry, which survives on peoples' fears and engenders mistrust.

Sharing our faith in this conscious contact brings us together to commit ourselves to one another. From this commitment we can create realistic ways of dealing with our addictions as well as our fears. We, like any addict, can develop an attitude that states: "I don't know about tomorrow. But I have made a choice to be sober today and I believe God will be with me to help me to be faithful."

We can make a similar choice to be free from our racism and our sexism, our clericalism and our consumerism, *today*. We also can choose to help free others from those addictions and their structural consequences today. Hearing our God-parent assure us in personal contemplation and communal prayer of the divine presence with us, and remaining in contact with this dynamic reality through a reflective attitude, continually invites us to make the beatitudes part of our life and good news for the world. From this contact, this experience of God, we will become gradually transformed in the transfiguring power of God (17:1–6). We can say to others who despair: "Get up! Do not be afraid" (17:7).

12. *Having had a spiritual awakening as a result of these steps, we tried to carry this message to compulsive cultural addicts and tried to practice these principles in all our affairs.*

Carrying this message is part of the evangelization process. It demands daily practice to resist those addictions over which we otherwise would be so powerless.

Since everything in this world is interconnected, our addictions, and the need for a market to reinforce them, are nourished on the exploitation of others. Just as we do not want to be manipulated by a force more powerful than ourselves, such as the researchers and the marketers, so the cry of other exploited poor must echo in our lives. Rather than just respond by simplifying our lives against the consumer ethic, we are also called to a new form of resistant lifestyle that will address such grave sins against God's plan for the world.

Trying to create basic communities wherein we can celebrate our efforts to be freed from these addictions is not enough. We must move, with the support of the basic communities of conscientization, to bring this message of conversion to others who also contribute to the pain of the world by their addictions. Pope Paul VI said that the disorder in our world (which is reinforced by the nation into which we have been born) demands that we awaken consciences to the drama of misery our addictions create. We are equally demanded to work for a total reordering of society in the power of God's spirit, so that we might resist this sin of our world.[12]

All those who strive to bring their lives to that order which reflects God's plan for the life of the world will have to become poor in spirit. All those who are poor in spirit realize their obligation to make come on earth that reign of God that is in heaven (6:10).

CHAPTER FOUR

Blessed Are Those Who Mourn; They Shall Be Comforted

Jesus, the Compassionate Healer, Touching a Broken World

In many ways, the second beatitude fulfills more messianic hopes than any other. Probably no beatitude more fully expresses Isaiah 61 than this bit of Jesus' wisdom that touches the core of the human condition. What was fulfilled of Isaiah's theology in Jesus' biography is to be realized within the community's spirituality for all time. Like Jesus, all the members of the church are to become ministers of messianic restoration within the world. This ministry is to flow from that experience of *exousia* which enables each member of the church to say:

> The spirit of the Lord God is upon me,
> because the Lord has anointed me; . . .
> To announce a year of favor from the Lord
> and a day of vindication by our God
> to comfort all who mourn;
> To place on those who mourn in Zion
> a diadem instead of ashes,
> To give them oil of gladness in place of mourning,
> a glorious mantle instead of a listless spirit [Isa. 61:1, 2–3].

So much in our lives—our relationships in family and community, our local churches and congregations, our dioceses and orders—points to a kind of listless spirit and depression. This listlessness and sense of alienation are other words for mourning. Mourning continually touches all levels of life. At the same time, many people are witnessing to the anointing they have experienced in their mourning. In turn, they are ministering consolation, healing, and restoration. In place of the listlessness, brokenness, alienation, and division that too often characterize the mainline churches and communities, they are bringing comfort to the world.

Matthew presents Jesus as the fulfillment of this beatitude. Jesus is the one who took on the sins of the world (1:21). In embracing the world's brokenness and mourning (8:17) he was able to cure all who were still under the authority (8:16) of that alienation. In taking all the forms of alienation of the world upon himself, rather than running from them, Jesus redeemed and healed them. This salvation from sin in all its forms opened the possibility for all people to be restored to the original goodness intended for them by God.

The fact that Matthew's Jesus exercised a new authority over the power and control of chaos evidences God's reign breaking into the world. Bringing the comfort of God's restoration (Isa. 40) to the community is the key to Matthew's Gospel.

Matthew presents Jesus exercising God's power through miracles and exorcisms. Above all, Jesus manifests God's care by touching the lives of ordinary people through healings. Matthew shows that, in Jesus' person, God's *exousia* enabled Jesus to be the divine fulfillment of the entry and presence of the messianic presence of God promised by the prophets (8:16–17; 11:2–5; 12:17–21).

One of the depictions of Jesus of most significance for the lived experience of the church occurs in the Beelzebub controversy (12:25–37). Here Jesus declares: "But if it is by the Spirit of God that I expel demons, then the reign of God has overtaken you" (12:28). Commenting on this passage, Donald Senior states:

> God's saving action on behalf of his people—the coming of the Kingdom—is also the ultimate significance of the miracles of Jesus, to which Matthew gives considerable attention (see the whole of chapters eight and nine). The political dimension of the Kingdom motif means that God's saving activity challenges every structure and system of values which threaten human life and the beauty of creation. Jesus' healing activity and his exorcisms mean precisely this.[1]

The healings, the exorcisms, and the nature miracles proclaim the inbreaking of God's reign. This reign must touch every dimension of the world so that creation might be restored to its original purpose.

The miracle stories in 8:1–9:34 represent part of the "works Christ was performing" (11:2) which were restoring creation to its original "work" (see Gen. 1:1–2:4). They represent part of the constitutive dimension of God's reign of power (8:1–9:34). The other part of the "works Christ was performing" refers to the teaching of the Sermon on the Mount (5:1–7:29). With the beatitudes as its prologue (5:1–12) the Sermon serves as the normative dimension of God's reign. These two sections (5:1–7:29 and 8:1–9:34) are bracketed by 4:23–25 and 9:35–9:37. These latter two passages show that the goal of making broken, mourning people whole and comforted was the core of Matthew's spirituality for Jesus as well as the community:

Matthew 4:23–25	*Matthew 9:35–37*
Jesus toured all of Galilee. He taught in their synagogues, proclaimed the good news of the kingdom, and cured the people of every disease and illness. As a consequence of this, his reputation traveled the length of Syria. They carried to him all those afflicted with various diseases and racked with pain: the possessed, the lunatics, the paralyzed. He cured them all. The great crowds that followed him came from Galilee, the Ten Cities, Jerusalem and Judea, and from across the Jordan.	Jesus continued his tour of all the towns and villages. He taught in their synagogues, he proclaimed the good news of God's reign, and he cured every sickness and disease. At the sight of the crowds his heart was moved with pity. They were lying prostrate from exhaustion, like sheep without a shepherd. He said to his disciples: "The harvest is good but laborers are scarce. Beg the harvest master to send out laborers to gather his harvest."

Healing was at the core of Matthew's theology of Jesus. Since his christology was inexorably shaped by his ecclesiology, Matthew immediately connects 4:23–25 and 9:35–37 (and later 11:1, 5) with the disciples and the whole church. He shows how Jesus summoned the twelve disciples (10:1) and the whole church (28:16), empowering both with his authority that they might continue his ministry. The silence about Jesus teaching and preaching after 11:1 seems to indicate that the church's ministry of healing was considered part of the "authority to expel unclean spirits, and to cure sickness and disease of every kind" (10:1).

Nowhere is the centrality of healing brokenness of all kinds in Matthew's christology and ecclesiology so clear as in 9:1–8. After portraying Jesus having authority *(exousia)* not only to forgive sin, but to heal paralysis itself (9:6–7), a change of referent makes it clear that Jesus' ministry has become normative in the ministry of the church. "At the sight, a feeling of awe came over the crowd, and they praised God for giving such authority to *men*" (9:8; emphasis added). What Jesus did is what the church is to do.

Matthew 5:1–7:29 (the normative dimension) and 8:1–9:34 (the constitutive dimension) represent the two halves of Jesus' circle of care. These must be extended through us into the world. Matthew shows the importance of these two sections by having each begin with a reference to the mountain, the symbol of God's presence-in-authority. Jesus, the Wisdom Teacher, went up the mountain to share God's plan of living with his disciples (5:1f.). Now, as Caring Healer, he leaves the mountain (8:1f.) to manifest in deeds that plan of living which restores people, groups, and the world to their original purposes.

The first cure of a person, one also considered outside the community (8:1-4), shows how God's reign is to break into the whole world. Jesus *sees* a leper in need, *cares* for him, and *calls* him to wholeness. Just as God had seen the affliction of the people in Egypt, heard their cry of complaint, cared for them, and called them to liberation (Exod. 3:7-8), so now from another mountain the liberating presence of God will be felt in the world through Jesus-Emmanuel and that church in whose members he dwells. As Jack Dean Kingsbury makes clear:

> Implicitly, the introduction of this story is also of considerable christ-ological importance. For one thing, it fixes attention on Jesus from the outset. . . . For another thing, by noting that Jesus descends from the mountain on which he has been teaching, it alludes to the circumstance that the unparalleled authority with which Jesus has taught there is also the authority with which he is about to heal this leper. Just as Jesus was made to stand above Moses in his teaching, so he will likewise stand above Moses in the mighty works he does.[2]

This initial miracle story (which is the first of ten in this section) provides a kind of summary statement showing how Jesus used his authority to establish God's circle of care within the human condition. Coming down the mountain (8:1) empowered by his God, Jesus shows how the divine presence is to be experienced: among the crowds, on behalf of the people. In Jesus, God has come to be with the people, aware of their need for healing.

Matthew shows how Jesus was first approached by a world in need in the figure of the leper. In Jesus and Matthew's time, the leper was considered both physically and socially separated from society. Even religion considered the leper someone to be rejected. Somehow, this leper sensed Jesus was different. He was approachable. "Suddenly a leper came forward and did him homage, saying to him, 'Sir, if you will to do so, you can cure me' "(8:2).

The encounter between the leper in need and Jesus with the hoped-for resources shows in a striking way Matthew's link between prayer and minis-try. In recognizing Jesus as the one with the authority of God to heal, the leper comes forward (see Num. 18:4) to quite literally worship Jesus (see Exod. 4:31; Ps. 5:7); he paid Jesus "homage."

The use of such a word by Matthew is almost liturgical. It indicates that the leper recognizes Jesus as having power previously equated with God. He addresses Jesus as "Lord." As Israel appealed to Yahweh (Exod. 3:7) during its time of need, so the leper prays to Jesus: ". . . if you will to do so, you can cure me" (8:2). If Jesus willed to do so, he could deliver the leper as God did Israel.

As God's presence with the people, Jesus-Emmanuel is invited to faithfully incarnate in the leper Israel's central religious experience. At the time of the exodus, God saw the affliction of the people and heard their prayer for restoration. Saying in response to their call, "Therefore I have come down"

(Exod. 3:8), God became present in Moses' life to free the people of their brokenness. If, in the former process of deliverance God's name and identity were revealed (Exod. 3:12–14), could Jesus, whose name means deliverance (1:21), do any less? Now, whenever these same conditions of need are present can any of those who are baptized in that same name not respond (28:16–20) in the power of that name (19:19–20)?

In this first request that the reign of God be manifest in the world, Matthew's leper recognizes Jesus as one with God's authority, able to have sovereignty over everything as God does (see 11:25; 19:26). In light of Matthew's further discussion (see 9:8; 11:27–28), the whole community shares this power too. As we see people who are in need and who are broken, we too can hear their prayers and cries of complaint. We too can heal sicknesses and diseases of every kind: internal and external, as well as personal, interpersonal, and infrastructural. Our response to this need demands that we no longer remain deaf to the calls of people who suffer. In Jesus' name we can stretch out our hands, touch that pain in all the ways it may be manifested, and say, "I do will it. Be cured" (8:3a).

In the Greek, Jesus' response to the leper's call for healing reflects an almost natural disposition of availability that is triggered by anyone in need. "I do will it" means "I am inclined." When we say "I am inclined," it means something within us makes us act or think the way we do. God's power within Jesus disposed him, by nature and by name, to save the people from their needs. As image of God, Jesus would always respond in care when he saw need. Because he cared about everyone, he would be open to being called upon for healing.

With this power of Jesus within each of us, by nature and name, we too should be inclined to respond in care to the needs of the world. If we do not evidence this spontaneous, automatic care of God, we will not see God. The pattern of God's life in Jesus will not be in us.

The call addressed to us by all those seeking deliverance from their need demands the same response from us that Jesus made to the leper's prayer for healing. As Jack Dean Kingsbury notes:

> The miracle as such takes place upon Jesus' utterance of the healing word: "I will; be clean!" (v.3b–c). The fact that Jesus appropriates the words of the leper in giving reply to him (cf. v.3 to v.2) reveals that the response of Jesus to the leper is to be construed as merciful in character and as confirming the resolve to heal he displayed already in stretching out his hand (cf. v.3a). In Jesus, his Son, God the Father manifests his will to save (cf. 18:14).[3]

We have received God's response to our personal calls for healing; now we are empowered to respond to the cries of the world. We are commissioned in power to proclaim to the world the good news of what God has done in us. "Then Jesus said to him: 'See to it that you tell no one. Go and show yourself to the priest and offer the gift Moses prescribed. That should be the proof they need' " (8:4).

The Mosaic law stated that only a priest could declare a leper cleansed (Lev. 13:2; 14:2–32). Since the leper was considered both a physical and social outcast, the leper's physical healing by Jesus could not remain isolated from society. Thus the individual healing would serve to manifest healing in the social realm as well.

A community is more enriched when one of its members is made more whole. In the strength of this greater wholeness, it can evidence greater solidarity as it ministers healing to a broken world. Just as the leper was able to be restored to the community, making it more whole, so the church (healed in the saving waters of baptism and ongoing reconciliation) is to minister to the needs of the whole world. In this way it contributes to the reordering of creation itself.

Matthew seems to have wanted to stress this universal dimension of Jesus' healing. The first three healings all refer to people in one way or another considered outside the particularist Jewish community. Immediately after cleansing the leper—an outcast from the community—Jesus healed two more representatives of groups not considered by the structures of Judaism to be fully part of the community: the centurion's son (8:5–13) and Peter's mother-in-law (8:14–15). God's authority in Jesus and the community must break into the whole world. It is to touch any group not part of the mainstream. It cures any pain to bring about restoration. This action fulfills what had been promised through the prophet Isaiah:

> It was our infirmities he bore,
> our sufferings he endured [8:17].

What are these infirmities of ours that he bore? They are our brokenness and tears, our anxiety and guilt, our experience of rejection and separation, as well as our loneliness and depression. What are these sufferings of ours that he endured? They are our alienation and grief, our anger and fear, our experience of pain and disappointment, as well as our sadness and, even, our death.

In healing sickness and diseases of every kind by bearing them in his own body, Jesus brought healing to all levels of life, not just those in our own personal lives, but in our groups and infrastructures as well. In taking on these infirmities and sufferings instead of running from them, in taking authority over them instead of being controlled by them, Jesus' ministry proclaimed what the words of this beatitude proclaim. Infirmities and sufferings must be taken on; they must be embraced before comfort and consolation can be experienced. By facing the brokenness and admitting the depression in his own life, relationships, and world, Jesus showed clearly that wholeness and healing come only when we enter into the *tohu wabohu* and bring light out of its darkness and despair.

What is this wholeness Jesus offers? It is the unity and joy, the security and peace, the experience of acceptance and restoration, as well as the new sense of meaning and enthusiasm that comes in a new, risen life. What is this healing he promises? It is the reconciliation and warmth, the comfort and consolation, the experience of tenderness and compassion, as well as the understanding and love that comes in a loving, caring relationship. If Jesus bore our infirmities and sufferings it was to bring wholeness and healing. The same mission is ours.

The rest of this chapter will show how Jesus took on brokenness in his own life, relationships, and society in such a way that comfort rather than mourning became the new dynamic for life. Bringing wholeness where infirmities once held reign and healing, where sufferings were in control, can now become the pattern for the spirituality of those who share in the *exousia* of Jesus.

Mourning and Comfort in Our Individual Lives

Matthew shows Jesus entering into this beatitude in his own individual experience of mourning. At the beginning of his public life, because he allowed himself to experience the temptation and mourning symbolized by the desert, Jesus received the comfort of angels (4:11). At the end of his life, Jesus experienced a succession of brokenness, from the agony in the garden (26:36–46) to the moment of his death (27:45–54).

In the garden with his disciples, Jesus voiced the depth of his pain: "My heart is nearly broken with sorrow " (26:38). The disciples' unconcern, despite earlier professions of care (26:31–35), failed to bring any comfort in his mourning. Comfort would come to Jesus only in understanding he had been faithful to God's plan by trying to heal a broken world. "My Father, if this cannot pass me by without my drinking it, your will be done!" (26:42).

In his agony Jesus did not run from pain. Rather he took it upon himself; he owned the brokenness and depression. Even though he admitted he did not want the pain or depression (26:39), by embracing them, Jesus received a deeper experience of inner peace as a reward for his fidelity. It offset the pain of the disciples' insensitivity and the world's hate. Comfort came to him in his mourning; he was blessed because his consolation had been ultimately in God.

Matthew's beatitudinal spirituality demands that we own our own personal brokenness, especially that which occurs because of our own sin. It demands that we confess that we have betrayed our call to be faithful to God's plan. If we do not admit that sin is part of our experience and mourn over it we will remain controlled by it. But, to the depth and degree that we own the brokenness in our individual lives, to the same depth and degree we will experience the blessedness of God's comfort, healing, and consolation. Only when we are willing to face our own inner alienation from God will we be able to experience the sense of wholeness that expresses messianic peace and fulfillment. An example from my life might illustrate what I mean.

I was becoming quite sensitive to the fact that there were areas in my life that exclude God. While not actually "sinning" all that much, I sensed that a deeper form of alienation controlled me. My gnawing sense was reinforced by the prayer that seemed to be coming to my lips with growing frequency: "From my inmost sin, O Lord, deliver me." More and more I was becoming conscious that this inmost sin did not really refer to what I was or was not doing externally. It referred to that part of my life where God was absent. My real self was alienated from the other, from God.

External sins did not matter that much to Jesus, although he brought healing to them. What concerned Jesus about them was that they revealed brokenness at the base of life. There God could not be found. "From the mind *(kardia)* stem evil designs" (15:19), Jesus had said. My *kardia,* or heart, was the center of my life; there I was alienated from God. From this underlying root of separation from God were stemming all sorts and forms of curiosities and phantasies, questions and doubts. The more I reflected on these roots, the more I realized that they could be given the traditional names of the capital, or underlying, sins: envy, avarice, lust, sloth, jealousy, gluttony, and anger. Our underlying capital sins (as persons, groups and societies) point to where we are alienated from God, each other, and ourselves.

As I reflected on my life, I had to admit that, within my depths, one, two, or three of these underlying attitudes were deeply affecting my drives, my wonderings, and my preoccupations.

Often during such times of reflection we also discover that our external "sins" or orientations are the symptoms of our inner disease. These symptoms usually reflect those inner realities we fear to face. For instance, our seeking affirmation and acceptance can expose our pride and jealousy. Our consumerism and materialism can unmask our gluttony and avariciousness. Our daydreams and fears about our sexuality can reflect our lust (and, perhaps, our pride or jealousy). These underlying fears and drives are the target for the ideologies of the advertisers. They realize how central such emotions are to our motivations. Whoever controls the motivations controls the behavior (see 6:21).

When we become aware of these points of alienation and mourning in our lives, we can do one of two things. We can deny they are there in various ways: increasing our work; getting more distracted. We can even submit to their control in our phantasies, relationships, and actions. The other thing we can do is to face them head-on.

I was becoming increasingly aware that as long as I was refusing to deal with these underlying areas of my life, what Jesus said to his disciples would be totally applicable to me: "The eye is the body's lamp. If your eyes are good, your body will be filled with light; if your eyes are bad, your body will be in darkness. And if your light is darkness, how deep will the darkness be! No man can serve two masters" (6:22–24). As the awareness of my darkness increased, so did the realization of my need to be delivered from my inmost alienation from God. This realization of my need to do something was further heightened when two ·friends of mine told me about events connected to their experiences with the charismatic renewal.

The first story that made me anxious and somewhat fearful (a sure sign, I had begun telling myself, that I was not yet as free as I thought I was) was shared with me by Fred Just. At that time Fred was a member of the Capuchin Order from another province. He told me about going to a healing retreat at Mount Saint Augustine on Staten Island.

The leaders of the retreat had decided to bring to the retreat center a woman from New England. She was supposedly suffering from demonic possession in six or seven different forms. The effort to free the woman of that evil had a deeply moving effect on Fred.

Listening to Fred talk of his experience and noting that never was a word mentioned there about the powers and principalities affecting social structures, I realized that I was concerned about structures and social sin. But was I addressing the devil, the sin in me as an individual? Was I not just the opposite of what I had criticized in so many charismatics? I had found fault with parts of the movement because so many charismatics seemed so uncaring about the dignity of all people and the need to work for a reallocation of the earth's resources. But, I was beginning to realize, equal fault could be found with me because I was not letting the Spirit of Jesus take full authority over my whole life.

The next story that challenged me was told by Werner Wolf. Werner loved to relate what took place during the annual National Catholic Charismatic Conference for Priests and Deacons at Steubenville, Ohio. It seems a priest to his right was "slain in the Spirit," an expression used to describe being totally taken up in God's power and loving presence. At the sight of the priest, fainted away, everyone praised God.

On Werner's left, a deacon was not quite so fortunate. The deacon was not possessed like the lady from New England; he was obsessed. This means that, although he did not directly will any evil in his life, some evil still controlled him. Sin had authority over him. The underlying control of his obsession now was externalized. The deacon had fallen down and was groveling like a dog. The people nearby knew they had to take authority over that controlling force in the deacon's life in the name of Jesus. In order to do so, they first needed to discover the nature, or the name, of the power that had so much authority over him. The name of the underlying control or obsession usually reveals one of the capital sins.

These two experiences made an enormous impression on me. The depth of their influence, however, became quite evident to me when Werner and some other men if our province started asking me, "Mike, why don't you come with us to Steubenville?" Little did they know why their invitation was making me so nervous!

I was quite aware of my own inmost sin, where I was not allowing God to take authority over my thoughts and behavior. My immediate emotional reaction to their invitation represented a classic defensive position. "Oh, no, I can't go," I remember saying to myself. "What would happen if I got zapped?" As my defensiveness increased, so did the realization that my fear and anxiety, as well as my growing feeling of guilt, would control me if I did not do something. At that point I began telling myself, "You phony. Here you go around saying with St. Francis that you want God to be your All. And you know very well that that very defensiveness shows that there is an area of your life where you aren't free. And you know that unless you deal with it and convert from it, you are going to remain under its control."

Around this same time, I was also developing a theory that went something like, "If you get defensive about anything, it means you are afraid to face something. If you fear anything it means something controls you. And if you do not face what controls you—your hurts, your anger, your underlying alienation from God—you will never be free. And if you are not free, the Spirit of the Lord cannot be there, because where the Spirit of the Lord is, there is freedom (see 2 Cor. 3:17)." So, quite aware of the inmost sin controlling me, it seemed my theory was apropos to my situation. Either I would continue to deny what was going on in my life or be invited to conversion by addressing it. Consequently I forced myself to say, "I am going to Steubenville!"

Before going to Steubenville, however, I knew I had to prepare myself for the eventuality of getting zapped! I would admit my mourning, my inner alienation, to another. Realizing the admission of what is deepest within us can be done only with a total stranger or a complete friend, I decided I would share this area of my life with Fred Just. Fred was more than my Capuchin Franciscan brother. He was a friend. Fred fulfills the definition of a friend: one who knows everything about you and loves you just the same. He would be God's angel sent to comfort me in my mourning. Fred would be God's minister sent to heal my brokenness.

The moment for this restoration to take place occurred at a time when we were both in New York. We decided to take extra time to be together.

The first thing we did was to see Liv Ullmann, my favorite actress, in Eugene O'Neill's play, "Anna Christie." Anna had been sent, as a motherless child, from Boston to a Minnesota farm to live with her cousins. After running away from the farm she went to St. Paul to become a prostitute. In the city she became very ill. Not wanting to go back to the farm, she had nobody to turn to except her father in Boston. So she returned, not wanting him to know about her past and her inmost sin. Her father, meanwhile, had been living on the barges in the harbor with one woman after another.

As the play begins, he is reading Anna's letter telling him that she will be coming. He immediately gets rid of the last woman who shared his barge. As the play develops, these two needy humans, with their brokenness and hidden sins, their alienation and their hurts, start healing each other. By the end of the play they have developed a process of mutual restoration. They have created a deep bonding of personal care that enables them to touch others.

After the play, Fred started to tell me things he had been discussing with a counselor. He shared experiences from his past and present life, telling me about experiences he had had at different stages in his life. Listening to his story, I was able to understand and accept not only the experiences, but Fred himself.

Sharing his mourning with me became an invitation to reveal and admit similar areas from my own past and present life. So I started talking to Fred, admitting my inmost sins, revealing those areas of my life that had been controlling me. I told him about my cowardice in grade and high school, those sexual fantasies you get when you are growing up (which never seem to leave!), and my hidden fears. Since it was a year before our Provincial Chapter and because various brothers had been telling me they thought I might become provincial, I was able to share my emotions about that. Did I want the job or not? Was it something I coveted deep down or was I fearful of failing in this ministry as I became more and more aware of my limitations?

Whatever came to my mind, I was going to share with Fred. I was not going to leave one stone unturned. I was going to be delivered from the depth of my sin. As I shared these drives and fears, these hurts and hopes, Fred was accepting the reality of their existence. But even more so, he was accepting Michael Crosby. He was touching me as a minister of healing in the deepest part of my mourning. In Fred, Jesus was saying "I do will it. Be cured" (8:3).

As I shared my mourning I realized what it meant to be having "the Spirit of the Lord God" come to anoint me. My growing release and joy gradually announced "a year of favor from the Lord." I was being restored to my original goodness; the tears, the forms of brokenness were giving way. In their stead was "the oil of gladness" (Isa. 61:1, 2, 3).

The experience of God's vindication of my sinfulness in Fred's acceptance brought back a line from "Anna Christie"—the only line I can remember. As we sat talking after the play and as my joy increased, I recalled a line toward the end of the play. Anna was on the boat by herself. She had her arms wrapped around herself in a hug, symbolizing a "glorious mantle instead of a listless spirit" (Isa. 61:3). I could identify with her emotion as she repeated over and over again, "I feel so clean; I feel so clean!"

Fred enabled me to experience this second beatitude in my depths: Blessed are those who mourn; they shall be comforted. Fred's ministry of care enabled Jesus-Emmanuel to cleanse me. As a leper I had come to Jesus saying, ". . . if you will to do so, you can cure me." Now, through the warmth and affection of Fred, "Jesus stretched out his hand and touched him and said, 'I do will it. Be cured' "(8:2–3). Now I would be able to go back and report my cleansing to others, not by broadcasting it (like I am doing here!), but by being a better minister of healing, a more sensitive angel of comfort to others.

This experience made me realize the absolute need every person has, in ongoing ways, of dealing with those fears and anxieties, those forms of guilt and pain, that mask anger and resentment and that create mourning and brokenness in our lives, memories, and relationships. Wherever the alienation and emptiness exist, in the power of Jesus' name, we are invited to deal with the mourning in order that we might experience comfort. From and in this experience of our own cleansing we can become angels of comfort who seek to affirm and restore the lonely lost sheep. In this way we further God's plan that not "a single one of these little ones shall ever come to grief" (18:14).

In the garden Jesus entered deeply into the experience of sorrow and mourning, depression and pain. This was the conclusion to the life process wherein he took all our infirmities upon himself (8:17). Open to this process, he was raised to a new, risen life. He was made whole in the resurrection.

Until we admit those areas of sorrow and loneliness, depression and pain, resentment and anger, that are deep within us—especially from the ways they express themselves in our inmost sins—they will continue to control us. They will have authority over us, and our relationships. Consequently, we need to enter the process of dealing with our mourning.

We need other angels, like Fred, to bring comfort to our mourning through the forgiveness of our sins. Whoever these angels may be, we are told they are the ambassadors, the alter egos of that God who brings us restoration. "I assure you, whatever you declare bound on earth shall be held bound in heaven, and whatever you declare loosed on earth shall be held loosed in heaven" (18:18; cf. 16:19). Experiencing forgiveness and reconciliation of our own sins, we can become better ministers of forgiveness and reconciliation. We can rejoice with Paul, saying to others as he said to the Corinthians:

> Praised be God, the Father of our Lord Jesus Christ, the Father of mercies, and the God of all consolation! He comforts us in all our afflictions and thus enables us to comfort those who are in trouble, with the same consolation we have received from him [2 Cor. 1:3–4].

The consolation "we have received from him" is God's healing, forgiving *exousia.* It is the power of the Holy Spirit given to us in healing which enables us to share this Spirit with all others in need.

As this beatitude was experienced by Jesus in his own individual life it can be experienced in ours as well. At the same time this beatitude can be something that each of us, in imitation of Jesus, can bring to the next dimension of reality: the interpersonal level.

Mourning and Comfort in Our Relationships

Matthew does not elaborate on Jesus' grief at the death of a close friend like the Baptist. He does not comment on the tears Jesus showed at the death of Lazarus (John 11:35ff.), which we read about in the Fourth Gospel. Yet, anyone who has just heard of or experienced the death of a loved one, can identify with the emotions and grief that must have enveloped Jesus upon being informed of John's death. "When Jesus heard this, he withdrew by boat from there to a deserted place by himself" (14:13a). When we lose such a loved one, we just want to be alone in our pain and loss.

Jesus would not remain immobilized by his sense of loss. The brokenness of others again invited him not to be controlled by his own pain and grief, but to continue a ministry of alleviating the hurts of others. "When he disembarked and saw the vast throng, his heart was moved with pity, and he cured their sick" (14:14).

The power to heal others is a gift the apostles were given for the sake of announcing the good news (10:1, 8). Matthew's theology shows that the disciples were not given the power to teach until chapter twenty-eight. Furthermore, they did little actual preaching (10:7). Especially from 11:2ff. on, Matthew shows that almost all of the disciples' exercise of power revolved around healing. Matthew seems very conscious of the human and psychological fact that barriers and controls must be broken and healed before people can be open to preaching and teaching. When we are in pain we cannot easily be taught or sermonized.

The healing power of the disciples flowed from the same *exousia* that enabled Jesus to heal. Yet, while they shared the same *exousia* to heal, the disciples were not always able to heal as Jesus healed. The difference was the disciples' lack of faith (17:14–21). When our healing of others does not measure up to the healing power manifested by Jesus, it is important that we examine our faith and that of the people with whom we minister. Because the disciples lacked faith, they were unable to implement the normative dimension of the circle of care even though they had been constitutively established to do so.

If we are to bring comfort, consolation, and restoration to those who mourn, healing must be central to our lives, as it was the core of the lives of the disciples and Jesus. It was the realization of the centrality of healing in the Scriptures that finally prompted me to go to Steubenville. I was becoming increasingly aware, applying Saul Alinsky's terminology to Jesus,[4] that the vested interest that led people initially to Jesus was their need for healing. Meeting that need, Jesus then invited them to go further in faith by his preaching and teaching (11:1).

I had become convinced that healing was *the* basic characteristic of God's care in Jesus. Whenever I would open the Scriptures to a non-infancy or non-passion-death-resurrection section I would always find a story of healing. One time I might open it to an example where Jesus healed individual people, such as the leper (8:1–4) or the possessed mute (9:32–34). At other times, Jesus' healing might be related to the second level. A group might be cured, like the two men possessed by demons (8:28–34) or the two blind men (9:27–31). One time I even opened to an example of restoration on the third level of what we would call part of the infrastructure, with the cleansing of the temple (21:12–16).

Not wanting to place any barrier to the expression of a possible gift of healing in my life, I went to Steubenville. I asked for the gift of healing there, but I came back without experiencing it in any manifest or extraordinary way. Because healing was so central to Jesus' life and the acts of the early church (1 Cor. 12:9), I remained haunted by the thought that it should be more evidenced in my life. So I continued to search, wondering if and where this gift might be some power the Spirit shared with me. Not until a year later did I realize that healing cannot be so limited to the level of extraordinary gift that it no longer represents the normative expression of our faith.

While visiting De Kalb, Ill. in September 1978, I decided to do some spiritual reading from one of the books I found in the apartment of my host, Chuck Walters. I picked up one by Barbara Schlemon: *Healing Prayer.* The title of one of its chapters immediately captured my interest: "Who Has the Gift of Healing?" In this short work Barbara Schlemon discussed three passages. The first (whose equivalent can be found in 28:20 and 10:7–8) stated: "Signs like these will accompany those who have professed their faith; . . . the sick upon whom they lay their hands will recover" (Mark 16:17, 18). Jesus was saying, I discovered, that healing is not so much connected with any gift; it is related to faith in Jesus' power in us which accomplishes that healing! The next passage (with its parallel in 7:7) again connected healing to faith rather than to some extraordinary gift: "I solemnly assure you, the man who has faith in me will do the works I do, and greater far than these. Why? Because I go to the Father" (John 14:12). Again, the Scriptures were making it clear that the works, *erga,* could occur if we but believed. (John uses *erga* here just as Matthew used it in 11:2 to describe Jesus' *exousia* of healing and teaching and their extension in us, the church.) In the final passage (with its equivalent found in 18:19–20) John and Jesus continued: ". . . and whatever you ask in my name I will do, so as to glorify the Father in the Son. Anything you ask me in my name I will do" (John 14:13–14).

Reading these three passages made it clear that healing is normative for the ordinary life of faith. I thought to myself, "I *do* have faith. I believe that Jesus is Lord; now I must develop that faith and not have my lack of faith control me."

Once we believe we share in God's power we must always be open to let that power become manifest. The invitation to do so continually presents itself. Little did I know how soon this fact about faith would be tested!

That afternoon I talked to the priests of the Diocese of Rockford. I drove home in a very thankful, joy-filled mood. Besides the gift of the morning reading, I was eagerly awaiting the next day's meeting with our Provincial Council.

In June of 1978 our Province had held an extraordinary Chapter to elect a new Council. Like every congregation of men in the United States, we had come to that Chapter with ten to fifteen years of upheaval behind us as we attempted to re-create a form of Capuchin Franciscan life that would be relevant to the needs of our era. The effort had taken its toll in numbers and enthusiasm. Studies showed that many of us sensed a need to begin a process of re-membering ourselves in prayer and concern for justice to deepen our unity. The unity we were seeking to deepen, I thought, took place when Ron Smith, a man of deep prayer and concern for the poor, was elected Provincial Minister on the first ballot. This was the first time in our modern history that a non-incumbent was elected on the first ballot. Then I was elected to the Council, followed by Keith Clark. Then the next two councilors were chosen. The whole process was a source of deeper bonding for many of us.

The unity we wanted to experience as a whole Province was something we sensed possible in the microcosm of our five-man Council. The June experience fired my anticipation for the Council meeting set to begin in Milwaukee the next morning. When I got home, however, the first words that greeted me came from one of our candidates. "Mike, the Council meeting has been cancelled. Ron's been taken to the hospital in Detroit. He's been having trouble seeing and they think there's an aneurysm on his brain. So they're going to have a brain scan tomorrow in the morning and will be ready to operate tomorrow afternoon."

Thud! My first reaction was: "God, what are you up to now? You just gave him to us; what are you trying to pull now?"

It happened that this same night, Evarist Bertrand was to talk to the candidates. Evarist had been deported from Nicaragua by the Somoza regime. He had been harrassed for forming basic Christian communites of conscientization. He had gathered young people in communities and they, in turn, had committed themselves for extended periods of service to the church and community. Since such new forms of religious dedication were considered subversive, Evarist had been harrassed by U.S.-trained military in Nicaragua, as well as El Salvador, before being put on a plane and sent to the United States with $5.00 in his pocket. Now he was touring the Midwest sharing his faith and experiences with different Capuchin fraternities.

As inspiring and interesting as both he and his message were, I was preoccupied with thoughts about Ron. When Evarist finished, I voiced my concern and said, "I really feel like praying for Ron." About ten of us, including Evarist, went to chapel to pray.

I began by recalling the Scripture passages I had read that morning in De Kalb. Then we all recalled that Jesus had said: "Again I tell you, if two of you join your voices on earth to pray for anything whatever, it shall be granted you by my Father in heaven" (18:19). Here were the ten of us. We were gathered together in chapel sharing God's word as well as our tears and hopes.

Confident that Jesus had meant what he said about asking for anything in his name (18:20), someone prayed, "Lord, we're asking for healing for Ron. And we're expecting that you are going to give him healing!" Another brother recalled the centurion pericope, where Jesus healed the official's son, even though the son was a distance away (8:5–13). We were in Milwaukee. Ron was hundreds of miles away in Detroit. Yet the same God was present to him in his hospital room as was here in our gathering (18:20). "Jesus," someone prayed, "just as you did it for the centurion, in the power of your name, we ask that you heal Ron."

After songs and silences and more prayers of thanks and praise, Matthew also seemed to speak to those doubts that crop up at a time like this: "What if nothing happens?" Someone recalled how Jesus seemed to understand this fear by saying, "Your heavenly Father knows all that you need" (6:32). Even though God sees us in need and cares about us, as a loving parent, God also wants us to be poor in spirit.

> Ask, and you will receive. Seek, and you will find. Knock, and it will be opened to you. For the one who asks, receives. The one who seeks, finds. The one who knocks, enters. Would one of you hand his son a stone when he asks for a loaf, or a poisonous snake when he asks for a fish? If you, with all your sins, know how to give your children what is good, how much more will your heavenly Father give good things to anyone who asks him! [7:7–11].

Like any caring parent who respects our integrity and freedom, God knows what we need. But when we recognize ourselves and others in need, Jesus tells us, we have to admit this dependence in poverty of spirit. "This is how you are to pray: 'Our Father in heaven, hallowed be your name, your kingdom come' " (6:9–10a). So that night the sense of our prayer was: "May that reign of wholeness, of healing, of restoration, and peace come into Ron and into the life of every person, every group, and every structure. And tonight, Lord, let it touch your minister Ron in a special way. May 'Your will be done on earth as it is in heaven' (6:10b). Certainly you have revealed your will in Jesus' words that you want us to ask for whatever we need. Lord, you can't let us down."

With the Scriptures, prayers, and psalms we encouraged each other's faith. This form of prayer itself ministered healing among us, lessening our fears in a powerful way. We left that prayer expecting great things to happen.

I went to work Tuesday morning to catch up on some things before the Council meeting. But I was too preoccupied with Ron. It was a sunny day, so I thought I would go to the lake for some sun and a swim. On the way to pick up a couple of the brothers at the Capuchin Fraternity House, I had a feeling that seemed to say, "Things are going well in Detroit." So I told the brothers about my thought. We went to the lake and, about the time we decided to return home, I had another reflection that simply said: "Ron is all right." As my heart got a little bigger in hope, I was tempted to keep the reflection to myself. "Who knows, I thought; it might not be from the Lord." But then, with equal insistence, something told me: "If you believe in your heart, confess it with your lips; you must give in to what seems to be the operation of the Lord." So I said to the others, "You know, I just had a thought that tells me Ron is okay."

As we got out of the car at home, I fully expected that God had heard our prayer. Walking into the house, Perry McDonald, our superior, said, "We've had good news from Detroit. Ron is all right. They don't know what's the matter, but there is no aneurysm so they don't need to operate."

"Wow, is that great!" I said. (This was my own version of "Praise the Lord!") As I started to walk away, another thought challenged me. "You've got to own this too." So I went back to Perry and asked, "When did that call come in?"

"About a half hour ago," he responded.

It was around the same time (see 8:13) that I heard, "Ron is all right." We had asked. We had received.

I've shared this faith journey because it seems we all need to be invited to submit ourselves and our sins and relationships to ever-deepening forms of healing. With the power of healing comforting us, we can become healers of others. We are called to be open to the myriad ways we can extend this expression of our faith, not just to the Rons in our life, but to those in our lives whom we have hurt and who have hurt us.

This kind of healing can restore the brokenness that comes from our hurt memories, can heal the pain that comes from mistrust, and can bind up our wounds. By baptism every one has the power to become a healer. Everyone has the power to experience this beatitude and to touch the lives of others and the whole world with its comfort.

Mourning over Structures to Bring Comfort

In facing head-on the various aspects of brokenness and depression in his own life and relationships, Jesus experienced the comfort of experiencing the fullness of the reign of God's perfection and wholeness. But, besides experiencing this second beatitude on these two levels, Jesus also evidenced it in the way he brought healing to the third level, the infrastructures of his society.

Probably the most poignant section of Matthew's Gospel comes toward the end of Jesus' life. Jesus is at the end of his rope trying to get his institution to convert. Time after time the leaders refuse to convert. Instead they place one roadblock after another in the path of Jesus' ministry. Overtaken with frustration, the only thing Jesus can do is vent an emotion of utter futility. His diatribe unleashed against the scribes and Pharisees represents one of the most pathos-filled statements in the Scriptures: "O Jerusalem, Jerusalem, murderess of prophets and stoner of those who were sent to you! How often have I yearned to gather your children, as a mother bird gathers her young under her wings, but you refused me " (23:37).

Although Jesus worked throughout his life for communal restoration, the infrastructure would not budge. Unable to bring about conversion because of society's sluggishness of heart (see 13:14–15), Jesus could do nothing else but mourn over his people. By admitting his brokenness and frustration at society's intransigence Jesus owned the grief from his apparent failure; yet comfort would come to Jesus in this realization that he had been faithful. A restored community would be announced by an angel of comfort (28:1–7) at the resurrection, after Jesus would be taken to the depth of despair.

Jesus mourned over his own institution's infidelity. Today Jesus' Spirit in us invites us to grieve, mourn over, the brokenness and alienation within our institutions. But, we might ask ourselves, "When was the last time we really grieved over such things as the sexism in our churches, the consumerism that tears apart our families, or the ideology that justifies destruction of whole peoples and the environment in the name of freedom?" Healing will never come within the infrastracture until we first admit the existence of the sins and cultural addictions that contribute to human and societal brokenness, and then mourn over them.

When our province came together for the 1978 Chapter, we had to admit that, as an institution, we had brokenness among our members. Despite the great efforts made since the Second Vatican Council, to achieve unity, a study showed we had not yet achieved the agreement we seemed to have had before the Council. We did not agree on which model of church we favored, how we were to live, which ministries were primary, and whether we sensed a need for a common goal. Faced with these facts about our dis-memberment some of us sensed we could no longer continue to live with our heads in the sand. We had to own the very real differences that are part of the reality of every group in the church-in-transition. We sensed a need to begin healing the wounds from that dismemberment. Admitting our dismemberment could lead to re-membering ourselves. From a re-membering we could then develop new forms of care with which we could initiate a process of patterning our lives in more unified ways for the good of society.[6]

For a week in June 1978 we gathered together under the theme: "Re-Membering Our Spirit and Life." We did not seek to achieve any great decisions or resolutions. We wanted to let the Holy Spirit, the real minister general of our province,[7] bring comfort to those areas over which we mourned.

At the liturgy celebrating the twenty-fifth and fiftieth jubilees of our brothers, the homilist was Rupert Dorn, a previous provincial. I never remembered Rupert as an exciting preacher. His charism seemed to be administration. During those tumultuous years, 1967 through 1973, his steady, low-keyed approach as provincial kept the province on an even keel. After leaving office, Rupert became a rural pastor and got involved in the charismatic renewal.

Rupert spoke on that occasion about the biblical concept of jubilee—the "year of favor" that Isaiah promised to those who were poor in spirit and who mourned (Isa. 61). Rupert noted that biblical jubilee contained elements of reflection, reconciliation, and freedom. He observed that we had taken time off that week for reflection. We were reflecting together on the future of the province. This reflection, the first step in bringing about a jubilee (see Lev. 25), would lead to the realization of our collective need for the next dimension of jubilee: reconciliation. Only if we sought reconciliation, Rupert urged, would we be able to experience the final gift of jubilee: our freedom as individuals and as a province.

Toward the end of the homily, Peter Kutch started to play gently on the pipe organ. The music and Rupert's words began to touch many hearts. As brothers put their heads in their hands, with some allowing the tears to roll down their faces, letting their mourning take hold of them, the once-average preacher built in *exousia*. Inviting us to conversion in the power of God's word he had let touch him, Rupert concluded:

> So during these days let us in the spirit of reconciliation and unity, while we will be different in age and shapes, in thinking and lifestyles and ministry, let us be united in our expressions of love. Let us be soaked in love these days. Soaked in love.
>
> In the spirit of jubilee, we pray that through our reflections and reconciliation we will feel a new freedom. We will feel that truly the bonds that are holding us down, that are impeding the progress of our beloved province will be cut. Jesus, you said at the resurrection of Lazarus, "Unbind him, let him go free." Unbind us and let us go free. Cut the bonds of bitterness and resentment that we may harbor. Cut the bonds of self-pity and mistrust and fear and false respect.
>
> Cut the bonds that keep us from truly loving our brothers and telling them so. Lord Jesus, heal all divisions in our lives. Let us now move into that gesture of reconciliation, the sign of peace, with a warm hand clasp or, if we feel comfortable, a hug and embrace. Let our brothers know that we are happy to be present to each other. My brothers, peace be with you. My brothers, I love you.[8]

For the next ten minutes or so, the whole chapel seemed to move. Brothers sought each other out, seeking reconciliation and peace. A couple of friars came up to me saying, as they hugged me, "Crosby, I really need reconciliation with you." I did not even know there had been alienation between us! But it did not matter. That afternoon a beautiful experience of comfort touched the mourning that had formerly controlled our province as an institution. We experienced the second beatitude: Blessed are those who admit their mourning; they shall be comforted with a new-found freedom and power.

This beatitude, however, cannot be restricted to our own limited institutions, be they local church or province. It must touch the total religious institution, as well as our economic and political institutions. In order to bring conversion to them, we must first admit the disorder that is being perpetuated by many social arrangements that are protected with ideologies (often in the name of God).

Martin Luther King, Jr., said he grieved over the sluggishness, the sloth of the church. This capital sin of sloth is deeply rooted within the churches regarding efforts to bring about social justice between the races. What King said regarding the "ism" of race can be applied to sexism in our church institution. This sin of sexism is alienating more and more women *and* men from the church. Yet, protected with our ideologies, it seems we still will not listen, lest we be converted (13:15).

This fear of conversion became very clear to me on one occasion as I shared a reflection week for campus ministers. The dynamics of the group revealed a growing awareness of problems stemming from a clerically controlled ministry in the Roman Catholic Church. On one side were clerics; on the other were non-clerics: religious women, married couples, and single people. All of these depended on clerics for their jobs and paychecks.

One particular problem involved a very friendly, but threatened young priest. A young couple had shared ministry with him at a particular Midwest campus. They were more successful than the priest in their programs and in getting students involved. To top it off, she was a feminist. By the time they came for this study week, the handwriting was on the wall. He who had the power could make the rules. And since this cleric not only had the power but the pursestrings, he could fire the couple, with the bishop's backing, if need be. The hatchet was about to fall.

I had done much sharing with the group during the week about the new directions for community-conscientization-conversion that I outlined earlier in this book. In a particular way, I talked about sexist structures and the need to convert from them. When the last morning arrived, I sat in the back of the group listening to their reflections on what their next steps would be.

They admitted my analysis of the sexist situation in the church was correct. That was an intellectual conversion. They even agreed that Genesis 1:26–28 cannot show the Scriptures supporting, as God's plan, a form of oppression for a whole class of people. That was a moral conversion. Yet, as I saw the members of the group discuss everything else but their sexism and elitism, I suddenly realized that this very way of discussing was a way of keeping them from a religious conversion. This religious conversion would have been an invitation to let an old form of ministry die in order to give birth in reconciliation to new power and possibilities for the good of God's whole church.

I had been under a lot of pressure previous to that week. I had also worked hard to share with the group. Thus, when I realized that all I had done was to no avail, I sensed what was about to happen to me, emotional person that I am. I quietly departed from the room and went outside. And I broke. Having spent myself intellectually and emotionally, my tears reflected the only emotion I had left within me.

At that point of tears, the image of Jesus weeping over Jerusalem came into my mind. As immediately as I had let myself enter into this mourning, the image of the weeping Jesus became an instant angel of comfort in my grief. It brought a consolation into my depths the likes of which I had rarely experienced. I had been faithful to the process, I seemed to sense. I did whatever I could; I could do no more. That was also the pattern of Jesus' life. He had nothing to show as he went to death; yet he had remained faithful. That realization brought comfort and peace.

At that point, I experienced Jesus' theology; my spirituality was founded in his gospel. Jesus could do nothing but weep when the leaders in his structure refused to convert. Now he was consoling me in my grieving over my unsuccessful efforts to bring care into the clerical structures of the church. Comfort came to my mourning; I experienced the blessedness of the second beatitude.

Almost at the same time I was experiencing this deep inner peace and joy, I realized that the priest in question was standing next to me. He must have watched me, as I slipped from the room. He said (with no solicitation on my part), "But Mike, I can't change."

His statement was almost a plea for understanding. Even though I had said little that morning, we both recognized the unwillingness to change that had become part of him and the group. My reply to him might be restated here to say: "If we don't change, then we will remain controlled. And, if we remain controlled in our fears and mourning, we will never experience the hope and comfort of the resurrection of God's power in us that has been promised."

Another part of the world we are called to mourn is creation itself. At the time of Jesus and Matthew, spirituality assumed the comfort of being part of an ecological balance. Today, we cannot afford to make the same assumption. Part of life's unity came from the birds in the sky (6:26); today oil slicks wash them ashore, and we are broken. Wild flowers and grass in the field (6:28,30) brought spontaneous joy; today the fact that chemicals leave the land barren makes us weep. Jesus spoke in parables about picking grapes from thornbushes, figs from prickly plants, and good fruit from decayed trees (7:16–18); today cash crops from the poor nations support the lifestyle of rich nations like ours and create for us a harvest of shame. Jesus assumed the foxes had lairs (8:20); today we cannot assume that many species of fox will survive, and we experience guilt as we wear our fur coats. Jesus multiplied loaves and fishes and brought comfort to the crowds (14:13–21; 15:32–38); today malnutrition and hunger increase on a global scale while acid rains suffocate streams and lakes as far north as Great Bear Lake.

We have become alienated from creation itself. What Hosea said of general infidelity to God's plan can be applied to this ecological situation:

> There is no fidelity, no mercy,
> no knowledge of God in the land.
> Therefore the land mourns,
> and everything that dwells in it languishes:
> The beasts of the field,
> the birds of the air,
> and even the fish of the sea perish [Hos. 4:1,3].

However, where mourning once controlled the earth, a restored people seeking first God's reign can take a new authority over creation itself. Creation can stop quaking in death (see 27:52). Instead it can proclaim a new solidarity with humans who realize creation too has rights that must be respected as part of God's plan. Extending care to inanimate creation brings good news into the whole world.

CHAPTER FIVE

Blessed Are the Meek;
They Shall Inherit the Land

Jesus, the Meek One, Inheriting the Land

An incident in Jesus' life that shows him fulfilling the third beatitude can be found in Matthew's portrayal of Jesus' triumphal entry into Jerusalem. Here Matthew quoted a section from the post-exilic prophet Zechariah. Zechariah had tried to get the people of the fifth century to identify the coming of the messiah with the restoration of the temple. The messiah's coming to take possession of the temple would signify God's *shalom*.

> Rejoice heartily, O daughter Zion,
> shout for joy, O daughter Jerusalem!
> See, your king shall come to you;
> a just savior is he,
> Meek, and riding on an ass,
> on a colt, the foal of an ass [Zech. 9:9].

The messianic king entering the city would come, not in violence, but in meekness. This meekness would find him inheriting the land.

When Matthew wrote his Gospel, Jerusalem had already been destroyed (see 24:1–2). Up to that time, however, Jerusalem had been recognized as the center of Jewish institutional life. It was the arbitrator of the people's social arrangements or "isms." It also served as ideological link with God. The real political, economic, and religious power in the Western world at that time may have been in Rome. Yet, just as in the case of dominated people today (the Poles, for instance, who consider their infrastructural identity in terms of Warsaw rather than Moscow), so the people in Matthew's time considered Jerusalem as the center of their universe instead of Rome. Whoever would be given Jerusalem would inherit *all* the land—the whole infrastructure containing all the institutions, "isms," and ideologies. Those who would give up Jerusalem would be relinquishing their authority (in its forms of love and loyalty, reinforcement and acclamation) to the new authority.

"The groups preceding him as well as those following kept crying out: 'Hosanna to the Son of David!' " (21:9). In entering Jerusalem, the center of the Jewish world, the shouts of the people proclaiming Jesus as the Son of David echoed the very first chapter of Matthew's Gospel. In his genealogy (1:1–17), Matthew tried to show the church that, in the person of Jesus, God's plan for the whole world would be fulfilled, just as it was fulfilled for Israel in David. Matthew portrays Jesus as new David and new Emmanuel, as the one coming with the authority of God's presence and power to take possession of the world itself: "Blessed is he who comes in the name of the Lord!" (21:9)."Blessed is he who comes" *to be with us!*

Recalling the image of the Emmanuel prophecy (1:21–23), Matthew assured his searching community that God can be found at the center of life. The God who comes, comes to be with us in every generation. This God comes to be at the center of our lives, our communities and families, as well as our institutions, their social arrangements, and ideologies. This God comes to take authority over all creation. Just as Jerusalem was once the center of the peoples' lives and loyalties, so now this God-in-Jesus-in-the-church takes authority to reorder all creation.

"As he entered Jerusalem the whole city was stirred to its depths, demanding, 'Who is this?' " (21:10). Earlier in Matthew's Gospel the disciples of John had asked who Jesus was: was he the messianic one who was to come (11:3)? Their question was precipitated, we have surmised, because the prisoner John had been going through the stages of the hermeneutic circle. Now "the whole city" (all of creation), also began to question previously cherished ideologies. The city was shaken to its depths just as creation itself was shaken at the divine presence (27:52). So deeply shaken would those in the infrastructure be at the coming of true authority that they would collectively ask, "Who is this?" Jerusalem's question reflected the world's hermeneutic query of Jesus and the church. It meant: "Are you the blessed one who is to be present with us; are you the one who is going to restore our relationships with God and one another with a new healing? Or do we have to look for another? The crowd reported back to Jerusalem's question of Jesus and society's hermeneutical query of the church: "This is the prophet Jesus from Nazareth in Galilee" (21:11).

Matthew shows the crowd letting itself be evangelized by Jesus. The average Jew was very willing to accept Jesus' power. This power was manifested in Jesus' healings and miracles, his preaching about God's reign, and his teachings, which offered a new way of wisdom. The crowds followed him; they were healed and fed by him; they joined him. The ones who were unwilling to accept the implications of Jesus' authority over them were not the average Jews or Christians for whom Matthew was writing. They were the leaders of both groups who had let power and authority go to their heads. They who had become the leaders within the traditional or newly emerging structures could not in meekness, submit their authority, their land arrangements, to the power of Jesus. That is why Matthew explains that:

> The chief priests and the scribes became indignant when they observed the wonders he worked, and how the children were shouting out in the temple precincts, "Hosanna to the Son of David!" "Do you hear what they are saying?" they asked him. Jesus said to them, "Of course I do! Did you never read this: 'From the speech of infants and children you have framed a hymn of praise'?" [21:15–16].

The average Jew and Christian as well as the leaders had one of two ways of reacting to the need to convert all land arrangements to Jesus' presence and power: meekness or violence, peace or indignation. Violence reflects an attitude that is unwilling to submit reality, or land arrangements, to the power of God. A defensive and protective posture is taken against any potential threat that may invite change. If the threat to change comes from a person, an ideology will often be created to delegitimize the authority of that person.

On the other hand, meekness reflects an attitude based on the discovery of Jesus' power in our lives. This helps us experience and understand God's plan. Meekness creates within us a desire to live according to that plan which calls into question our previously cherished land arrangements. The average Jew and Christian generally responded to Jesus' authority in an unthreatened spirit of meekness. Many of the scribes, Pharisees, chief priests, and other leaders responded in a defensive spirit of indignation (21:15) and violence to Jesus' authority.

Matthew's portrayal of Jesus' triumphal entry into Jerusalem thus lays the groundwork for considering how we can try to let the third beatitude be fulfilled in our lives. The depth of our experience of this beatitude will depend on how we regard the "land"—in meekness or in violence. To understand which of these two attitudes will dominate our behavior, we should first determine what Matthew meant by "land." From this we can consider the implications of land for our own situation.

Spirituality: Integrating Word and World, Prayer and Ministry

The history of spirituality, like Israel's own history, revolves around two themes: God and the Land, the Word and the World. To the degree that these two dimensions were integrated as fully as possible in Israel's life they created as much significance for the historical Jewish community as the Trinity does for the Christian community. Israel-Yahweh-Land were to come together around the Torah. The Torah, with its commands regarding worship of Yahweh, life in the land, and relations to others would help enable Israel to live authentic spirituality. Spirituality brings God, the land, and people together in a triangle. Israel's spirituality, as well as ours, must keep a proper balance between Yahweh and the land.[1]

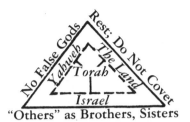

"Others" as Brothers, Sisters

In the law the Jews were shown a way of not allowing the land to become an end in itself. This would insure that Yahweh would remain central to Israel's existence. Because humans are always tempted to make the land the dominant force in their lives as people, families, and nations, the Torah told Israel not to covet resources. To remember that Yahweh was the source of all those resources, Israel was also commanded to take a sabbath rest one day each week, and a year each fifty years. This would provide the Israelites the chance for reflection to determine if they might be coveting power, possessions, and prestige. These manifestations of the land might otherwise tempt Israel to let power, possessions, and prestige become ends in themselves.

Because Israel was part of a wider world, the nation would be continually tempted to cultural addictions. It would be tempted to serve the world's gods rather than the word of the one God. To be free from being seduced by this temptation, the Torah warned Israel not to have any false gods take the place of Yahweh in its institutions, social arrangements, or ideology.

Finally, because of Israel's unique self-understanding of its relation to God and the land, the nation might be tempted to forms of exclusivism, elitism, and separatism. It might begin to think God wanted the whole world to exist just to support its land arrangements. This temptation could easily become an ideology reinforced by false gods to protect the nation's social arrangements within its institutions. Such a way of thinking could create the potential for Israel to become an elitist group of peoples with a highly nationalistic attitude. The attitude could easily legitimize Israel's direct and indirect rejection of other people. Therefore, the Torah showed that the aliens, all those outside community, were to be regarded as brothers and sisters.

The commandments were the normative dimension offered Israel that it might express fidelity to its constitutive religious experience. As the Israelites fulfilled the commandments, through obedience to the norms by their lives, they would become more constituted as the beloved people of God, a covenanted people of the word. On the reverse side, the more God and God's word became central to the way Israel lived in the land, the more easily the people could live under the norms of the Torah.

Israel is archetypal of us all. The history of Israel's spirituality is characteristic of all spirituality. It reflects the need for balance between responsibility toward Yahweh and the Land, the Word and the World. When we, as Israel, do not integrate expressions of Yahweh and the land, our spirituality will manifest one of two extremes.

The first happens when the land becomes an end in itself. Then, an idolatry becomes part of our ideology. It makes God support our individual, interpersonal, or infrastructural land arrangements. God's blessing is equated with "making it" on the land. At the other extreme, if our spirituality is so oriented to Yahweh that we assume no responsibility toward the land, we will personally covet the land, or allow it to be coveted. Under this extreme we do not assume responsibility for the correct use of land through stewardship of its and our resources. Consequently we will not be able to rest in the land even as we pray to God for peace within our borders.

Excesses around these two poles of the Land and Yahweh, the Word and the World, outline the biblical history of Israel's spirituality. These excesses can also be applied to contemporary approaches in spirituality today.

The first irresponsible form spirituality can take happens when we develop a notion of God that removes us from responsibility toward the land, toward power, possessions, and prestige. If we observe a problem or are told about some difficulty beyond us that affects others, we may pray to God to do something about it. Even though our land arrangements might be contributing to the surface problem we hope God will alleviate, we refuse to consider those parts of our relationships and structures that *cause* the pain! This attitude seems to say that if something is wrong in God's world, God will intervene in the land to do something about it. We do not see that, as images of God in the world, we are to care about these deviations of God's plan by using our resources to bring healing to them. This one-sided form of spirituality is called angelism or pietism.

An expression of this excess can be found in early stages of the conversion process. Enthusiasm about manifestations of religious experience can so predominate that we spend an extraordinary amount of time seeking union with God. Meanwhile, we neglect responsibility toward others in our immediate community and family, or concern for a world beyond immediate experience. Such an attitude can often be found in many prayer movements.

We go to a prayer meeting aware, from the evening news and daily papers, that all sorts of problems are fracturing our world. But even though this is God's world and, therefore, part of God's care, its problems do not seem reflected in our prayerful concerns. While we may pray that God will do something about these problems, we never consider changing our lifestyle or our structures, each of which may be reinforcing those problems. We will continue to eat this or wear that even as we know both may be the result of exploitative practices. We will continue to bank at a financial institution that discriminates or redlines. We say to ourselves, "If God wants things to be different, God will do something about it or reveal to us what we should do. So, until this is done we're just going to pray that God's *will* be done. If God wants this done, God will see to its accomplishment."

Such an attitude fails to see that God's self-revelation and will for us is usually mediated through normal historical experiences. If concern for others is not part of our normal care system, the concern will not easily be normative of our prayer forms either. Unconsciously, even as we spend more time in prayer, we may be praying to a God of our own experience, limiting this God to our small world, reinforcing our ideology under the guise of religion. We may even have prophecies that reinforce unjust social arrangements such as sexual domination and false use of power. Thus God's name is used to legitimize what is against the divine nature.

The God of Jesus insists that, if our religious experience of God's care is authentic, it will manifest itself in deeds of care toward others in need:

> None of those who cry out, "Lord, Lord," will enter the kingdom of God but only the one who does the will of my Father in Heaven. When that day comes, many will plead with me, "Lord, Lord, have we not prophesied in your name? Have we not exorcized demons by its power? Did we not do many miracles in your name as well?" Then I will declare to them solemnly, "I never knew you. Out of my sight you evildoers!" [7:21–23].

In some prayer groups there may be a desire to do God's will by being concerned about the poor or others in need. However, this concern is often limited to members of the particular group. This was the case in a prayer group I attended for a time. A great amount of solicitude and help would be shown members who lost their jobs, needed babysitters, were in poor health, or needed rides. Rarely, if ever, was any practical concern shown regarding problems in the wider parish proper or the surrounding city, much less the economic and political structures that reinforced the lifestyles of many of the members at the expense of others. As a result, their brothers and sisters whom they were to love as a way of fulfilling the command to love God totally (22:36–40) continued to be hurt and broken. To be concerned about structures and the way they systematically create obstacles to God's plan would take a special revelation for the prayer group. We forget that the perennial revelation had been given years ago regarding anyone in need: *Where* did I see you?

In an effort to show my concern for a spirituality in the charismatic renewal that reflects a fuller integration of the Word and the World, I talked at length with one of the movement's leaders. After her initial negativism I discovered she was not very open to my thoughts. She seemed to have me in a bag with other "social justice folk" whom she saw as unconcerned about prayer.

After listening to my concern, she implied that she would be praying for me that someday I would be able to be touched by God to really accomplish God's designs in the world.

While this incident does not reflect the attitude of all the leaders in the charismatic renewal, too often concern for the world is limited to just the individual or interpersonal levels of life. One time, for instance, I listened to a national leader in the healing ministry discuss evangelization, healing, and social structures. Using the example of wealthy women relating personally to poverty-stricken women in Mexico, he insisted that this one-to-one approach was *the* way to deal with social structures. His insufficient social analysis neglected to consider the fact that these wealthy women were central to the systematic continuation of those forms of oppression that kept the poor women in misery. The rich remained rich; the poor got a hand-out.

In the late 1970s, I discovered that what the rich women were doing toward the poor in Mexico we as the Midwest Capuchin Province were unknowingly doing toward the people of Nicaragua with our investment portfolio.

By 1976 many of the laity along Nicaragua's Atlantic coast had become quite conscientized about their rights as images of God through pastoral courses given by our brothers (as well as through other means). As a result they began to call for the implementation of their civil rights, especially related to the distribution and control of the land. The result was a growing suspicion of the Capuchins by the United States-backed political and military leaders, along with a growing harrassment of the laity.

In some areas *la guardia* began to torture the peasants and interrogate those who had become leaders. In response, thirty-one of our Friars sent a letter to President Somoza decrying the violation of human rights that existed. Within a short time they were joined by all the bishops of Nicaragua. They wrote a pastoral letter on the situation and called for the restoration of peace and civil rights. Commenting on the role of the province in this part of Nicaragua's revolution, the November 1977 issue of *Maryknoll* noted:

> After a decade of work in the Zelaya region, U.S. Capuchin priests were beginning to see the fruits of their labor in rural schools, agricultural clubs, homemakers' associations and medical units. The Capuchin message was very simple: people who work together and pray together are able to achieve a better life for themselves and their community.
>
> In some areas such as the districts along the Prinzapolka River, this message has saved the people from the National Guard. There are no *orejas,* or informers, to tell lies, and when a member of the community is falsely accused by the military or a large rancher, people unite behind him. Thanks to the Capuchins, these peasants are beginning to have greater awareness of their legal rights.
>
> In other areas, however, many of the community structures built up over the years have been destroyed by the National Guard. All but 5 of the 30 agricultural extension clubs in the rural area around Siuna have been closed on the grounds that they might be "subversive."[2]

As tensions rose in Nicaragua as the result of such activities and the growing power of the National Sandinista Liberation Front, Somoza hardened his political position, backed by many U.S. congresspeople. He renegotiated debts, backed by U.S. monetary agencies and banks. He strafed his own civilian population, backed by U.S.-trained armed forces. Meanwhile, in the United States, we had been lobbying Congress and praying mightily for peace in Nicaragua.

In late 1978, during a chance conversation, I discovered that one of the banks that had loaned Somoza millions of dollars was Bankers Trust in New York. Much to my surprise, the province, whose portfolio exists to help our brothers, including those in the Nicaragua ministry, had 500 shares in Bankers Trust! While the province was ministering and praying for justice on the level of the individual and group, it was unwittingly investing monies to reinforce the third level of the infrastructure, which systematically countered our part in the efforts to bring justice and peace to Nicaragua!

Immediately we began a process with Bankers Trust. After initial dialog proved futile, we filed a shareholder resolution asking the bank to disclose its loans to Somoza and to make no more loans to Nicaragua until the Somoza regime and ideology would be replaced. Had we not taken this action (which subsequently resulted in Bankers Trust agreeing to our proposal), we would have been praying and ministering with one institutional hand, while our other hand benefited from structures of oppression. Had we remained uninvolved on the structural level, as an institution, we would have been saying, "Lord, Lord."

The other form irresponsible spirituality often takes occurs when our notion of God isolates God's activities to working for a just order in the world of individuals, interpersonal relationships, and infrastructural levels. Consequently, little or no room is left for transcendent religious experience. One time picketers protested outside a cathedral of a Midwest diocese. They were concerned that the diocese was not sufficiently involved in racial issues. Inside the cathedral people were meeting for their all-night vigil. One of our men went outside to ask the picketers to join the group inside for the prayer service. "I don't need to go in there," one demonstrator responded, "I experience Jesus in the picket line, the soup line, and among the poor." Jesus will be found in such places, where two or three are gathered. Yet, his presence cannot be limited any more to the welfare rows than to the rows of people making Holy Hours of Reparation, as long as their motivation is correct.

Many times people working to change structures and promote justice seem embarrassed to pray together, yet they quote the Scriptures to justify the kind of just world they struggle to create. It almost seems that God and the Scriptures are often used to justify a certain world order. Particular economic structures which are based on a concrete economic or political analysis, become ends blessed by God. Neoconservatives and Marxists alike can do this.

We need social analysis. We need to admit that certain political economies must be endorsed and supported as more closely approximating the justice of God in the Scriptures. Yet, the very misunderstandings and obstacles we face in our ministry to bring about a just political economy demand more than social analysis; they call for depth in religious experience and opportunities for shared faith. They demand both an incarnational and transcendent dimension.

Some may be doing everything possible and at all levels to fulfill the plan of God that clearly shows the need to promote the dignity of all peoples through a more equitable sharing of the earth's resources. Yet if one's life is totally given in this direction, what the Spirit said to the Church at Ephesus can be apropos to this situation:

> I know your deeds, your labors, and your patient endurance. I know you cannot tolerate wicked men; you have tested those self-styled apostles who are nothing of the sort, and discovered that they are imposters. You are patient and endure hardship for my cause. Moreover, you do not become discouraged. I hold this against you, though: you have turned aside from your early love. Keep firmly in mind the heights from which you have fallen. Repent, and return to your former deeds. If you do not repent, I will come to you and remove your lampstand from its place [Rev. 2:2-5].

As we try to make sure we do not put our lamps under a bushel, but in the open so that all the world can see (5:14-16), we also must continually return to the transcendent experience of that light within our depths, which manifests the presence of God (6:21-23). Our lamps should not go out because of our failure to wait for our God (25:1-13) in the solitude of prayer.

Prayer and ministry are equal dimensions of spirituality. Jesus' spirituality was no more authentic when he healed the sick than when he departed to be alone with God. Both had their proper time and place in his spirituality. When either prayer or ministry absorbs the one without enabling the other to be given its proper order, unsound biblical spirituality results.

We can no longer afford to say which takes priority—prayer or ministry, religious experience or social justice, charismatic activity or ethical obedience. From the example of Jesus, Matthew articulates the need for his community to develop a spirituality that integrates both the Mount of the Transfiguration (17:1-8) and the Mount of Final Commissioning to bring God's total plan into the whole world (28:16-20). The need for such balance is particularly acute today as we reflect on our past history as people who say we are committed to Yahweh.

Biblical Spirituality in Our Land

We are the inheritors of a spirituality that subtly reflects a civil religion. Civil religion tends to equate religion with "making it in the land."[3] We have created institutions to enable a faster and more secure access to the land's limited resources. We have justified our actions in the name of God. We reinforce this ideology, with God on our side, supporting our social arrangements. Ads in our diocesan papers and religious magazines often seek to convert us to the "American Way" of consumerism. This ideology is also reinforced when we often spend over fifty percent of our parish budget on schools that help our children make it in the land, even as we say that these schools are an alternative to the "American Way."

We seem afraid to criticize seriously either our own forms of media or education from the viewpoint of that justice which reorders all institutions to reflect the divine will. Yet the Synod of Bishops in 1971 made such a critique—which we have yet to apply seriously to spirituality:

> Part of the human family lives immersed in a mentality that exalts possession. The school and the communications media, which are often obstructed by the established order, allow the formation only of the man desired by that order, that is to say, man in its image, not a new man but a copy of man as he is.[4]

This statement from the 1971 Synod of Bishops addressed the ideology in media and education which, in effect, often reinforces the attitudes of our nation's infrastructure. When this mentality or ideology, which supports consumption, is questioned, it is interesting to note the cancellation of subscriptions that takes place in magazines like *Maryknoll*. Some come from those who sign their letters as "True Catholics."

Interesting, too, are the numbers of parents who threaten to pull their children from our schools, once these institutions develop a curriculum geared to education for justice and nonviolence. Even though the 1971 Synod of Bishops said this is the purpose of Catholic education and even though the 1977 Vatican decree on the proper purpose of Catholic education and schools stated the same, the average U.S. Catholic does not seem ready to financially support such a biblical base for our schools. Nicholas von Hoffman commented on the decree:

> The Vatican says that church schools ought to be helped "in face of materialism, pragmatism and the technocracy of contemporary society." According to Rome, parochial education is alive with "those who are building a new world—one which is freed from a hedonistic mentality and from the efficiency syndrome of modern consumer society."
>
> Any school system dedicated to imparting such values is worthy of support. But by their fruits you shall know them, and the products of Catholic education in the United States seem as enslaved to hedonism and the efficiency syndrome as Jews, Baptists and pagans.
>
> The failure of American Catholic education is that it has made its students socially docile and politically conventional persons, far from being models the rest of us can look up to, they bear a depressing resemblance to everyone else.[5]

Even though the 1971 Synod of Bishops said we must develop forms of conversion on the individual and social levels in face of the infrastructural use of the media and education, Catholic behavior, as noted by von Hoffman shows how little we have moved.

In light of the third beatitude we are finding it increasingly difficult to criticize honestly the consumeristic lifestyle that we, our families, our neighborhoods, our dioceses, and religious orders evidence. Consequently, manifesting the attitude of meekness in the land is a problem. To aid our critique and need for conversion on the individual and social levels, we might do well to examine further how Israel was warned by God to view the land it was about to inherit.

Israel was about to cross the Jordan. Moses realized the nation needed to remember its past so that it could live securely with Yahweh in the future. Realizing the human tendency to make the land an end in itself and to make gods to support that idol, Moses said:

> These then are the commandments, the statutes and decrees which the Lord, your God, has ordered that you be taught to observe in the land into which you are crossing for conquest, so that you and your son and your grandson may fear the Lord, your God, and keep, throughout the days of your lives, all his statutes and commandments which I enjoin on you, and thus have long life. Hear then, Israel, and be careful to observe them, that you may grow and prosper the more, in keeping with the promise of the Lord, the God of your fathers, to give you a land flowing with milk and honey [Deut. 6:1–3].

Once in the land, it would be difficult to seek Yahweh first. So that the people would depend on God's word to have all the resources they needed in the world (6:33), Moses stressed the need for symbolic reminders. These symbols would help the community always to remember, from its past experience, that its ultimate security had to be placed in God's word. To help it never forget its need to base its love and loyalty ultimately in God (see 6:4–5), Israel was given no less than nine different ways to remember not to forget:

> Take to heart these words which I enjoin on you today. Drill them into your children. Speak of them at home and abroad, whether you are busy or at rest. Bind them at your wrist as a sign and let them be as a pendant on your forehead. Write them on the doorposts of your houses and on your gates [Deut. 6:6–9].

Once we get into the land of the condominium, the job, the position, the neighborhood, the education degree, the second and third car, the honor, the tenure, it will be easy to forget that it was God, not ourselves, who *brought us* to this form of the land. The land is always inherited; it is not taken. It is not ours to take, but God's to give. Thus we have no absolute right to it. What individual rights we may have must be subordinated to the rights of everyone in the community:

> When the Lord, your God, brings you into the land which he swore to your fathers, Abraham, Isaac and Jacob, that he would give you, a land

with fine large cities that you did not build, with houses full of goods of all sorts that you did not garner, with cisterns that you did not dig, with vineyards and olive groves that you did not plant; and when, therefore, you eat your fill, take care not to forget the Lord, who brought you out of Egypt, that place of slavery [Deut. 6:10–12].

In the eighth chapter, Moses made it clear that all resources of the earth that were considered fundamental, basic human needs of that era (such as food, water, and mineral resources), would be given in enough abundance so that no one would lack anything. God would provide in a way that no one would need to have more than enough at the expense of others:

Therefore, keep the commandments of the Lord, your God, by walking in his ways and fearing him. For the Lord, your God, is bringing you into a good country, a land with streams of water, with springs and fountains welling up in the hills and valleys, a land of wheat and barley, of vines and fig trees and pomegranates, of olive trees and of honey, a land where you can eat bread without stint and where you will lack nothing, a land whose stones contain iron and in whose hills you can mine copper [Deut. 8:6–9].

We are all tempted to say: "It is my own power and the strength of my own hand that has obtained for me this wealth" (Deut. 8:17). Moses made it clear, however, that the one who made every person as God's image is also the one who enables every person to have access to the resources:

Remember then, it is the Lord, your God, who gives you the power to acquire wealth, by fulfilling, as he has now done, the covenant which he swore to your fathers. But if you forget the Lord, your God, and follow other gods, serving and worshiping them, I forewarn you this day that you will perish utterly. Like the nations which the Lord destroys before you, so shall you too perish for not heeding the voice of the Lord, your God [Deut. 8:18–20].

Israel was told to remember. We need to remember our history and roots as well. Deuteronomy says we should never forget: "It is the Lord, your God, who gives you the power to acquire wealth" (Deut. 8:18). Such a statement directly contradicts the myth, the ideology, that declares, "We did it; why can't they?"—whoever the "they" may be.

The power to make it "into a good country" (Deut. 8:7) came to us because our ancestors, like Israel's, were at a unique place at a unique time. Many of them entered the land as immigrants before the racial minorities were given full political and economic freedom. Our ancestors had skills. The land was open. Their labor was needed. Today, with structured unemployment and technology that is both capital- and energy-intensive, the frontier that once welcomed our ancestors is closed to aliens, minorities, and women. The very conditions that created the wealth we have "inherited" are not structurally possible for "them." Yet, we have the nerve to question, "Why can't they pick themselves up by their own bootstraps?"

The unique history which we have inherited from our ancestors came home to me when I was in Ireland in late 1978.

It had always been very important for me to be Irish. My family attended St. Patrick's, the Irish parish in Fond du Lac, Wisconsin. I went to St. Pat's grade school for eight years. I was part of the annual St. Patrick's Day play. During those years I even dreamed of marrying Kathleen McKelvie.

In 1978, at the request of Pax Christi, I went to Ireland to give workshops on corporate responsibility and the future of religious life.

At the end of one seminar in Dublin attended by major superiors from many orders throughout Eire, I was principal concelebrant of the liturgy. During the period of silence after communion, I was distracted with the thought: "Wow, Crosby, do you realize what's going on here? Here the leaders from all these orders have come to listen to what you've been saying. They're accepting it. You aren't just the first from the family to come back to Ireland like any tourist; the leaders of its church have come here to listen to your thoughts!"

At that point in my distraction I mused: "Wouldn't it be great if I could go back and tell Mother and Dad about this and share this great experience with them, knowing how proud of me they'd be." My musing turned into a deep religious experience. "But you are here aren't you? You've seen it all. You're in the communion of saints that have gathered around this altar!" At the realization of my parents' presence, the role they played in my past life came to me as a gift: "If it weren't for you I wouldn't be here. If it weren't for the way you shared your life with me, I wouldn't have the educational and psychological background that brought me to this point in my life."

I said to myself: "You can't take credit for anything in your whole life; it's all been one big gift. How stupid to think you've made it by yourself. You may have tried to be faithful to the process, but it certainly wasn't your power!"

It was my parents; it was their parents; it was their brothers and sisters; it was all the ancestors. It was the genealogy of those instruments of God's plan from Cork and Mayo, Donegal and Kilkenney who came across the ocean to the towns of Colby and Mitchell, Wisconsin. Somehow that genealogy resulted in two unbelieveable people, Blanche Bouser and Hugh Crosby. They came together from all "those others." From their love I was born in Fond du Lac. There they nourished me and my three brothers. With their blessing I had moved from home. Now, with thirty-eight years of more people and many other experiences, I was at this time and place in Dublin.

This whole collage of people in my history, events that molded me, family experiences, and brothers the province had given me, all became present in the silence of that communion meditation. The awe with which it over-powered me brought me to tears of deep thanks and joy, especially for my mother and dad. The fact that all these forms of land were now part of my life—my abilities, my resources, my honors, all these inherited gifts— has now made me continually ask: "By what right do we, who have come from ethnic stock, dare to reject any of our brothers and sisters who, because of flukes in history, were born at the 'wrong time'? By what right do we descendants of those who freely came to Boston and New York dare pre- sume that the same results of historical opportunities given our ancestors and us can now be predicated of the descendants of enslaved peoples?"

Now that I am in a leadership position in the province, the realization of brokenness in some of our men, which can be traced all the way back to infancy and destructive family relationships, has made me also realize the gift of my very warm extended-family background. My sisters-in-law, Sue and Carol, love me. So do my four nephews and my niece. I have had caring aunts, uncles, and cousins. Even the fact that I lived on shady Bank Street has put me years ahead of many others. While such gifts have been given me, others, I have discovered, have had to work for years to be freed of negative childhood and adolescent experiences. These emotional scars have taken such authority over them, that they have been inhibited from advancing as rapidly as I have been able to.

Returning from Ireland in early December, I was more conscious than ever that just the way I had celebrated Christmas in Fond du Lac helped provide me with attitudes that were very different from a black kid's in the ghettoes of Milwaukee. I shared this realization one evening with Tim Elms, one of the Capuchin candidates. He was also from Fond du Lac and was working at St. Elizabeth's in the youth program among blacks as I had done six years before. Tim knew exactly what I meant when I said, "You know, Tim, when we look at the way Christmas is celebrated in the poor community around St. Elizabeth's, it's so different from what you and I ever experienced. From the very beginning of our childhood, we lived in the land in such a way that we just expected gifts to come. Baby Jesus was as much a part of this as Santa Claus. We knew something was behind it all, but we never had that sense of fear that we wouldn't be getting anything because the welfare check might not come or because the case worker might make it hard to get extras. It's just something beyond our experience."

Caring about the poor and the oppressed from a deep poverty in spirit helps us understand how history has worked in our lives and how we have become rooted in the land. Without such a realization we can easily continue to use the land of our power, possessions, and prestige to legitimize the continued non-participation of our brothers and sisters in the mainstream of life.

If we are the meek in this land, we have to be the ones who change the direction of spirituality in our country that legitimizes, by its violent silence, the continued division among social groups. We have to be the ones who convert so that we never forget that we are no more the images of God than anyone else, and that our stewardship of the earth's resources cannot support structures and relationships that deny others their right to those resources. We have to be the first ones who no longer wonder why the poor might need what we want. Instead we should begin to ask ourselves if we really have a right to what the poor may need. We have to be the first ones who understand the connection between the land and wealth. We should be the first to realize that we have been invited, as was the rich young man, to use our resources on behalf of those without the land who are in poverty (see 19:16–22). We have to be the ones who bring the full implications of this beatitude to bear upon every level of our lives.

Our Wealth and Biblical Land

In discussing the land, it is important that we consider it in the context of our nation's terminology, especially the way land is perceived in the ideology of our political economy.

In his book *The Affluent Society,* John Kenneth Galbraith offers an interpretation of what the Bible called "land" in his notion of contemporary *wealth.* Wealth is the sum total of all our financial resources; while income is that which we derive from our wealth. Thus, when we speak of land, we are talking about all financial resources, about wealth. "Broadly speaking," Galbraith writes:

> there are three basic benefits from wealth. First is the satisfaction in the *power* with which it endows the individual. Second is the physical *possession* of things which money can buy. Third is the *distinction* or *esteem* that accrues to the rich man as a result of his wealth.[6]

Following Galbraith's definition of wealth as power, possessions, and prestige, "the land" becomes much more extensive than private property, although private property is part of our preoccupation as well.

In considering whether we as individuals, families and religious houses, parishes and provinces, dioceses and congregations, are inheriting the land, we should consider whether or not we are meek or violent in the way we use our power, possessions, and prestige.

Everyone has some degree of wealth. Therefore it is important for us in the United States (which has the highest amount of accumulated wealth in the world), to bring a biblical spirituality to bear upon life—individual, communal, and collective. In this way we determine the degree that God's word is the ground of being for us as we dwell in this world. An understanding of the power-possessions-prestige dimensions of wealth becomes all the more relevant in discussing spirituality. The Spiritual Exercises of St. Ignatius considers their equivalents (riches-honor-pride) to be the tools that the powers and principalites use to try to lead people astray. "From these three steps," Ignatius wrote, "the evil one leads to all other vices."[7] In our wealthy society, power, possessions, and prestige continually tempt us to submit to these forms of control used by the evil one, or the powers and principalities of this world.

Matthew presents the powers and principalities offering Jesus a similar temptation to live under the world's influence rather than under God's will for the land. Building on themes discussed earlier from Deuteronomy, Matthew has Jesus (and the church) "led into the desert by the Spirit to be tempted by the devil" (4:1). Moses and the Israelites spent forty years in the desert, trying even there to be in control of God. Matthew presents Jesus and the church facing the continual temptation in every era to promote a spirituality wherein God reinforces the power, possession, and prestige needs of the infrastructure.

The first temptation outlines how Jesus and the church should consider possessions themselves. Offered a spirituality that makes economic considerations (such as providing bread from stones) the goal of fidelity, Jesus reminds the tempter, as Moses reminded the Israelites (Deut. 8:3): "Not on bread alone is man to live but on every utterance that comes from the mouth of God" (4:4).

Jesus and the church are also tempted to seek prestige the way society might interpret it (even if it be by some dramatic gesture such as leaping from a precipice to be borne up by angels). Spirituality based on such dramatic forms of religious experience can be spurious. To seek these extraordinary experiences so that others might hold us in awe puts "the Lord your God to the test" as the Israelites did in the desert (Deut. 6:16). Jesus rejects the spirituality of pietism and angelism that keeps us from getting involved in the world (4:6).

The final temptation, which reinforces society's values, involves the use of power itself. On the mountain, the two authorities, the two manifestations of power, would meet:

> The devil then took him up a very high mountain and displayed before him all the kingdoms of the world in their magnificence, promising, "All these will I bestow on you if you prostrate yourself in homage before me" [4:8–9].

Because Jesus remained conscious of the power he experienced in the depth of his prayer (4:2), Satan was unable to seduce him to live by land arrangements that would be contrary to that experience. Thus, Jesus said, "Away with you, Satan!" Quoting Deuteronomy again (6:13), Jesus made clear that all spirituality is to manifest a lifestyle that submits every land arrangement to the power of God: "Scripture has it: 'You shall do homage to the Lord your God; him alone shall you adore' " (4:10).

The violent way that the powers and principalities deal with power, possessions, and prestige stands in sharp contrast to the meek way in which spirituality should deal with wealth. In this sense we can understand more fully Psalm 37, which served as the foundation for Matthew's understanding of this beatitude.

Psalm 37 discusses two ways that people seek security in the land: through violence or meekness. Seeking security in excessive power, possessions, and prestige results in various forms of jealousy (Ps. 37:1), anxiety (Ps. 37:1, 7), anger, and wrath (Ps. 37:8, 12). This false security leads to evildoing and various forms of wickedness as a way of protecting the position of individuals, groups, and society. The psalmist warns against making such land-based attitudes the foundation of our lives. Rather, the psalmist urged, "Trust in the Lord and do good, that you may dwell in the land and enjoy security" (Ps. 37:3).

We manifest that trust by our fidelity to the Lord's covenant. Fidelity to our part of the covenant makes us want to use our power, possessions, and prestige in the way of meekness, or under the authority of God's plan. Such trust and commitment to do what God wants leads to a way of living in society that evidences the deepest form of security, inner peace. In this security we can "leave it to the Lord, and wait for him" (Ps. 37:7).

Despite God's promise to be with us to meet our needs, we still seek to find security in our own resources. Often we are so controlled by our need to be in charge that we make ourselves gods. We cannot leave anything to God's provident care. We have to be *sure.* We cannot trust that God will be faithful to these promises. All these attitudes evidence some lack of faith.

These attitudes also show how much we try to make God image ourselves. Because we are often unfaithful and cannot be trusted to keep our word, we unconsciously do not believe God will be faithful to the divine word and promise. Instead of finding our ultimate security in God's reign and eternal plan, we run after all those things the land holds up as the gods that give us security (6:32). Despite our protestations about trusting in God, we cannot place all our security and trust in God as we enter the land of power, possessions, and prestige.

When we face the possibility of losing these forms of wealth, we suddenly "get religion" again. Suddenly, we discover our dependence on God. Such a religiosity fulfills Thomas O'Dea's sociological definition of religion as the human response to our breaking points. When our power, possessions, and prestige are slipping away, we "get religion." We discover our need for God. Then, when we are secure, power, possessions and prestige become our gods again. Our security rests in them.

When we face our breaking points, our limitations, our disillusionment, our *tohu wabohu,* we get God. We do not "need" God when we are not breaking, unless, of course, we have discovered the true God of religious experience. This God empowers us to want to do good toward others as an expression of our experience of God's goodness in and to us. This attitude is what Matthew saw to be essential for spirituality in society.

Such spirituality is an invitation to conversion. But the experience of conversion will be possible only if we seek God, find God, and submit our security needs to God's authority. Seek first this reign over you, God's way of holiness, and all these things you've been running after will be given you besides (6:33). Our religious experience of God will establish us securely in God's way of holiness as we do good to others, by working for justice. As we promote justice, God will be with us in the land, meeting our needs.

Meekness and Violence: Two Ways of Living in the Land

Jesus is simply saying that a life based on ultimate trust in God makes us poor in spirit in such a way that our basic wealth in all its forms rests securely in God. All the human expressions of wealth must be oriented to others to promote God's reordering of our world in justice. Manifesting such a spirituality brings about the reign of God's presence, which protects us securely. If, for the sake of this divine plan, we orient our wealth on behalf of the poor, God will always provide. In our traditional spirituality we easily prayed the *Memorare,* which stated, "Never was it known that anyone flying to thy patronage was left unheeded." If God took care of all the needs of the people in the desert, will God not take care of our need for daily bread (7:7–11; cf. 6:30f.)? Somehow our spirituality has to reflect this rootedness, this confidence in God's promise.

When people are troubled hearing such thoughts, I ask them if they know people who (for the sake of God's reign) have oriented their lives to promote God's plan but who are now in need. I have never heard of anyone, who, for the sake of God's plan, has worked for justice, who does not have an inner security, in spite of external tensions. The psalmist says: "But the meek shall possess the land, they shall delight in abounding peace. . . . Neither in my youth, nor now that I am old, have I seen a just man forsaken nor his descendants begging bread. All the day he is kindly and lends, and his descendants shall be blessed" (Ps. 37:11, 25–26).

Blessed are the meek; they shall inherit the land. Meekness means committing our lives to fulfill God's plan. Since God's plan is inseparable from justice, those disciples will be blessed who promote justice. They may be persecuted; they may even break; but they have an inner peace, even in depression, that assures them of God's promise that their real needs will be met.

Meekness is the blessed way of dealing with the land of our power, possessions, and prestige. It brings us the reward of God's favor and peace.

Come to me, all you who are weary and find life burdensome, and I will refresh you. Take my yoke upon your shoulders and learn from me, for I am gentle and humble of heart. Your souls will find rest, for my yoke is easy and my burden light [11:28–30].

Each of us has been invited to come to Jesus in our weariness. Each of us can bring the burden of running after so many things, without finding meaning. Each of us can walk through our first steps of the hermeneutic circle and admit that we are not really trusting in God's word as in the past. Each of us again can be touched by the refreshing, the strengthening experience of God's presence. In saying, "Come to me," Jesus is saying we do not need to go to the power, the possessions, the prestige of our society and above all to the empty promises of an ideology that has held us in its yoke.

Jesus also says, "Come to *me*" instead of to the Torah. Life cannot be found in a law, only in a person. Come to me, not to your elites, to your scribes and Pharisees with their theologies, their academic controls, and their teaching. Come to me for the wisdom that has been revealed to me by my God and yours (11:25–27). Come to me and be refreshed with the plan of life for yourself and the world. I have received this plan from God; now I freely share this plan with you.

In coming to Jesus, to that Jesus whom we have sought and found, we can more easily sell all those things—those institutions, isms, and ideologies—whenever they do not reflect God's plan. We can be free of their yoke by submitting to a new authority, a new yoke. In taking the yoke of Jesus upon our shoulders we learn from him in religious experience everything that has been revealed to him (11:27). This revealed way of wisdom becomes a norm we can follow in our nation.

In the past, farmers would take wet clay and fashion a yoke around the shoulders of their oxen. Once the clay hardened, the animals were without pain, for the yoke was made to fit the unique shoulders of each ox. By saying, "Take my yoke upon your shoulders," Matthew's Jesus is asking us to shoulder a unique plan for ourselves, our communities, and our world. Even though there may be difficulties in implementing this yoke of God's will, God's plan is fitted for each of us; therefore we are able to bear the burden. Following that plan will find us on the road to meekness.

Meekness, such as Jesus exemplified, demands total dedication to God's plan for the world. Meekness is the attitude of those who are poor in spirit. These *anawim* have abandoned themselves to implement God's provident plan for creation. Meekness arises from our experience of God's power within us. It makes us willing, in that power, to touch all forms of wealth. The meek ones are those who, like Jesus, are totally dedicated to orient their world to God's word. Because of his meekness, which showed his concern for everyone, Jesus was blessed. Because his authority-in-meekness makes us concerned for the world and for what God wants for the land, we too will be blessed. As a result, John Meier notes, we are assured that we also will inherit the land:

Jesus the Son, the apocalyptic revealer, the Wisdom of God, will give these poor the eschatological rest promised to God's people by his prophets, promised to those in need of instruction by the wisdom-teachers of Israel. Instead of the yoke of the Mosaic Law as interpreted by the overbearing Pharisees, the poor are to accept the yoke of Wisdom's apocalyptic revelation, which, as we have seen, is reducible to the relation of the Father and the Son. That is why Jesus can say "Learn from me," without bothering to state any direct object of the learning. He is both teacher and content taught, the very basis and embodiment of the morality he demands. This yoke of apocalyptic Wisdom will, despite the designation "yoke," mean liberation and relief after the legalistic yoke of the Pharisees. For Wisdom in the person of Jesus is not a harsh task-master and a casuistic hair-splitter. Rather, he is the archetypal poor man of the beatitudes, meek and humble of heart, patient and kind toward sinners, totally dedicated and obedient to God.[8]

If meekness means total dedication to God's plan, the meek person reflects a whole reversal of attitudes toward power, possessions, and prestige. In taking on the yoke of God's plan for the world, meekness reflects a nonviolent way of dealing with wealth in all its forms. A meek person has an entirely new way of dealing with power through service (20:20–28), with possessions by using them on behalf of the poor (6:19ff.; 19:16–22), and with prestige by avoidance of any show or titles:

> As to you, avoid the title "Rabbi." One among you is your teacher, the rest are learners. Do not call anyone on earth your father. Only one is your father, the One in heaven. Avoid being called teachers. Only one is your teacher, the Messiah. The greatest among you will be the one who serves the rest. Whoever exalts himself shall be humbled, but whoever humbles himself shall be exalted [23:8–12].

If meekness reflects the way God's word in us enables us to relate to the land, then violence is the way society's word deals with power, possessions, and prestige. This fact is very important to consider when we try to develop biblical spirituality for the United States. Our land was conceived in violence related to property rights and their unequal distribution among people.[9]

Bill Cunningham, the former Director of Justice Education for the National Catholic Education Association, used to say: "If you and I are alone on an island and you have the loaf of bread, you will never sleep." In other words, to protect our consumer-selves, we must keep our defenses up. The link between consumerism and militarism can be extended beyond individuals to groups. It affects races and sexes, the rich and the poor, the North and the South.

If wealth (or land), in Galbraith's terminology, is not approached with an attitude of meekness, it will generate mistrust and divisions. "Where do the conflicts and disputes among you originate?" St. James asked:

Is it not your inner cravings that make war within your members? What you desire you do not obtain, and so you resort to murder. You envy and you cannot acquire, so you quarrel and fight. You do not obtain because you do not ask. You ask and you do not receive because you ask wrongly, with a view to squandering what you receive on your pleasures. O you unfaithful ones, are you not aware that love of the world is enmity to God? A man is marked out as God's enemy if he chooses to be the world's friend. Do you suppose it is to no purpose that Scripture says, "The spirit he has implanted in us tends toward jealousy"? Yet he bestows a greater gift, for the sake of which it is written, "God resists the proud but bestows his favor on the lowly" [James 4:1–4:6].

Since God's favor rests on the meek, the lowly ones, Matthew offered the third beatitude as a way of nonviolence to help his community live in the violence of their society. Since violence is the reaction when power, possessions, and prestige are threatened, nonviolence can become an attitude that can be brought to all situations.

Matthew's Jesus urges a new way of reconciliation instead of anger (5:21–26). Nonviolence should touch every level of life with a forgiving, understanding, caring attitude toward everyone, especially oppressors. When I was a teenager, the pastor would ask me at the end of each confession: "You don't have any hard feelings against anyone now, do you?" I would quickly respond "No." Now that I have grown, I cannot so simply reply that I have no hard feelings against others.

Matthew's Jesus urges a new way of reconciliation instead of retaliation (5:38–42). Jesus urged, "when a person strikes you on the right cheek, turn and offer him the other" (5:39). However, from Jesus' own spirituality, we know that this way of nonviolence does not mean sitting back without a response. While we do not know from Matthew how Jesus responded when he actually was slapped (26:67–68), John tells us (John 18:22–23) that Jesus used it as an occasion to begin a dialog with his oppressor.

Matthew's Jesus urges a new way of reconciliation that even includes loving and praying for our enemies (5:43–47). Reconciliation proves we are sharing in God's life and want to extend God's loving plan for everyone. As I have reflected on my life, I have found that I stew about those who are against me. Rarely do I bring my stewing to solid prayer, seeking to love and forgive those whom I consider to be my enemies.

Finally, Matthew's Jesus urges a new way of reconciliation in which we even try to avoid judgment (7:1–5). We are asked to be aware that all people have a history that they express in attitudes and actions we so easily reject. Too many times others elicit violent attitudes from me. I discovered once how easily this happens to me. A young nun at a retreat I was giving spoke very muffled English. I thought to myself, "Is this Order that hard up for recruits that they'll even take someone like her?" I continued to think this way, growing in anger toward her and the Order, until I discovered that the young nun was deaf and dumb.

The way of nonviolence is the way of care. It can do much to heal an uncaring world that busily runs after power, possessions, and prestige. Nonviolence should be able to touch every aspect of our lives. It can enter our attitudes and our behavior. It can reflect a new way of wisdom and meekness that arises from our sense that God is God, we are God's people, the land is God's, and the land is ours to use responsibly.

Meekness can extend itself as stewardship for the resources of the land itself in contrast to the violence we have done to the earth.

Injustice and disorder in the way we pollute land, sea, and sky point to desecration of God's plan for all creation. The central good news of Matthew's spirituality tells the world that God is with us (1:3; 28:20). Yet, we often fail to evidence this fact of God's presence in our midst in the way we exercise stewardship over the land and the whole ecosystem. Instead, we violate the command given Israel by Yahweh as it came into the land: "Do not defile the land in which you live and in the midst of which I dwell; for I am the Lord who dwells in the midst of the Israelites" (Num. 35:34).

If we honestly believe God is with us, our spirituality will reflect that faith in meekness toward God, humans, and the land itself. It simply is unrealistic to believe we can continue to exploit false gods, dehumanize people, and pollute the earth without suffering consequences. Therefore, wisdom would tell us more than ever that we need a good dose of spiritual realism as we consider how we will live on the land within a limited ecosystem.

This nonviolent attitude of meekness best reflects one of the two poles needed for both the mystical life and solid spirituality. The fourteenth-century English mystic Walter Hilton based the spiritual life on the twin virtues of meekness and charity. Meekness and charity were to become normative or practical in such a way that they would gradually come to constitute God's reign within each person. Hilton called meekness "spiritual realism." Spiritual realism, or meekness, meant the simple understanding of the way God wanted humans to live on earth. Hilton considered this kind of meekness so beatitudinal that he urged, "Therefore shape thee for to be arrayed in His likeness, that is in meekness and charity, which is His livery; and then He will homely know thee, and show to thee His privity."[10]

If we are meek, we have learned the wisdom way of Jesus. If we are meek, we will be arrayed in the likeness of Jesus as he revealed the likeness of God (11:27–30). If we are meek, we will have been faithful to God's word in our land.

CHAPTER SIX

Blessed Are Those Who Hunger and Thirst for Justice; They Shall Be Satisfied

---

The Constitutive and Normative Dimensions of Justice

The fourth beatitude expresses concepts faithful to the Old Testament notion of justice. In a special way, it reflects the understanding of justice that runs throughout Isaiah 61. As this messianic passage about Israel's restoration indicates, the fullest expression of justice contains both a constitutive and normative dimension. With "the spirit of the Lord God" anointing us (Isa. 61:1), we are clothed with a robe of justice; we are wrapped in a mantle of justice (Isa. 61:10). The robe and the mantle of justice enable us to experience God in the depths of our being as *our* justice. With Mary we rejoice heartily in the Lord who has become the joy of our very being (Isa. 61:10; cf. Luke 2:46–47). Constituted in God's justice, God uses us to "make justice and praise spring up before all the nations" (Isa. 61:11).

Justice is God's authority, which must be manifested in the world. The goal of justice, people like Jeremiah believed, was to reorder the world's alienation of *tohu wabohu*. At Jeremiah's time the chaotic situation was reinforced by Israel's leaders, who lacked genuine care for the community. Consequently,

> Behold, the days are coming, says the Lord,
> when I will raise up a righteous shoot to David;
> As king he shall reign and govern wisely,
> he shall do what is just and right in the land.
> In his days Judah shall be saved,
> Israel shall dwell in security.
> This is the name they give him:
> "The Lord our justice" [Jer. 23:5–6].

Jeremiah and Isaiah show that the constitutive dimension of justice begins with a personal experience of God's care for us in our disorder and need. In our need, God empowers us so that we can complete the circle of care by living under the normative ethic of justice.

God will always raise up people, who become ministers to others of the same justice they have experienced from God. When God intervened in the life of the community that suffered the injustice of its clerical class (23:1–4), the community experienced Yahweh as "our justice" (Jer. 23:6; 33:16; cf. Isa. 11:1–11). In the power of that experienced justice, Israel was called to a similar ministry of justice. Since Israel's religious experience and ministry is the archetype of our spirituality, when the world sees our ministry of justice it should also be able to say of us "our justice":

> They will be called oaks of justice,
> planted by the Lord to show his glory.
> They shall rebuild the ancient ruins,
> the former wastes they shall raise up
> And restore the ruined cities,
> desolate now for generations. . . .
> Like a bridegroom adorned with a diadem,
> like a bride bedecked with her jewels.
> As the earth brings forth its plants,
> and a garden makes its growth spring up,
> So will the Lord God make justice and praise
> spring up before all the nations [Isa. 61:3–4, 10–11].

Matthew's Jesus declares blessed those who hunger and thirst for justice. In promising satisfaction (5:6) to those who hunger and thirst for God's power in them, Jesus speaks primarily of the constitutive dimension of God's order for our life. Whoever hungers and thirsts for justice recognizes their absolute need to share in God's forgiving love. As affluent North Americans, we do not easily hunger and thirst. The obsession that hunger and thirst create was obvious in *The Holocaust*. From the way the people besieged the man they discovered with bread, we can better understand what it means never to be satisfied, to be obsessed, to hunger and thirst for something above any other thing.

Hunger and thirst reflect the two basic needs of the human race. In the desert, without productive land, Israel depended on Yahweh to satisfy hunger and thirst. In the desert, the Israelites experienced their absolute dependence on God, yet they were continually tempted to run the show. The people were not content to live in that triangle of integration that brought them, as Israel, into dependence on *Yahweh* as they shared the resources of the *land*. Wanting to control the land rather than depend on God who had promised always to be with them (Exod. 3:12), Israel grumbled. The people said to Moses and Aaron: "Would that we had died at the Lord's hand in the land of Egypt, as we sat by our fleshpots and ate our fill of bread! But you had to lead us into this desert to make the whole community die of famine!" (Exod. 16:3).

At this moment of weakness, the Israelites said they would have been happier with the security of enslavement. At least they could rely on a structure of oppression to feed them. Despite their grumbling (and their poor theological and political analysis!) God showed fidelity to the promise to be with them. Yahweh's word promised to satisfy their hunger for bread: "I will now rain down bread from heaven for you. Each day the people are to go out and gather their daily portion; thus will I test them, to see whether they follow my instructions or not" (Exod. 16:4). In Egypt, the Israelites relied on the inconsistent word of an oppressor to give them bread each day. In the desert, the Israelites would have to rely on the ever-faithful word of their Liberator to give them their daily bread.

As we saw in the last chapter, we are always tempted to let the land—even in its oppressive forms—control us. There is a need in us for assurance that we will always have bread. God structured Israel's dependence on the divine promise to give the ultimate resource of life, bread. God would give Israel daily portions so that the community continually would realize its need for God. Israel would be assured God would give enough bread. But just enough.

> They so gathered that everyone had enough to eat. Moses also told them, "Let no one keep any of it over until tomorrow morning." But they would not listen to him. When some kept a part of it over until the following morning, it became wormy and rotten [Exod. 16:18–20].

The bread became wormy and rotten because Israel did not need it. Enough was enough! Yet we always want more than enough. Recalling this experience, Matthew's Jesus said,

> Do not lay up for yourselves an earthly treasure. Moths and rust corrode; thieves break in and steal. Make it your practice instead to store up heavenly treasure, which neither moths nor rust corrode nor thieves break in and steal. Remember, where your treasure is, there your heart is also [6:19–21].

The history of Israel in the desert is repeated in the lives of each of us. God does not want us to lack for any resource. The God who responds to our need asks only that we never store up. God asks us not to live in excess so that others in need may have enough. If we try to get more than enough, we become less than God's images. As Denis Goulet says, we are called to live by a new moral order: we are to seek just enough in order to be more.[1]

Another basic human need the Israelites experienced in the desert was thirst. Rather than be meek in the land, secure in Yahweh, they let the land control them and became violent. "Here there was no water for the people to drink. They quarreled, therefore, with Moses and said, 'Give us water to drink' " (Exod. 17:1–2). The Israelites let the land create in them an attitude of violence by their quarreling and grumbling (Exod. 17:2, 3). Despite this,

> The Lord answered Moses, "Go over there in front of the people, along with some of the elders of Israel, holding in your hand, as you go, the staff with which you struck the river." The place was called Massah and Meribah, because the Israelites quarreled there and tested the Lord, saying, "Is the Lord in our midst or not?" [Exod. 17:5,7].

"Is the Lord in our midst or not?" This is the perennial question arising from the human condition that needs to be sure and to control. Yahweh has shown throughout Hebrew history, and Matthew makes clear for our histories, that God is in our midst (1:23) for all days (28:20). In response God asks us to believe our needs will be met: "Your heavenly Father knows all that you need" (6:32). God knew what Israel needed when it was in the desert; God knows what we need. We do not have to imitate the Israelites, who grumbled and were anxious about life's basic resources. Just as God gave enough each day to the Israelites, so God will do the same for us:

> Seek first his kingship over you, his way of holiness, and all these things will be given you besides. Enough, then, of worrying about tomorrow. Let tomorrow take care of itself. Today has troubles enough of its own [6:33–34].

The word Matthew uses in urging us to seek first God's way of holiness is *dikaiosyne,* or justice. This use of *dikaiosyne* in 6:33 is one of the seven times in his Gospel that Matthew employs this particular word. The other time he uses it in quite the same sense as 6:33 is 5:6: "Blessed are they who hunger and thirst for *dikaiosyne;* they shall have their fill."

In using *dikaiosyne,* Matthew does not seem to have appropriated the word from the traditional sources available to him. Rather, he inserted it in the Gospel in each of the seven instances (3:15; 5:6, 10, 20; 6:1, 33; 21:32). In examining these insertions we find that Matthew has developed both a constitutive (5:6; 6:33) and normative (5:10, 20; 6:1) dimension of justice.

To achieve the constitutive experience of God's justice in us, we are to hunger and thirst for God's life, saving power, and care for us. We are never to be satisfied until we experience these manifestations of God's justice. We are to ask for justice in prayer, seek its power in reflection, and knock until we have opened for us ever-deepening experiences and understandings of this liberating presence of God-with-us. Aware that the same God, who sees us in need and who cares for us as divine images, will also respond to these calls, we gradually experience ourselves being constituted, provided with everything that is good. The "good thing" that we especially experience is the *exousia* of God's spirit (see 7:11). We become blessed with justice, we share in God's life, which empowers us to be faithful.

The way we show our fidelity to this presence of God within us and our communities is to complete the circle of care by living under the norms of justice. The last chapter will discuss the consequences coming from society to those who witness to justice's normative dimension (5:10–12). The next part of this chapter will elaborate on the other two normative uses of *dikaiosyne* (5:20; 6:1). Here the word is used to describe the kind of ethic that should guide the Christian community in its individual members, its groups, and its own institutional life.

"I tell you, unless your holiness," your *dikaiosyne,* Jesus said, "surpasses that of the scribes and Pharisees you shall not enter the kingdom of God" (5:20). Matthew gives the warning of Jesus to the community after talking about the need to fulfill in its life everything found in the Scriptures (5:17–19).

Jesus came to evidence within his spirituality everything found in the Hebrew Scriptures, the law and the prophets. To stress the theme of continuity for his community-in-tradition, Matthew used the word *plerosai* to refer to Jesus' *fulfilling* the law and the prophets. He would use the same word a total of twelve times throughout his Gospel; all referring to the fulfilling of the Scriptures in Jesus' spirituality. Matthew shows Jesus using it one of these times in his inaugural address (3:15). At the time of his baptism Jesus said: "We must do this if we would fulfill *(plerosai)* all of God's demands *(dikaiosyne)."* Justice fulfills God's whole plan for the world. Justice is essential to spirituality. This spirituality of justice is expressed in fidelity to law; yet all law must serve justice. Unless our justice exceeds pure legalism we cannot be part of God's reign (see 5:20).

Throughout his Gospel, Matthew presents Jesus as the one who interprets law in light of the demands arising from human need. In two key passages about the standing grain (12:1–8) and the cure of the man with the shriveled hand (12:9–13), the author of the First Gospel presents Jesus as the one who bends laws to serve justice and people rather than the other way around, the way of the scribes and Pharisees. He shows Jesus' truth standing in contrast to that of the leaders.

In the face of Jesus' growing threat to their legitimacy, these authorities "began to plot against him" (12:14) for his deviations from their interpretations. While Jesus' way of truth addressed the needs of the people (12:15–16), it deviated from the hypocritical practices of the leaders (12:17–21). Recalling the authorities' increasingly violent attitudes toward him, Matthew again shows Jesus fulfilling the messianic promises that spoke about persecution for those promoting justice (Isa. 42:1–4):

> Here is my servant whom I have chosen,
> my loved one in whom I delight.
> I will endow him with my spirit
> and he will proclaim justice *(krisin)* to the Gentiles.
> He will not contend or cry out,
> nor will his voice be heard in the streets.
> The bruised reed he will not crush;

the smoldering wick he will not quench
until judgment *(krisin)* is made victorious.
In his name, the Gentiles will find hope [12:18–21].

The word Matthew uses for justice and judgment that is "made victorious" is *krisin*. In other places, *krisin* (or *krisis*) is translated as truth. Truth is the foundation for the justice, or *dikaiosyne*, of Jesus. At the same time it unmasks the hypocrisy of the so-called justice of the scribes and Pharisees (5:20). In this sense it is clear that the battleline between Jesus and the leaders of his day was the issue of truth. "I assure you," Jesus said, "on judgment day *(krisin)* people will be held accountable for every unguarded word they speak. By your works you will be acquitted, and by your works you will be condemned" (12:36–37).

Even though Matthew's Jesus hardly uses the word, the issue of truth and its violation was central to the whole approach of the scribes and Pharisees, which Jesus most abhorred. While they paraded as models of holiness and justice, many of the leaders of the Jews (and the church) were nothing but hypocrites. Jesus saved his most extensive condemnations for such leaders. They were stumbling blocks for the community (23:1–36). Their lifestyles contradicted what they taught. They used their elite status as interpreters of the law to reinforce their own needs, rather than the peoples'. "This religious split in them," John Meier says of the scribes and Pharisees,

> is seen in two basic forms: they say but they do not do (v.3), and what they do they do only for external show, not as an expression of interior reality (vv. 5ff.; cf. 6:1–18). One is reminded very much of the problem of the false Christians in 7:21–23: they say "Lord" but do not do the will of the Father. What they do do are showy, flashy religious deeds (miracles) which lack interior substance. In both cases, we have the fundamental split in professionally religious man which is hypocrisy: saying but not doing, or exterior show with no interior substance. Interestingly, this split is also called by Matthew, in both cases, *anomia*, "lawlessness" (7:23; 23:28). . . . In the Septuagint, *anomia* often is used, not for theoretical opposition to Law or particular commandments, but rather for that fundamental rebellion against God's will which marks the truly evil person.
>
> The fascinating point here is that both the legalistic Pharisees and the free-wheeling charismatic Christians could be equally guilty of *anomia*. The "life-styles" may be different. But the rejection of God's will for the sake of one's own will is the same, and the resultant split is the same.[2]

Challenging the Lie, the Obstacle to Justice

In general, inner alienation or separation from God's plan was structurally manifested in the chaos of the community. Such chaos, sociologically speaking, is also called *anomia. Anomia* reflects the lawlessness that results from *tohu wabohu,* or injustice. In contrast to the teaching of Jesus, that of the scribes and Pharisees was untruthful because it did not promote justice (see 16:5–12). Such hypocrisy was contributing to spiritual as well as sociological *anomie,* or lawlessness within the community.

The antitheses (5:21–47) showed a new way of interpreting the law so that its underlying truth would promote the justice that exceeded that of the scribes and Pharisees. Immediately after these antitheses, the community was warned to avoid those forms of piety *(dikaiosyne)* that say one thing externally but internally reflect another dynamic (6:1). Whether the practice be almsgiving (6:2–4), prayer (6:5–15), or fasting (6:16–18), no religious exercise could mislead people; none could be untruthful or hypocritical.

Spirituality cannot be a sham; if so, it denies God's truth. The word *hypokritoi* means ungodly in the Septuagint. It is just the opposite of *dikaiosyne,* or godly, which practices what it preaches. Hypocrisy gives mere lip service to God's plan as it follows its own plans.

The need for truth-in-spirituality today is no less urgent than our current need for truth-in-government or truth-in-packaging. We should never be satisfied until we make truth the foundation of our lives, our relationships, and our society in all its institutions, social arrangements, and, especially, its ideology.

While in the novitiate, I began to realize how I was violating justice by my untruth. As a teenager I justified lying to my parents because I said they were too strict; but now I could not afford the luxury of such a rationalization. I discovered I was keeping God's justice from possessing me as fully as it might by the sin of my lies. I was also failing to promote honesty in relationships with others. I was misleading them. My dishonesty was taking all sorts of forms: misstatements, distortions, exaggerations, half-truths and, at times, outright lies and denials of truth itself.

I found myself embellishing a story, wanting others to get a certain impression. I discovered it was quite easy to manipulate words or facts in such a way that the desired effect would take place. By controlling the disclosure of truth, I could order life the way I desired. The more I discovered I was withholding facts and truth, the more I realized that, small or large as these various lies might be, they all were evidence of a lack of conversion. The more I admitted this, the more I also knew I had to take charge over these sins, little as they might be. If I did not, they would control me, keeping me under their authority.

I recall telling myself: "Here you are, Crosby; you're in the novitiate and you're trying to say you want God to be your all. But you get so concerned about doing big things, which will make God your all, that you don't see it's the little things like those lies that are really keeping this from happening." The more I thought about this, the more sense it made. Gradually I realized my forms of untruth were separating me from God. Furthermore, I was telling these lies for varying motivations, all related to human respect.

I had to make a choice. I could either rationalize my actions and remain controlled by this deviation from God's reign in me; or I could submit to conversion's call. I was weighing alternatives: continue to lie and, in that measure, keep from growing in God's life or live in truth and, to that same degree, risk possible negative reactions from others. I decided, "I think I want to practice a little violence toward myself because I want to be converted from this sin." Then and there, I made a structure for that commitment. I decided that, whenever I would catch myself in any form of a lie, I would correct the false impression as soon as possible.

I started to practice my resolve. Soon I discovered two things. First, I always knew when I was lying. Secondly, I discovered that whenever I caught myself lying and corrected myself (sometimes in the very same sentence), I never once was rejected.

As a result of this decision, I have come to hunger and thirst for truth in my life. I want it to characterize the way I relate to others and my world. At the same time, I must add, I expect the same honesty from others as well.

I have tried to temper my obsession for truth with care. I have tried to be less brutal and violent in my desire for honesty. While I remain committed to honesty, I have discovered my absolute need to ask myself a question before sharing some truth or fact with another: "Do you really like her or him?" If I cannot answer my question positively, I have discovered I have no right to share my "truth" with such a person. Rather, in the appeal to being honest, I will really be trying to control and dominate in an uncaring way. If I do not care about some people, I have little right to ask them to convert. Furthermore, if they do not first feel my care, they will never be open to my call for conversion anyway.

I still come off like a sledgehammer and am especially threatening to people who are defensive about their negative self-images. Yet I remain convinced of Paul's wisdom in urging the church "to profess the truth in love and grow to the full maturity of Christ the head" (Eph. 4:15). In care we can speak the truth. If we want to build up relationships in justice, we must "see to it, then," as Paul urged the Ephesians, "that you put an end to lying; let everyone speak the truth to his neighbor, for we are members of one another" (Eph. 4:25).

My obsession for truth is both an asset as well as a frustration. In a special way, I have discovered this fact as I try to bring my hunger and thirst for justice-built-on-truth into the infrastructural level of our nation's institutions, "isms," and ideologies.

The disorder and injustice in our society is often founded on and legitimized by distortions of truth.[3] Nowhere is this form of biblical hypocrisy more evident than in the industry that exists to manipulate words in such a way that people will be led to act on assumptions based on distortions of truth—the public relations industry. In late 1978 *The Wall Street Journal* ran a front-page background story under the following headlines:

The Image Makers
In Public Relations, Ethical Conflicts Pose Continuing Problems
Lies, Stonewalling, Cover-Up to Protect the Company Often Are a
    Way of Life

Reinforcing what we have already said about the market economy, which subordinates people to the goals of production, the article stated:

> Pressure to produce, even if it means compromising personal moral standards, is perhaps greatest at the middle-management level. But nowhere do the ethical conflicts come into sharper focus than in the corporate public-relations departments.[4]

Whether it be government, business, the military, or even ecclesiastical institutions themselves, words can be manipulated by the powerful. People can be led to act on false impressions. The lie can become the means for effective control.

Toward the end of the war in Vietnam the Pentagon deliberately reduced the previous figures of enemy forces from 600,000 to 300,000. In this way, U.S. citizens would not realize how outnumbered our forces were. During this same time, seven to eight thousand U.S. soldiers were killed, not counting those from other countries. The reason the Pentagon gave for this deliberate lie was simple: "Otherwise those who have an incorrect view of the war will be reinforced." Truth can be called incorrect when you control the ideology, even at the expense of human life.

"To Some at Harvard, Telling Lies Becomes a Matter of Course," another front-page article in *The Wall Street Journal* declared. The article (which resulted in denials by Harvard as well as a "we stick to our story" by the *Journal*) explained:

> Gerald M. Thomchick got the highest grade in part of his Competitive Decision Making course at Harvard Business School because "I was willing to lie to get a better score."
> That's fine with Prof. Howard R. Raiffa, whose course is designed to teach budding businessmen to negotiate in the real world. Like it or not, Prof. Raiffa says, lying—or "strategic misrepresentation," as he calls it—is sometimes resorted to in business negotiations.[5]

There are subtle ways institutions and social arrangements use ideology to be protected from criticism. One way will be by the lie. At other times it will be inadequate analysis or perception of the social structure itself. This ideological control becomes evident, for instance, in writings of the neoconservative school or when we demythologize the statement that "the church is not to be political."

I was with someone who had just finished a speech calling on an audience of churchpeople to begin lobbying government to promote justice. "But," I said, half-cynically and half-seriously, "the church is not supposed to be political." In unbelief, he looked at me and said earnestly: "Was there ever a time when the church was *not* political? It's been political since it was born. It's just a matter of whose politics you are talking about. *That* defines whether the church will be considered political or not!"

The institutional church is continually political. In Poland it must be political to survive. In Italy it decided to battle a divorce law and to let contemplatives leave their convents to vote against the communists. In Nicaragua it understood the rights of the people to "give in to the temptation" to revolt against the "manifest long-standing tyranny" of institutionalized, structural violence under Somoza.[6] In the United States, it spends monies to lobby on abortion, federal aid to private schools, and other issues.

A problem arises when well-meaning people have been led to think that the institutional church is not being political. Even as it professes so-called neutrality when an "alien" party or economic system is dominant, the institutional hierarchy can covertly support a political party and economy more to its liking. This support can continue even as the church makes statements about the need to remain uninvolved. This hypocrisy came to my attention regarding the institutional church in Chile.

In March 1977, a Jesuit acquaintance, Brian H. Smith, published an article in *Theological Studies* with T. Howland Sanks, S.J. It described the role of the bishops of Chile during 1960–1974 under the title "Liberation Ecclesiology: Praxis, Theory, Praxis." Using the sources available at that time, Smith and Sanks showed how the Chilean hierarchy

> had to adapt the Church to three very different political regimes since 1964: a reformist Christian Democratic government (1964–1970), a Marxist-socialist coalition administration (1970–1973), and an authoritarian military regime since September 1973.[7]

The authors spent a good portion of the article discussing "the contention that the Church can have no neutral political position in the struggle for justice and that elements of Marxist analysis provide a useful method and strategy to make a political commitment by the Church effective."[8]

Smith and Sanks analyzed *Gospel, Politics, and Various Brands of Socialism*, written by the Chilean hierarchy in 1971, eight months after the election of Allende. It discussed the issue of the church's relationship with the political economy. The Jesuits explained:

> The bishops emphasized that the Church is not bound to support any political or economic system or party but rather encourages "Christians to struggle for those socioeconomic structures which make more effective all the gospel values of personal and social liberation, justice and

love." They admitted that there are various possibilities for implementing these values even in different types of socialist regimes.

The hierarchy stressed, however, how important it was for the official Church to maintain a public position independent of all political parties and movements. Concretely, this meant that official representatives of the Church—bishops, priests, deacons, as well as religious and lay personnel in positions of pastoral responsibility—could not publicly identify with a party.

Such neutrality in partisan politics by its official spokesmen, claimed the bishops, not only enables the Church to perform its primary pastoral mission but in itself can be a positive contribution to secular society.[9]

The closest the bishops came to permitting support by the "faithful" of Marxist parties or movements was to offer guidelines which could be used to judge a political or economic system. The bishops wrote a pastoral letter around the same time entitled *Christian Faith and Political Activity*. This document was written primarily to address a group called Christians for Socialism. The authors of the *Theological Studies* article state:

> . . . the bishops again stressed the importance and possibility of a neutral political position for the official Church, but they distinguished between "politics insofar as it underlies every social reality" and politics as "partisan activity." They admitted that the official Church enters into politics in the first sense of the term and tries to influence public policy by educating "its lay sons in a faith that does not lack a social dimension" and "insofar as its social teachings can and hopefully will be heeded by society." The Church, however, is not guilty of playing politics in the partisan sense of the term, since it does not offer any political model that is "properly its own" and because it eschews that mode of action which characterizes partisan political activity—the pursuit of power. The most significant political impact of the Church is indirect, inasmuch as its "aim is to renew human beings interiorly so that they may dedicate themselves to the struggle for social justice."[10]

People can argue with the conclusion of the Chilean bishops or with their line of reasoning. However, around the same time the *Theological Studies* article appeared, an event took place that showed that the Chilean hierarchy had indeed been playing covert partisan politics for years. This new piece of information directly contradicted theories such as those advanced by the hierarchy itself regarding the "role" Catholics could take in support of one or the other regime.

This new evidence revealed how one kind of political involvement supported the hierarchy's land arrangements (literally and figuratively). Therefore, actions used to support those forms of power, possessions, and prestige were not considered political. Thus, even though it practiced one thing covertly, the official church was overtly professing neutrality toward all political or economic institutions, or any theory used to legitimize them.

I had been involved in research related to the involvements in Chile of the International Telephone and Telegraph Company (ITT) during the crucial period between the transition from the popularly elected Christian Democratic regime of Eduardo Frei (1964–1970) and that of the popularly elected Marxist regime of Salvador Allende (1970–1973). During my research, I exchanged information with the former United States Ambassador to Chile (1967–1971), Edward Korry. According to the ambassador, as early as 1962 the CIA channeled federal monies through church-related institutions, with the support of the Chilean hierarchy, to keep Allende from defeating Frei in the 1964 election. Thus members of the Chilean hierarchy were covertly practicing the very partisan politics they rejected in their statements.

As Korry noted, the United States:

responded with public money to appeals from foreign Jesuits for federal help to combat not only "Marxism" but also "laicism" (theological term for the widespread Free Masonry movement in Chile) and "Protestantism" (a reference to the American Pentecostal missionaries then swarming across South America).[11]

The Chilean hierarchy was up to its neck in actions Sanks and Smith would never find in files. More frightening, however, the desperate actions of the bishops unmask what elites of *any* institution might do by using ideology overtly and covertly to protect their power. "I tell you, unless your holiness surpasses that of the scribes and Pharisees you shall not enter the kingdom of God" (5:20).

Desiring more truth about ITT's specific role in Chile, our province inquired into ITT's attempt to keep Allende from power during those crucial days in late 1970. Our questions were shared by many others. Some of those included the U. S. Justice Department and the Securities and Exchange Commission. Not getting anywhere through dialog, our province filed various shareholder resolutions with ITT asking it to disclose information about its political involvement abroad, especially in Chile.

In response, ITT began a covert investigation of the province in 1977. It told the Better Business Bureau that the company had received a letter from the province over my signature "requesting funds for an overseas operation." The BBB was asked to report back to the requesting person(s) at ITT with details about the province! When this was exposed as an outright lie (we had never sought ITT's financial help for anything), ITT found another means to try to discredit our province and the effort of church groups to call for corporate accountability. Its new tactic showed how easily the church and church people can be used by corporations against each other.

I attended the 1978 ITT shareholders meeting with our request for the truth about its political contributions, not only in Chile, but elsewhere since 1965. After I spoke, a priest from a large Eastern archdiocese approached the microphone in clerical collar to say (in ITT's edited version—again altered, it seemed to me, from original words!):

> When we talk about morality we have to use our brains as well as our emotions. Morality is a very complicated concept, especially when it is applied to major companies in underdeveloped countries. To harass a company that is doing very well by the people of that country is counter-productive. Morality has to be people-centered, and many theologians I've talked to have been very pleased with the fact that the people in underdeveloped countries have been taken care of by the shareholders and the management of this company. [12]

The moment this priest began his speech, I realized what was happening. ITT had succeeded in using this priest against the Capuchins. And, as Harold Geneen, the head of the Board of Directors, and John Navin, the secretary of the company, watched my reaction, I just shook my head. As the shareholders clapped for the priest (as they had previously murmured against the Capuchin), I realized more fully what Matthew's Jesus had said, "What I am doing is sending you out like sheep among wolves. You must be clever as snakes and innocent as doves. Be on your guard with respect to others" (10:16–17).

It did not matter that I recall this priest had said that *every* theologian he knew was supportive of ITT (his "many theologians" was an alteration in the final text); it did not even matter that he was unable to bring his "people-centered morality" to bear upon the activities of a corporation that actively tried to thwart the democratic processes of a whole nation. The real pain came with the realization that today in our church, as it was with Matthew's community, those who work for justice can often expect to be rejected by members of their own households:

> Whoever acknowledges me before men I will acknowledge before my father in heaven. Whoever disowns me before men I will disown before my Father in heaven.
>
> Do not suppose that my mission on earth is to spread peace. My mission is to spread, not peace, but division. I have come to set a man at odds with his father, a daughter with her mother, a daughter-in-law with her mother-in-law: in short, to make a man's enemies those of his own household (10:32–35).

Religious Acts and the Promotion of Justice

Another time Matthew uses *dikaiosyne* is after the command that follows the six antitheses: "In a word, you must be made perfect as your heavenly

Father is perfect" (5:48). Following that command, Jesus declared: "Be on your guard against performing religious acts *(dikaiosyne)* for people to see. Otherwise expect no recompense from your heavenly Father" (6:1).

Religious acts of justice should reflect God's justice. If we live under that normative ethic of justice which reflects our being constituted in God's justice, then the circle of care can become completed in us as we draw others into its warmth. We draw others into the circle of care by our piety or religious acts.

Traditionally, piety was considered a way of showing to others the love one received from God. Thus almsgiving, prayer, and fasting were common practices of justice. They were recognized as a way to reorder relations with those in need through alms (6:2–4), with God and neighbor through prayer that celebrates forgiveness (6:5–15), and with the oppressed through fasting that enables one to experience the depth of need to respond more easily to the cries of others (6:16–18). Jesus said that each of these three normative dimensions of justice had to be expressed beyond that of the scribes and Pharisees (see 5:20).

Matthew shows how this expression could go beyond that of the leaders in two ways. First of all, he prefaces each religious act by saying, "When you give alms," "When you are praying," and "When you fast." By using the word "when," Matthew seems to be operating from an important "given" about traditional spirituality. If God's justice, order, and life are within us, it should be normative that they are expressed automatically. Matthew simply assumes that a person experiencing God's presence, energy, and power will give alms, pray, and fast. As a consequence, Matthew's Jesus does not say, *"If* you give alms, pray, or fast," as though we have a choice.

Secondly, our motivation must exceed that of others. If we give alms, pray, and fast for others to see we "are already repaid" (6:2,5,16). But if our deeds of justice reflect an attitude of poverty in spirit, "your Father who sees in secret will repay you" (6:4,6,18). A sure test determining if these words will find us judged positively or negatively is to ask ourselves if we continue our acts of piety when no one is around.

Spirituality cannot give double messages. If God sees our heart inwardly dedicated, wanting to live only for God's glory, our eyes shall see that glory. We will come to the experience of God's justice; we will *know* Yahweh contemplatively. Without this attitude, we will bring into our acts of piety a competitive spirit that will bring upon us the same rejection given to Jehoiakim:

> Must you prove your rank among kings
> by competing with them in cedar?
> Did not your father eat and drink?
> He did what was right and just,
> and it went well with him.
> Because he dispensed justice to the weak and the poor,

it went well with him.
Is this not true knowledge of me?
says the Lord.
But your eyes and heart are set on nothing
except on your own gain [Jer. 22:15–17].

The first form of piety Matthew discusses is the giving of alms. This admonition about almsgiving is best understood in light of a consideration found in the Book of Tobit. Tobit was a devout and wealthy Israelite living in captivity among the Ninevites after the fall of the Northern Kingdom in 721 B.C. The angel Raphael showed Tobit that almsgiving was to be more central to his life than prayer or fasting. What Raphael told Tobit became a lesson for Matthew's community:

> . . . Do good, and evil will not find its way to you. Prayer and fasting are good, but better than either is almsgiving accompanied by righteousness. A little with righteousness is better than abundance with wickedness. It is better to give alms than to store up gold; for almsgiving saves one from death and expiates every sin. Those who regularly give alms shall enjoy a full life, but those habitually guilty of sin are their own worst enemies [Tob. 12:7–10].

In the ancient eastern world, a tremendous gap existed between the rich who had power, possessions, and prestige and the poor who were powerless, without many possessions, and who were the "nobodies" of those cultures. The responsibility of the wealthy class toward the poor and needy was described in Hebrew as *sedaqa* (righteousness) and *sedek* (justice). When prophets and wisdom writers like Tobit spoke of the responsibility of the rich to hear the cry of the poor, they expressed themselves in terms of *sedaqa* and *sedek* rather than words meaning love. After the exile, *sedaqa* and *sedek* gradually took on the meaning of almsgiving. Often these words were translated in the Septuagint as *eleemosune* (mercy or care) and *dikaiosyne* (justice).

The root of the word "almsgiving" means social responsibility. Any excessive wealth in the form of power, possessions, and prestige must be given to or used on behalf of those who are in need. Giving excess is naturally expected. There can be no ifs, ands, or buts about it. The Hebrew Scriptures simply assumed that people, groups, and institutions should manifest this piety on behalf of the poor.

Almsgiving is not a matter of feeling. It cannot be arbitrarily cut off when it happens that the recipient of our alms might not manifest thinking or behavior akin to our own. In the same vein, alms should not be cut because they might go beyond a purely individual or interpersonal level to alleviate the structural injustice that often sustains poverty and brokenness. Alms cannot be geared only to band-aid approaches; they should also be geared to promote economic and political structures of justice. In this light, it is interesting to note how groups that call for structural changes in the power groups on behalf of the poor in cities rarely, if ever, receive United Fund monies.

While many North American Christians have been educated to show "charity" toward individuals or even groups, they cannot understand or support the growing involvement of a number of Catholic and Protestant institutions in the ministry of corporate responsibility, a contemporary way of "giving alms." This ministry finds denominations, dioceses, and orders such as our Midwest Capuchin Franciscans and the Sisters of Charity of Nazareth, Kentucky, using our stock in U. S. corporations to bring justice to their social arrangements and activities. One such rejection of this effort to promote corporate responsibility came to my Corporate Responsibility Office in a letter from a former secretary at the Securities and Exchange Commission. What we might consider a form of piety—our shareholder resolution with ITT—was alien to his understanding of piety. Furthermore, he added that as long as we continued to evangelize structures in this way, he would stop giving alms to the institutional church:

> I happen to have a couple of shares of ITT and also happen to be a good, traditionalist (that means no social gospeler) Catholic. I have been married for thirty-five years, so I suppose that also makes me a stodgy and non-chic Catholic.
>
> Well at first I believed all your pious nonsense, about wanting to prevent despoliation of the land and to help the beleaguered Indians, but your resolution to ITT vis-à-vis their supposed operations in Chile is nothing but a lot of palpable crap and nonsense and Christ must surely be turning over in his heavens at what is passing these days as "Christian" involvement.
>
> I personally don't think you or the good sisters from Kentucky have any damned business pestering the likes of ITT, which in my opinion does a helluva lot better at ITS JOB than you do at yours. That is, it provides jobs, it uplifts the economy, not only of the United States but other nations, and it has provided this country with the finest communications posture in the world. On the other hand, what are you doing about saving souls, which is precisely what you SHOULD be at, not running up and down working up a lather against ITT, or South Africa or whatever your current target.
>
> I personally feel you could care less about Chile; your objective, as well as that of the misguided Protestants and the others in your combine, is nothing more or less than the destruction of our free enterprise system and its supplanting by a Socialist, planned economy, all in the name of egalitarianism.
>
> If you think I am wrong, send me a resolution condemning any American company for doing business with Russia, Cuba, North Vietnam or Poland.
>
> You are one of the reasons why I don't give a red cent to the church

anymore. I give it to individual entities, the Catholic missions that feed the aged and give them a bed, the various Hospitality Houses and the Missions, but to the institutional church, not a dime until you people go back to doing what you were ordained for and that does not include trying to bring down the Chilean government or trying to create a heaven on earth.

Sincerely,
Theodore L. Humes

P.S. In my youth I used to attend St. Augustine, Lawrenceville, Pittsburg, where my recollection of those fine German Capuchins with their pity and deep concern for our *religious* needs is very vivid.

cc: Sister Margaret Ross
    Sisters of Charity Nazareth
    Nazareth, Kentucky

P.S. Sister Margaret. My sister was a devout member of the Sisters of Divine Providence in western Penna. She left the order after fifteen years because [of], precisely, this kind of worldly activism—your troublemaking shareholder resolutions.[13]

The next form of piety that promotes the normative dimension of justice deals with prayer and the attitude we bring to prayer. "Whenever you pray, go to your room, close your door, and pray to your Father in private. Then your Father, who sees what no man sees, will repay you" (6:6). In addition to the Our Father (6:9–13) in this section (6:1–18), Matthew's Jesus presents the proper way to pray in the form of a "do" and a "don't": do not babble (6:7–8) and do forgive (6:14–15).

When we examine much of the prayer offered in our daily lives, our families, and communities, as well as in our weekly liturgies, we have to admit there is a lot of babbling going on—many words without much meaning. For instance, in some churches and religious houses we see people performing many forms of piety that reflect a "sheer multiplication of words" (6:7) such as litanies or other devotions. At times, some of this piety is connected to themes supportive of capitalism, free enterprise, patriotism, and larger military budgets, and against those Russians we pray will be converted, as our Lady of Fatima promised. All the while, deep forms of anger and fear toward minorities often pervade the discussions of such groups at their coffees and socials. If anyone does address the lack of forgiveness at one of these devotions or holy hours of reparation, the challenge is rejected as out of place, or "political."

In many religious communities and families, efforts are being made to show deeper care and to celebrate this by bringing members together to share talents, ministries, and common concerns. Unfortunately, these forms of sharing are not often matched in deeper sharing of faith and prayer. Prayer is still considered to be personal and individual. It is not to be shared, except in words. For example, at one Marriage Encounter weekend the participants felt very free in sharing how they communicated, expressed themselves sexually, dealt with problem children, and even how they managed their finances. But when a leader suggested the group discuss their understanding of God and how they prayed, someone said, "Isn't that getting too personal?"

My feeling is that those fraternities in our Midwest Capuchin province with the least amount of problems go beyond the rote recitation of the daily Prayer of Christians and at least take time for pauses within it (to allow for the possibility of shared prayer and reflection), or adapt their common prayer to include faith and life sharing, or action/reflection forms. These communities are the ones most others want to join.

In communities where members get together to recite three psalms in the morning and then, again, in the evening (often scheduling the latter immediately after dinner and before the evening news), the door is hardly open for the possibility of any deep, shared experience of faith.

When I was young, our family—like many others—prayed the daily rosary. When the rosary was discarded as a family way of prayer it was replaced with little or nothing else except grace at meals. We have yet to reap the consequences of inadequate prayer forms in the contemporary family.

I discovered one re-institution of relevant prayer forms while visiting my brother and sister-in-law in Texas. They started praying the Scriptures with their children. While I was there Sue asked if I would like to say night prayers with my nephews. I read a little story to Shane and Kent that was designed to explain a Scripture passage in their terms, and said the prayer that followed. It took only five or ten minutes, but it helped them realize God's part in their lives. Today all families are called to find new forms of prayer, to share faith and God's word, if they are to grow spiritually.

Besides urging the community not to babble in prayers, Matthew places a great stress on forgiveness as an attitude necessary for strengthening prayer and community. Babylon was the sign of division and of alienation of the people not only from God but from each other. Not able to live in harmony with God's plan for their community, the people ended up babbling. When people come together in unforgiveness, uncare, and irreconciliation and recite words they call prayer, they may be fulfilling a law or obligation, but they are not fulfilling justice. Therefore, Jesus says, the prayer of the people in this community will not be heard (6:15).

Many leaders in the charismatic movement have long known that the obstacles to healing and to deeper experiences of God are very often related to alienation and unforgiveness. Time and time again, this is confirmed in speeches and books from people like Barbara Schlemon, Francis McNutt, Mike Scanlon, and the Linn Brothers (not to mention all the evidence from non-Catholic leaders such as Ruth Carter Stapleton). Story after story is told.

People come to prayer meetings seeking healing. They remain broken, only to respond affirmatively when someone asks: "Is there anyone here that you are angry with, or about whom you have hard feelings?" or "Is there anyone in your family, your work, or your past who has hurt you?" or "Do you still harbor anger and resentments and find it hard to forgive?" Brokenness grounded in divisions, resentment, and unforgiveness separates us from union with God. Alienation must always be healed; it can never be rationalized away (see 18:21–22). "If you forgive the faults of others, your heavenly Father will forgive you yours. If you do not forgive others, neither will your Father forgive you" (6:14–15).

As he discussed that justice that shows itself in prayer, Matthew included the Lord's Prayer as the model of prayer that does not babble, but forgives. As we pray these words in our concrete world of people, groups, and structures, we should realize that the words of the Lord's Prayer must relate to the reality of our time.[14] Its words invite all levels of the world to change whatever negates the fulfillment of those words on earth as they would be fulfilled in heaven (6:10). If we are not "trying to create a heaven on earth," by applying these words to all people and forces, we should stop praying the Lord's Prayer.[15] Our actions and lifestyle will show we do not mean what we pray when we say we want God's reign on earth as it is in heaven. We will have been babbling.

The final way justice is to be normative in the community is through fasting (6:16–18). While the bridegroom, Jesus, was on earth, there was no need to fast. A purpose of fasting is to help clear the mind in order to remember someone or something from the past. With the powerful experience of God-with-them in Jesus, the disciples had the living example of Jesus continually motivating them. They did not need to recall his deeds; they witnessed his *exousia*. They experienced Jesus' fast as reordering conditions of need and brokenness (see 9:14–15).

However, Jesus warned the disciples, "When the day comes that the groom is taken away, then they will fast" (9:15). With the commission to go into the whole world (28:18–20), fasting serves two purposes. We fast to remember the bridegroom and his ways. By practicing a kind of violence to our "surface self," our senses, we can be more fully open in our "real selves" to be constituted in religious experience. Secondly, having set priorities as to what is now truly important in life we can commit ourselves more fully to the ministry of Jesus. We can more easily give ourselves and our resources in greater solidarity with the poor and those in need of healing.

Fasting makes us more open to experience the transcendent. It also helps shape a vision whereby we can view our world with God's eyes. In the power of that experience, we can call for a reordering of those realities that contradict the reign of God.

Matthew did not elaborate on the concrete form our fast should take. However, because he presented Jesus fulfilling so many texts from Isaiah (especially Second Isaiah), it is safe to suggest the kind of fasting Matthew recommended for his community. Jesus viewed his ministry as fulfilling a fast (see 11:2–5). Following Second Isaiah, our fast, too, should reflect our fidelity to the task of reordering society:

This, rather, is the fasting that I wish:
releasing those bound unjustly, untying the thongs of the yoke;
Setting free the oppressed,
breaking every yoke;
Sharing your bread with the hungry,
sheltering the oppressed and the homeless;
Clothing the naked when you see them,
and not turning your back on your own.
Then your light shall break forth like the dawn,
and your wound shall quickly be healed;
Your vindication shall go before you,
and the glory of the Lord shall be your rear guard.
Then you shall call, and the Lord will answer,
you shall cry for help, and he will say: Here I am!
If you remove from your midst oppression,
false accusation and malicious speech;
If you bestow your bread on the hungry
and satisfy the afflicted;
Then light shall rise for you in the darkness,
and the gloom shall become for you like midday;
Then the Lord will guide you always
and give you plenty even on the parched land.
He will renew your strength,
and you shall be like a watered garden,
like a spring whose water never fails.
The ancient ruins shall be rebuilt for your sake,
and the foundations from ages past you shall raise up;
"Repairer of the breach," they shall call you,
"Restorer of ruined homesteads" [Isa. 58:6–12].

We too can be called "repairers of the breach" and "restorers of ruined homesteads" (58:12). If we receive such names, it will mean that we fasted so faithfully that the "spirit of the Lord God" constituted us "oaks of justice, planted by the Lord to show his glory" (Isa. 61:1, 3). Similarly, we will be those who "rebuild the ancient ruins" (Isa. 61:4).

Fasting helps us to be more open to the Spirit of God. In fasting we are inspired to reorder society to reflect God's plan. This is central to beatitudinal living. In a special way fasting is fundamental to the fulfillment of Isaiah 61 and this particular beatitude: "Blessed are those who *hunger* and *thirst* for justice."

Hunger and thirst are two global realities. Fasting from food and water can make us more aware of how hunger and thirst affect half of the world. By personal fasting we can experience, in a limited, temporary way, the all-pervasive, sustained hunger and thirst experienced by hundreds of millions. Our very resistance to fasting can become an inspiration to resist whatever in our lives, our relationships, and our structures, contributes to hunger and thirst in the world.

Often we flee from the only kind of fasting that has been asked of us (Isa. 58:5; Matt. 6:16–18). Our very lifestyle depends on others' hungers. Journalist Frank Aukhofer has illustrated how our lifestyle evidences misplaced values at the same time it ignores hungers of the world:

> Recently a wine merchant bought a full page of space in *The New York Times* to boast that he had drunk a bottle of 1865 Lafite Rothschild—and to offer for sale three other bottles at $15,000 each or $50,000 for all three.
>
> That same edition of *The Times* carried a front-page story by Seymour M. Hersh (of My Lai massacre fame), which said that 2.25 million people in Cambodia were facing starvation.[16]

It is good to fast from such material resources as food and drink. Yet we are also called to fast in a way that makes our power useful to those in need. We are called to fast from discrimination or any other attitudes and actions that create or perpetuate injustice. This manner of fasting will do much to untie the thongs of prejudice's yoke, which keep women, minorities and Third World peoples oppressed (Isa. 58:6).

Not Being Satisfied until Justice Is Fulfilled

The other two times Matthew uses *dikaiosyne* involve John the Baptist. "When John came preaching a way of holiness *(dikaiosyne)*," Jesus said to the chief priests and elders of the people, "you put no faith in him; but the tax collectors and the prostitutes did believe in him. Yet even when you saw that, you did not repent and believe in him" (21:32). Because the tax collectors and prostitutes repented, they experienced God's justice; in that justice they made the way of Jesus normative for their lives. Consequently, Jesus added, "I assure you that tax collectors and prostitutes are entering the kingdom of God before you" (21:31).

The other time Jesus uses *dikaiosyne* is connected to his "inaugural statement" in Matthew's Gospel. John's baptism was to be the sign of reform that would show that Jesus was committed to letting God's reign dominate his life. In submitting to John's baptism, Jesus said, "We must do this if we would fulfill all of God's demands *(dikaiosyne)*" (3:15).

Justice is the fulfillment of God's will, of God's demands. Jesus' words about the purpose of the baptism summarize everything we have said thus far. In commenting on 3:15 Donald Senior has shown that:

There are two key words in the sentence: To "do all" (literally to "fulfill," the same Greek word Matthew so frequently uses regarding Jesus' fulfillment of Old Testament prophecies) and "righteousness," or justice. The latter term has a double layer of meaning in biblical thought. *God's* justice is his saving activity on behalf of his people. *Human* justice, or righteousness, is the effort we make to respond to God's goodness by carrying out his will.

It is possible that both levels of meaning are present in this keynote statement of Jesus. God's justice, or plan of salvation, is fulfilled by the very presence of John and Jesus in world history. At the same time, Jesus is a model of *human* righteousness as well, because he carries out God's plan of salvation by his loving fidelity to his Father's will. This emphasis on obedience to the will of God, on obedience perfectly modeled by Jesus, is a hallmark of Matthew's portrait of Christ.[17]

All those who hunger and thirst for the justice Jesus personified in his life, all those who will not be satisfied knowing that God's plan for the world is still not fulfilled, will show in their spiritualities Matthew's portrait of Christ. Their biographies will become models of the theology of justice that Matthew found fulfilled in Jesus.

CHAPTER SEVEN

Blessed Are Those Who Show Mercy; They Shall Receive Mercy

Mercy: The Sign of God's Perfection and Care

An essential aspect of justice is *eleemosune*. *Eleemosune* is translated as mercy or care. Mercy is the outpouring to others of God's gift of mercy that we have experienced. When my spirituality expresses this fifth beatitude, I manifest compassion, concern, and care for every human being. This quality of mercy enables me to become a brother or sister to everyone in the world in such a way that I share God's very blessedness. "Blest are they who show mercy (*eleemones*); mercy shall be theirs (*eleethesontai*)" (5:7).

As with every beatitude, the fulfillment of this one is best evidenced in the way Jesus was merciful and thus received the favor of God's mercy (see 17:5). Rather than discussing different ways Jesus showed mercy through his teaching, preaching, and healing (which all signified mercy), suffice it to say that Jesus' mercy revealed a central characteristic of God's perfection (5:48; cf. Luke 6:36).

The perfection of God and the quality of mercy are almost synonymous. The more we express ourselves as merciful individuals, the more we become merciful groups, and the more mercy that flows from our institutions (especially through the so-called spiritual and corporal works of justice and mercy), the more fully we can experience God's perfection which is revealed in mercy.

The theme of showing mercy as a sign of God's mercy is part of wisdom literature. The one who knows mercy, especially in the form of forgiveness, builds up order in the community. Such a person stands in contrast to the one who is vengeful. Vengeance will receive God's vengeance, just as those showing mercy receive God's mercy. According to Sirach:

The vengeful will suffer the Lord's vengeance,
for he remembers their sins in detail.
Forgive your neighbor's injustice;
then when you pray, your own sins will be forgiven.
Should a man nourish anger against his fellows
and expect healing from the Lord?
Should a man refuse mercy to his fellows,
yet seek pardon for his own sins?
If he who is but flesh cherishes wrath,
who will forgive his sins?
Remember your last days, set enmity aside;
remember death and decay, and cease from sin! [Sir. 28:1–6].

Mercy is related to the forgiveness of failings, hurts, and sins. It reflects God's forgiveness of us and the way we forgive others (6:12). It is covenantal. It signifies, in its very manifestation, God's eschatological entry into whatever condition and situation may need reordering. As we show mercy, God becomes present. The more merciful we are and the more perfect we become, the more God's revelation affects all parts of the world.

Mercy is central to community living, as Matthew shows in Chapter 18. After outlining a way to make peace within his divided community (18:1–20), he concludes with a vivid example showing how members of the community should never stop forgiving and showing mercy: "Then Peter came up and asked him, 'Lord, when my brother wrongs me, how often must I forgive him? Seven times?' 'No,' Jesus replied, 'not seven times; I say, seventy times seven times'" (18:21–22). Thereupon Jesus told a parable (18:23ff.) that equated God's reign with mercy itself. The Wisdom Teacher declared, in effect: "That is why the reign of God is discovered in the quality of mercy."

In the parable about the merciless official, Jesus made it clear that the circle of care and mercy is essential to the spiritual life. The circle can be completed only if we respond to others in and with the divine mercy and care first shown us. In *seeing* the need of the official who was in debt (18:23–25), the king also heard his cry of complaint (18:26). The king *cared* for the official; he was "moved with pity." He *called* the official to be free of the debt and let him go (18:27). However the official failed to *respond* (18:28) by hearing the cry of complaint from someone else in debt to him (18:29). In fact, "he would hear none of it." The official refused to manifest a comparable *care* through his forgiveness of the lesser debt (18:30). Consequently, the king banished the official from his *sight* as unworthy to remain in the royal presence (18:32–34). Matthew would make clear later, in another story about the works of mercy (25:31–46), what Jesus concluded in this parable: "My heavenly Father will treat you in exactly the same way unless each of you forgives his brother from his heart" (18:35).

In an extended but inspiring exegesis of Matthew's parable about the merciless official, John Meier describes how the circle of care is to draw within it every level of our world. He writes:

> To limitless debt there can be no solution except limitless compassion. The master shows himself truly master by wiping out the entire debt with a sovereign act of grace.
>
> Fortunately, while the master's mercy changes the official's situation, it does not change the official. . . . A Christian cannot win God's forgiveness; but he can lose it by refusing to extend it to a brother. It is this theme of "brother" which gives the parable its ecclesial interpretation in verse 35. A pure act of mercy has made us all free sons of the Father of Jesus, and therefore we are all brothers in the church in which Jesus dwells. To refuse a brother the forgiveness which has made us sons is to rupture the family bond and to break the lifeline of mercy binding us through Jesus to the Father. The church was created by the mercy of the Father made present to us in Jesus. The church can continue to exist only if the men who were made brothers by this mercy continue to exchange it—not with an external ritual gesture, but "from the heart." That is Matthew's last word on life and discipline in the church.[1]

Whatever the debt may be—forgiveness of sins among individuals, healing of hurts in communities and families, or even restructuring of the foreign debt of Third World nations—we are called to manifest that lifestyle of jubilee which proclaims unlimited forgiveness (see 11:2–5). This lifestyle proclaims the year of God's favor and care to the world (see Isa. 61:2).

The quality of mercy outlines not only an essential dimension of spirituality but the nature of the church itself. The church is to manifest the reality of Jesus. It is to live the beatitude of mercy because it has been blessed in Jesus' mercy. Meier concludes:

> The mercy Jesus has shown them has made them the church. The survival of the church depends on their extending what they have received: mercy without measure. At this point, the nexus of Christology and ecclesiology is not just the dogmatic axis of Matthew's gospel; it is also the profoundest expression of his spirituality.[2]

Since God's perfection is revealed in mercy, our spirituality—which has perfection as its goal (see 5:48; 19:21–23)—is inseparable from mercy toward those in need.

Abraham Heschel said that mercy and care reveal God's pathos. This great Jewish philosopher wrote that pathos means God is never neutral, never beyond good and evil: "God is always partial to justice. The divine pathos is the unity of the eternal and the temporal, of meaning and mystery, of the metaphysical and the historical. It is the real basis of the relation between

God and humankind, of the correlation of Creator and creation, of the dialogue between the Holy One of Israel and His people."[3]

To be separated from God's mercy is to be a-pathos or without mercy. We are not constituted in pathos or care if we refuse to live by the norm of God's mercy in our sympathy and empathy toward others. If we do not care, we do not image God.

We do not care when we are apathetic about the hurts and pains of others. We do not care when we remain neutral in face of the systemic ways nations and races keep others in debt through fear and control. If we do not care, if we are apathetic and decide to remain neutral in the face of injustice, we are not manifesting the very way God has chosen to be present in life. Since pathos is God's revelation, not to care is to cut ourselves off from God's revelation and sight.

There can no longer be any excuses for uninvolvement, even including a lack of information or the need for neutrality. In a complex society we will never have all the information on any subject. As part of the network of injustice we are always involved in one way or another. We must choose to care as our own way of faithfully continuing the mercy and forgiveness of God in history.

As we saw in the last chapter, Matthew's Gospel reserves Jesus' greatest anger for uncaring leaders of the Jews and the church whenever they frustrated justice by professing one thing and practicing another. He called such a lifestyle "hypocrisy," or a lie. Truth and the lie were the issues at stake when Jesus and the leaders argued with each other over the breaking of laws. The uncaring leaders were misusing their power by not responding to the real needs of the people; they used their authority to keep the people bound up and indebted in one form or another (23:4ff.). Jesus invited the leaders to manifest a deeper form of authority, namely the quality of mercy, which would unbind the yoke by serving the people's needs (20:25–27).

Mercy flows from an inner disposition of covenantal fidelity or truth. More important than the observance of external laws, the ethical norm of mercy would evidence an internal dedication to live according to God's plan. This is the kind of mercy that God desires, even more than sacrifice, if the latter means a legalistic ritual void of covenantal care. Matthew desired to stress this inner quality of care for his divided community in a singular way. Of all the gospel writers, he alone quoted Hosea's words about mercy—not just once but twice (9:13; 12:7):

For it is love (*eleos*) that I desire, not sacrifice, and knowledge of God rather than holocausts [Hos. 6:6].

In each of the circumstances that gave rise to Jesus' application of the Hosean quote to himself, Matthew shows the leaders unable to move beyond their legalism to bend the law to meet human needs. The first time, it happened that, while Jesus was at table in Matthew's home, many tax collectors and those known as sinners came to join Jesus and his disciples at dinner. The Pharisees saw this and complained to his disciples, "What reason can the Teacher have for eating with tax collectors and those who disregard the law?" [9:10–11].

Tax collectors and "sinners" were typical of those rejected from society's mainstream by the leadership group. So when Jesus and his disciples would go so far as to have dinner (a sign of acceptance) with such rejects, that was pushing tolerance a bit far. Aware of their righteousness, Jesus said: "People who are in good health do not need a doctor; sick people do. Go and learn the meaning of the words, 'It is mercy I desire and not sacrifice'" (9:12–13).

The next time Matthew places Hosea's quote on Jesus' lips is in response to another situation of conflict with uncaring leaders: "Once on a sabbath Jesus walked through the standing grain." Matthew notes: "His disciples felt hungry, so they began to pull off the heads of grain and eat them. When the Pharisees spied this, they protested: 'See here! Your disciples are doing what is not permitted on the sabbath' (12:1–2)."

The Deuteronomic law, which forbade reaping on the Sabbath (Deut. 23:25), had been bent by David to meet the needs of his followers (1 Sam. 21:4–7). Even the priests themselves mitigated some Sabbath laws in order to carry out their liturgical duties in the Temple (Num. 28:9–10). Jesus recalled these cases (12:3–6). Yet the intolerance of the leaders deafened their ears to what Jesus was trying to convey about the quality of mercy.

The external action, which found the leaders and Jesus in conflict, related to two situations of eating with outcasts and plucking the grain on the Sabbath. These related to varying interpretations of the law. Especially in this second Sabbath controversy (12:9–14), Jesus shows that the law of love and doing good (22:39–40) is more important than the law of the Sabbath.

The very placement of the two Sabbath controversies, after the promise of rest in 11:29, cannot be isolated from the creation story of Genesis 1:1–2:3, wherein God's doing of good led to the Sabbath rest. The first Sabbath controversy showed that the law could be disregarded to meet one's own need (12:1–8); now in this second instance (12:9–14), the law could be lifted to *do good* to those precious ones who were in need. Doing good, from Genesis on must be the basis for all relationships, actions, and laws. All externals must be based on this fundamental dynamic.

The *internal* dynamic, which finally separated the leaders from Jesus, was his mercy and doing good versus their apathy and intolerance. So obsessed were they by their need to use the law to keep them in their positions of control, they could overlook the needs of human beings in the name of that law.

I discovered that the Pharisees' sandals fit my feet when I participated in a psychodrama at a Youth Convention of Secular Franciscans in Quincy,

Illinois. The activity centered around the "magical" gift of anything the participants needed or desired.

As I came on stage in front of the group, the group leader said, "What do you want?"

Since I had been seriously wanting to live in such a way that God would be able to be free to work in my life and ministry (but being afraid to say this), I responded, "I'd like to have the ability to communicate what I desire in such a way that people will accept what I'm trying to get across."

"Well, you certainly are in luck!" the magician said. "I've got a form of that behind each of those (imagined) curtains. If you choose the first, people will accept what you say and they'll accept you, even though they probably won't do anything about it. If you take the middle curtain they'll accept everything you say and they'll act on it, but they probably will reject you for telling them about it. If you take my final curtain they won't accept everything, just some. But they will continue to accept you." With this he concluded, "So, which one do you want?"

Without much hesitation I said, "I'll take the second one."

"Good," he responded. "Now what will you give me for it?"

Realizing the game was getting serious, I stalled by saying, "I'll give you a million dollars."

"Oh, no," he said. "We don't take any material things for things so important. So, what'll you give me?"

Immediately something flashed through my mind; it was what I would be very happy to part with: "I'll give you my intolerance," I said.

Intolerance, or lack of real care and mercy toward others, was the big obstacle in my life that kept me from fulfilling my dream. It was the plank in my life that kept me from being more sensitive to the needs of others (see 7:1-5). Of course, I would be happy to give up my intolerance.

Usually, when we examine those things about which we are most defensive, feel most guilty, or sense to be our chief faults, they stand as the greatest barriers to the goal we are trying to achieve. Because their intolerance refused care and mercy toward needy members of the community, the leaders found themselves threatened by Jesus' words and his lifestyle of mercy as well.

In his dispute with the leaders, Jesus judged them as wanting in two situations, both of which related to eating together (9:10; 12:1). The law, which had replaced the Temple sacrifice, was not being grounded in the people's need for compassion, mercy, and care. Originally, the Torah and its interpretation had been envisioned by the Jamnian Pharisees as a way of bringing about community order and unity from the disorder of A.D. 66–70. But now the law was becoming an end in itself; it was a source of disorder. It secured the leaders in their position as they stood intolerantly judging Jesus and the disciples for eating the grain. Inviting them to return to the original basis for all law, Jesus said: "If you understood the meaning of the text, 'it is mercy I desire and not sacrifice,' you would not have condemned these innocent men" (12:7).

Mercy: The Foundation for Word and Worship

Mercy is the foundation of both law and cult, Torah and worship. All our sacrifices, be they liturgical rituals or the ministry of our lives, should express mercy, forgiveness, care, compassion, sympathy, and empathy toward those in need. Otherwise they will not be part of God's pathos, care, and mercy.

The texts from Hosea reveal how Matthew weaved into his gospel fabric eucharistic threads which are colored with mercy. In each of the controversy texts regarding with whom and on what day the disciples shared a meal, Matthew quoted the text from Hosea (Hos. 6:6). It dealt with the inner disposition needed for true covenantal sharing of the sacrifice.

Besides these texts, Matthew makes other links between mercy and the eucharistic sacrament of sacrifice. In each of the instances in which he describes the multiplication of the loaves (14:13–21; 15:32–38), the condition that precipitated the ritual of taking, blessing, breaking, and giving the loaves (14:19; cf. 15:36) was the reality of human need that evoked Jesus' mercy.

"When he disembarked and saw the vast throng, his heart was moved with pity and he cured their sick," Matthew notes in 14:14. Similarly, after leaving Tyre and Sidon, Jesus

> passed along the Sea of Galilee. He went up onto the mountainside and sat down there. Large crowds of people came to him bringing with them cripples, the deformed, the blind, the mute, and many others besides. They laid them at his feet and he cured them. The result was great astonishment in the crowds as they beheld the mute speaking, the deformed made sound, cripples walking about, and the blind seeing. They glorified the God of Israel [15:29–31].

Both 14:14 and 15:29–31 show a merciful Jesus responding to the suffering of others by healing their brokenness. This signified part of the messianic fulfillment of the covenant. The other part of this covenant would follow immediately in the ritual sharing of bread. This meal would further illustrate Jesus' mercy (14:15–21; 15:32–38):

> Jesus called his disciples to him and said: "My heart is moved with pity for the crowd. By now they have been with me three days, and have nothing to eat. I do not wish to send them away hungry, for fear they may collapse on the way" [15:32].

Jesus did not wish that the crowds—a symbol for humanity in need—should ever be left without food. By extending to the community his power to heal broken humanity (9:8; 10:1, 8; 28:18–20), Jesus' power to feed a hungry world now has been given to us: "Jesus said to them (us): 'There is no need for them to disperse. Give them something to eat yourselves' " (14:16).

Hearing that they were to use their own resources on behalf of those in need, the disciples gave the same response we are tempted to give once we realize that we too are called to minister healing in our world of suffering and poverty: "We have nothing here" (14:17). We have only our limited resources and weaker faith. But Jesus' power can transform even that smallness into a miracle of care for the world.

The five loaves and a couple of fish (14:17) might be considered nothing in the eyes of the world. Yet we are continually invited to share even the little we may have with others.

According to scripture scholar George Lamsa, the fact that one person refused to be selfish and shared with others became the invitation for a community numbering well over five thousand to do the same. According to Professor Lamsa, people in those days carried their food beneath their cloaks; thus it was difficult for others to know who had what resources. The example of one or another person (14:17; 15:34) willing to share with others in need became the inspiration for others to share. In this way the disciples were able to help all the people eat. "All those present ate their fill" (14:20; 15:37).

In the community of Jesus, symbolized in the eucharistic gathering, resources should be used to respond to the people's needs for healing and sharing. There should be no discrimination. None should have more than they need, for this is a sign of that alienation from the covenant that perpetuates suffering and poverty.

Matthew presents the Eucharist as the manifestation of God's merciful covenant. In this covenant, wounds are healed and bread is shared. The eucharistic covenant is diametrically opposed to those conditions that create suffering and keep people in poverty.

From Matthew's understanding of the Eucharist and the human condition, we can create a model of mercy that contrasts the alienation of the world with the covenant of God's Word. The covenant should celebrate fidelity to God's revealed word in the ritual of healing and resource sharing on every level: individual, interpersonal, and infrastructural. However, this covenant can be celebrated only in the concrete reality of our world. The alienation, the *tohu wabohu,* of the world is rehearsed in the miserable ritual of suffering and poverty on every level. The eucharistic covenant and the world's

THE WORLD
Individual
Interpersonal
Infrastructural
ALIENATION
suffering   poverty
- -
healing   sharing
COVENANT
Infrastructural
Interpersonal
Individual
THE WORD

alienation cannot be celebrated together without some form of idolatry.

Because the ritual of our world should be celebrated in our words and worship, we must raise a serious question regarding the quality of mercy in much of our church. We must ask if what passes each Sunday for Eucharist might not also be criticized by Jesus, even though it fulfills every prescription of the liturgists and canonists. "Go and learn the meaning of the words, 'It is mercy I desire and not sacrifice.' I have come to call, not the self-righteous, but sinners" (9:13). If the creation and sustaining of our nation's reality unwittingly stands for a world of suffering and brokenness, how can we come together to celebrate in ritual those signs that witness to the opposite reality?

For Matthew's community and ours, the covenant of healing and sharing that is symbolized and established in the Eucharist should stand as a counter-sign to the world's suffering and poverty. It should stand as the triumph of justice and mercy over sin and brokenness. Consequently, Matthew's Jesus says, if we are approaching the altar to celebrate the covenant and there realize the ritual of our world manifests alienation from others, we must go and be reconciled by seeking to change the conditions that have created that alienation. "Then come and offer your gift" (5:24).

It is true that, left to our own resources, we will never be able to "give them enough to eat." Yet, to truly celebrate the Eucharist, we must feed as we are fed. The poor of our nation and our world who are affected by our infrastructural arrangements will never be filled from our resources if we do not show mercy by giving them something to eat ourselves. What we must give must come from *our* table—from our power, possessions, and prestige. If, with the *exousia* given us in the Eucharist, we still fail to give evidence of the mercy shown us, we too will find ourselves hungry. Because we have separated ourselves from our tablemates, the brothers and sisters of the earth, we will have separated ourselves from the table of Jesus.

Recalling that a lack of mercy separates us from our tablemates, as well as from the divine host, is helpful when we reflect on Matthew's narrative of the Eucharist itself (26:20–30). Matthew divides into two parts what took place around the table: the betrayal of Jesus by his companion and tablemate, Judas (26:20–25), and the actual sharing of the eucharistic meal itself (26:26–30).

To understand the implications of putting the betrayal before the sharing of the Eucharist, it is important to recall the previous Matthean use of Hosea (9:13; 12:7). Jesus used this text from Hosea in his disputes with the leaders of the community to show that the true worth of the ritual of sacrifice was to be measured not so much in fidelity to legal rules, but in the expression of covenantal fidelity in mercy or care. Jesus demanded that all ritual sacrifice, legal or cultic, had to be based on the dignity of every person. Because of this dignity, if any ritual sign of the covenant would be approved, it was primary that each person's needs be met.

Good deeds of mercy toward all people are the only God-requested resources we can bring as gifts to the banquet. At the Eucharist there can be no rejection or betrayal of any person. There can be no discrimination. This attitude of reconciliation and universalism stands as a total countersign to any lack of mercy shown on any level of life. Love denies exclusivism and separatism. By having Jesus eat with the tax collectors and sinners (9:10), who were society's rejects, Matthew offers us a model for every Eucharist. There can be no discrimination either in our lives or the ritual expression of our Eucharists. "According to this view," David Hill comments,

> the tax collectors and sinners who are welcomed by Jesus represent for Matthew the Gentile Christians in the Church. . . . Was the table-fellowship of Jew and Gentile in the Church an object of *Jewish* polemic? Was that issue of concern to the authorities of Jewry in the period after A.D. 70? If not, to whom is Matthew seeking to justify the reception of Gentiles? Was the issue of table-fellowship a live issue to anyone in the mid-eighties of the first Christian century, the period with which the emergence of Matthew's gospel is usually associated? . . . No evidence yet brought forward appears strong enough to overthrow the probability that the Church of the evangelist Matthew was a largely Jewish-Christian community struggling to find or to maintain its identity over against the new post-A.D. 70 (i.e., broadly post-Jamnian) Jewish establishment. Jewish Christians were about to be, if they had not already been, effectively banished from the synagogues. Matthew and his congregation are forced to regard the mission to Israel as a thing of the past and are now discovering an understanding of themselves and of the mission "to all nations," a mission in which "Israel" would no longer play a distinctive role. If then the Pharisees—and it is part of Matthew's redactional intent to make them as often as possible Jesus' enemies (to the extent that they become a kind of theological construct for "that rejecting generation")—have a contemporary application for Matthew, it is a *negative* ideal for Judaism as a whole. . . . In short, the situation in the Matthean Church may not have been very different from the one encountered by Jesus himself. The Pharisees of Matthew's day (influencing attitudes in the congregation, if not actually themselves within it) must go and learn—they must learn from the word of Scripture (Hos. vi. 6) and from the behaviour of Jesus and of his disciples, i.e., the Church, that loyalty to the divine will will cause the rupture of every social, cultic and religious barrier.[4]

Mercy is central to the way the eucharistic meal is shared among table-mates. It contradicts the intolerance, lack of forgiveness, and prejudice that otherwise create barriers to God's covenantal plan. Thus, to celebrate the ritual of the Eucharist appropriately, it is of primary importance that we first examine ourselves to determine if we are bringing to the Eucharist an attitude of separatism, rejection, or exclusivism. Such negative attitudes stand as the main obstacle to the mercy that is central to Matthew's spirituality and understanding of the Eucharist.

The Lack of Mercy and Eucharistic Fidelity

We are called to examine ourselves not only in the way we may be separated from God by our personal sins or from our neighbor by our family or community divisions; we also must be concerned about the way we bring to our assembly attitudes of rejection toward the poor. Since prejudice against the poor can be so subtle we must examine ourselves carefully. Prejudice against the powerless and those without possessions or "names" is part of our cultural addiction. Often we may be under its subtle influence even as we think we are doing good toward others.

I discovered once how subtle prejudices can be. I also discovered how far I was from showing true mercy and care toward my tablemates who are poor. I received a phone call from Catherine Cleary, one of the most powerful women in the United States according to *Fortune* magazine. She was president of the First Wisconsin Trust Company, and also on the Board of Directors of several corporations, including General Motors, Kraft, Northwestern Mutual Life Insurance, Kohler, and American Telephone and Telegraph.

She asked if I would lecture on corporate responsibility to one of her classes at the University of Wisconsin-Milwaukee. I went home that evening very enthusiastic about sharing the news. My enthusiasm immediately dampened when I realized who my tablemate would be. It was Kate.

I did not know Kate's last name, but I knew her background. Our fraternity had heard about Kate when the Capuchins at St. Benedict's Meal Program called asking if someone in our house could drive her to their daily meal because she was having serious leg problems. Since Kate lived a couple of miles from St. Benedict's and just a few blocks from us, it was decided to invite her to our fraternity for dinner. This was our inaugural meal.

While sitting next to Kate, I began to think: "What am I going to say to her? What a boring conversationalist she is. What a small world she lives in. What a sight she is, with her dyed red hair. I really don't like you, Kate." At that point I remembered Catherine Cleary, and her call that day.

When I had spoken to her, it was not "Kate Cleary"; it was not even "Catherine." It was "Miss Cleary." As I thought how easily I called my tablemate "Kate," I also remembered how enthusiastic I had been to tell the community that *the* Catherine Cleary had called *me* on the phone. Then it all became evident that I had two attitudes toward two Catherines.

Catherine Cleary was powerful, *Fortune* said. She had many possessions. She had titles. And then there was Kate without wealth in any form. There was Kate without a last name, who depended on us; without enough money left from her Social Security check to buy a meal; without any prestige and positive self-image.

The very fact that I had never really asked for her last name was a sign of my attitude of superiority over her. I had power, possessions, and prestige over her. I did not like Kate. And Kate was my table partner.

I suddenly realized what these thoughts revealed about myself. I thought: "You phony! You are doing to her exactly what you go around condemning. You are as prejudiced against the poor as anyone." In my admission of rejecting Kate, I discovered I was prejudiced against all the poor. I did not like the poor. Period.

That subtle attitude of prejudice I discovered in myself is one of the main structural barriers to more authentic Eucharists in our Church. We all seem to betray our tablemates in varying degrees. Consciously and unconsciously we discriminate between those with and those without wealth.

How far we are from Matthew's Jesus who ate with all kinds of people! We and our liturgies express those attitudes and practices that St. James found contrary to faith. In his epistle he said clearly that faith in Jesus negates any favoritism (James 2:1). Even more so, to celebrate the mystery of faith with an attitude of prejudice violates God's plan:

> Suppose there should come into your assembly a man fashionably dressed, with gold rings on his fingers, and at the same time a poor man in shabby clothes. Suppose further that you were to take notice of the well-dressed man and say, "Sit right here, please," whereas you were to say to the poor man, "You can stand!" or "Sit over there by my footrest." Have you not in a case like this discriminated in your hearts? Have you not set yourselves up as judges handing down corrupt decisions?
>
> Listen, dear brothers. Did not God choose those who are poor in the eyes of the world to be rich in faith and heirs of the kingdom he promised to those who love him? Yet you treated the poor man shamefully [James 2:2–6].

Matthew stressed the need to treat all people as images of God by sharing resources with them. This would be a sign of fidelity to the two great commandments (22:34–40). James expanded on this way of wisdom by adding: "You are acting rightly, however, if you fulfill the law of the kingdom. Scripture has it, 'You shall love your neighbor as yourself.' But if you show favoritism, you commit sin and are convicted by the law as transgressors" (James 2:8–9). For James, the sacrifice of obedience to the law of God must reflect an inner attitude of mercy: "Always speak and act as men destined for judgment under the law of freedom. Merciless is the judgment on the man who has not shown mercy; but mercy triumphs over judgment" (James 2:12–13).

Since favoritism toward those with power, possessions, and prestige on the one hand and separatism from those without these on the other are so linked to our present reality, it is important that we honestly investigate how this addiction may control us in our individual and social lives.

Alienation from our tablemates can take place in our individual lives with an external attitude of rejection, such as I expressed toward Kate. Individual rejection can be extended to a whole class. I did not just reject "Kate," but all the poor. When my rejection extended to a whole group it manifested my internal attitude of prejudice. Individual expressions of rejection and feelings of prejudice have counterparts on the social level. Individual rejection becomes social discrimination. Individual prejudice becomes social alienation. Society rejects whole classes of people through laws, forms of seniority, functions, and trade restrictions. These are forms of discrimination. The underlying, internal dynamic that legitimizes the discrimination, or that remains even when external forms of discrimination may be obliterated, is alienation. Non-whites, for instance, are welcome to be members in our assemblies. But if the membership is almost 100 percent white, or if the music remains limited to that of the Weston Priory or the St. Louis Jesuits, the alienation continues.

Mercy must be central to the spirituality of the church as it gathers for worship. This fact helps us understand why Matthew was so concerned that his church live under the universalism of the resurrection. The power of the resurrection in the energy of the Eucharist is to declare that here, in church celebrating Eucharist, every individual is equal. The Eucharist, the ritual covenant of mercy, is the symbol of what the whole structure of the church should be manifesting: equality of individuals made in God's image, sharing enough of all the earth's resources.

The reality symbolized by the Eucharist is to be normative of the church's life. All people are equal because all share in the one meal as tablemates.

Now that we have discussed the first part of Matthew's setting for the Eucharist—the notion of betrayal among tablemates (26:20–25)—we can reflect on the unique attitude Matthew brought to the institution of the Eucharist itself (26:26–30).

Matthew's redaction sets his account apart from the other gospel accounts of the Eucharist. After using the same words (took, blessed, broke, and gave) regarding the sharing of the eucharistic bread (26:26) as he did for the multiplication of the loaves (14:19; 15:36), Jesus said, " 'This is my body.' Then he took a cup, gave thanks, and gave it to them. 'All of you must drink from it,' he said; 'for this is my blood' " (26:26–27).

Exodus 24:4–8 referred to the ritual sharing of blood as the sign of the covenant between God and the people. Jesus' blood, like his body, represents his whole life poured out in sacrifice to establish a mercy-filled covenant of universalism for the whole world. By using this phrase referring to the blood of the covenant in that sacred room in Jerusalem, Matthew seems to have been making a link to the Prophet Zechariah as he did earlier regarding Jesus' entry into Jerusalem. According to John Meier,

> The phrase "the blood of your covenant (with me)" occurs in Zechariah 9:11, immediately after the prophecy of the meek King coming to Jerusalem on an ass as universal prince of peace (9:9–10). Because of the blood of the covenant, prisoners are released and return from exile as promised. Since Matthew quotes Zechariah 9:9 at the triumphal

entry (21:5), he may well intend the allusion to Exodus 24 to be coupled with an allusion to Zechariah 9.[5]

Next, by adding the words that define the purpose of the Eucharist itself—"for the forgiveness of sins" (26:28)—Matthew shows that God's covenantal mercy is primarily shown in the sacrificial death of Jesus. Jesus' death leading to resurrection brings salvation. This is the essence of the passover that is celebrated in the eucharistic ritual. The specific forgiveness of sins that is central to the Eucharist is God's merciful care. This care reorders whatever divisions and prejudices, brokenness and alienation may exist among tablemates on any level. As Donald Senior notes, Matthew's unique addition of the phrase "for the forgiveness of sins,"

> recalls what the Gospel had previously affirmed about Jesus: He is the savior who frees the people from their sins (1:21); he is the servant who lifts the burden of pain and death from the helpless (8:17; 12:18) and who gives his life in service for the many (20:28). This Jesus is the very one whose death is proclaimed as the final act of love which forgives the world's sin and frees those trapped in the vise of death [cf. 27:51–54].[6]

Freed from sin ourselves, we want our Eucharists to celebrate our efforts to free all others who remain broken in bondage.

To show that Jesus' appointed time of sacrificial death was not only drawing near (26:18), but was at hand at the time of the Eucharist, Matthew added a word to indicate the momentousness of the Eucharist. By being shared *"now"* (26:29), it became the sacred moment that celebrated the passover action of Jesus' death and resurrection, which would have everlasting consequences for the world.

The final unique redaction of Matthew's version of the eucharistic meal was his addition of the phrase "with you" (26:29) to show the sense of community between Jesus and his tablemates. Jesus' meal would be shared with all the "you's" of the world—from those disciples in Jerusalem to us disciples today—with all who gather to share in the bread and the cup.

By adding "with you," Matthew shows that the sacramental sharing of the body and blood of Jesus reinforces the central theme of his whole spirituality. Matthew added "with you" to refer to the eucharistic presence of Jesus vis-à-vis the disciples for all time. Its use cannot be divorced from that similar phrase Matthew used at the beginning of the Gospel to refer to Jesus-Emmanuel (1:23) as God-with-us. At the end of the Gospel he uses "with you" to indicate the abiding presence of Jesus with us always (28:20).

Matthew also uses "with you" indirectly by alluding to God's presence in Jesus with the church at various other times. He identifies concern for the poor as a sign that the messiah has come to be with us (11:3). Jesus exercised the messiah's authoritative presence and power over the society that proclaimed his presence (21:9–10). Jesus also promised that in every gathering of the assembly he would be with us in our midst (18:20). It is little wonder, then, that the Eucharist includes that phrase in which Jesus makes a covenantal promise to be present with us always. As Meier notes:

> Since all these references are to a presence of Jesus among believers in the church this side of the parousia, the addition of "with you" in 26:29 makes a reference to the eucharist likely. "From this moment on"—a Matthean addition stressing the pivotal eschatological turning point of the passion—Jesus will not enjoy tablefellowship with his disciples until the sacrificial death is accomplished; then renewed fellowship will be possible at the eucharistic banquet which gives a foretaste of the final banquet after the parousia. In the eucharist, the Son of Man who gave his life as ransom continues to grant forgiveness of sins, fellowship, and a pledge of his parousia.[7]

Through the sharing of the bread and wine, we celebrate the sign of what authentic spirituality should proclaim. Experiencing Jesus' mercy with us as we share in the one bread, we become a mercy-filled community respecting the dignity of all our tablemates. The way this bread is shared in the sacrament is the way life's resources are to be shared.

In another place where Matthew presents Jesus talking about the giving of bread, his eucharistic overtones are also quite clearly present: "Give us today our daily bread" (6:11). Matthew's use of the word *epiousios* for "daily" has a unique meaning. In the Eucharist, every person stands equally in need. All of us are powerless around the table. We need the bread of life. This bread that is so necessary, as the word *epiousios* indicates, is mercifully given us by God. God not only gives us what we need; God gives *enough* of what we need. But God does not give more than is necessary. Enough is enough.[8]

Again, this dimension of Eucharist symbolizes wisdom's way about life: more than enough of any resource is unnecessary. To have more than enough is to lack the quality of mercy toward tablemates. Living in excess violates the covenant. In the Eucharist all are called to be faithful disciples who believe Jesus' words that our God will always be with us to feed us. We too can eat all that we need. But all of us who eat are to be satisfied with just this much (see 14:20; 15:36) and no more.

The Lack of Mercy, Anger, and the Quality of Care

This understanding brings us to another occurrence of *eleos,* or mercy, in Matthew's Gospel (23:23). As it was uniquely used by Matthew in 9:13 and 12:7, so, in 23:23 the word also appears in the context of a dispute between Jesus and the intolerant leaders. An examination of Matthew's unique use of mercy should throw more light on our understanding of the fifth beatitude: blessed are the ones who show mercy because mercy will be shown them

(5:7). Jesus' anger, reflecting God's anger, was directed to the leaders precisely because they did not show covenantal mercy:

> Woe to you scribes and Pharisees, you frauds! You pay tithes on mint and herbs and seeds while neglecting the weightier matters of the law, justice (*krisis*) and mercy (*eleos*) and good faith (*pistin*). It is these you should have practiced, without neglecting the others [23:23].

The triad of justice, mercy, and faith were to be the underlying covenantal attitudes used to interpret all law. Matthew's triad seems to allude to a similar trinity found in Micah, a contemporary of Isaiah. Like Isaiah, he tried to inspire a community restoration after the exile. Israel's restoration, however, could not be accomplished through rituals of sacrifice without the accompanying reality of a caring community:

> With what shall I come before the Lord,
> and bow before God most high?
> Shall I come before him with holocausts,
> with calves a year old?
> Will the Lord be pleased with thousands of rams,
> with myriad streams of oil?
> Shall I give my first-born for my crime,
> the fruit of my body for the sin of my soul?
> You have been told, O man, what is good,
> and what the Lord requires of you:
> Only to do the right and to love goodness
> and to walk humbly with your God [Mic. 6:6–8].

Micah, like Isaiah, tried to bring a message of hope and meaning to a community experiencing disillusionment. He found that personal, familial, and communal meaning results when life reflected God's purpose for life as outlined in Genesis 1:26–28. Since God looked and saw creation's meaning in its goodness, meaning comes only when we do what is good and what is required of us. In this light Matthew saw doing the right (justice), loving goodness (mercy), and walking humbly with God in faith as the triad essential to his spirituality.

Matthew's whole spirituality concretely spells out what is good and what is required of the community for all time. Doing what is good and right fulfills the law and the prophets not only for Jesus but for each of us. Thus, David Hill explains, the need for justice, mercy, and faith (23:23), is essential to the spiritual life:

> This triad is the third expression in Matthew's gospel of Jesus' understanding of the essentials of the law (and therefore of obedience), the

other two being the formulation of the Golden Rule (vii.12) and the twofold love-commandment (xxii.40). It is perhaps by this kind of emphasis that Matthew attempts to give content to the "righteousness" that surpasses that of the scribes and Pharisees, and that is demanded of disciples for entrance into the kingdom of heaven (v.20). Three times in controversy with the Pharisees, Matthew has Jesus point to the neglect or absence of *eleos*; it is part of the evangelist's redactional intent to affirm that *eleos*—the constant love for God that issues in deeds of compassion—is at the heart of the better righteousness that is essential for admission to the kingdom?[9]

Fidelity to the covenant means doing good through justice, mercy, and faith. Whoever does good enters the circle of care and walks with God as disciples following Jesus. We walk with God and experience divine mercy to the degree that we express to others the mercy that has constituted us in God's favor. Such mercy is not shown so much by fasting one or three hours from food or water before the Eucharist (although it can help set a reflective mood in us); the fasting that is required of us is to abstain from forms of rejection and prejudice. We are to fast by working to overcome discrimination and alienation in our world (see Isa. 58:3–7).

In a special way Matthew's Jesus warns us that mercy means avoidance of anger and the need to seek forgiveness (5:22–26). As we approach the altar where we celebrate God's mercy, mercy toward our tablemates must accompany us. Jesus' words about seeking mercy imply that the spirit of anger is diametrically opposed to the quality of mercy and the circle of care.

There is nothing wrong with the emotion of anger. The emotion of anger is something spontaneous, beyond our control. This is not the kind of anger Jesus rejects. The Scriptures show anger being justified when it reflects a break in promised covenantal relationships. God became angry only when the people broke the covenant. Fidelity to the covenant restored God's mercy:

> For a brief moment I abandoned you,
> but with great tenderness I will take you back.
> In an outburst of wrath, for a moment
> I hid my face from you;
> But with enduring love I take pity on you,
> says the Lord, your redeemer.
> This is for me like the days of Noah,
> when I swore that the waters of Noah
> should never again deluge the earth;
> So I have sworn not to be angry with you,
> or to rebuke you.
> Though the mountains leave their place

and the hills be shaken,
My love shall never leave you
nor my covenant of peace be shaken,
says the Lord, who has mercy on you [Isa. 54:7–10].

Truth is always basic to covenantal fidelity. Because the leaders were untruthful by not practicing what they preached and by using their power for their own ends, Jesus became angry. Jesus showed that God's anger is thus the divine reaction to our lack of genuine mercy. Once we realize that only a lack of mercy justifies anger, we also realize how seldom our anger reflects the divine motivation for anger.

Not too many years ago I was a very angry person. I was angry at the province, at the parish, at white people, at the corporations, at the United States, at the pope. I was angry at basically everyone (including myself). I justified my anger. I told myself that all these "others" should be more just and should convert from their ways. Many reacted to my anger with their own anger. Others just avoided me. Still others feared me.

One day I said to myself: "Who do you think you are that you can go around (especially in the province) implying people should change to *your* ways. You justify this because you think your ways are the right ways. Don't you think that other people can justify their ways? Don't they believe you ought to think and act the way they do? Why don't you see that they see no reason to convert to what you think is right because you are not ever open to what they think may be right?"

As I had these thoughts, another insight flashed in my mind. It proved to be the underlying reason for my anger: "And besides you don't really care. You don't care about them. You probably don't really care about anyone."

Once I realized that my anger was based in a lack of pathos, I discovered that care, mercy, and genuine understanding must be at the heart of evangelization that invites people, groups, and institutions to conversion. Care or mercy must be the basis for any invitation to change. If we do not care, we have no right to ask anyone to change. If we lack mercy, we have no right to get angry when people do not change. Only God has the right to get angry whenever we do not change, because only God always cares. Our anger will be justified only when it reflects God's wrath. God's anger is shown only when people refuse mercy and covenantal fidelity.

Once I started to be converted, by honestly caring about the brothers in the province, it seemed that the men in the province started to change and show more care as well. Perhaps it was just a case of the plank being removed from my own eye (see 7:5). At any rate, a feeling of mutual care gradually replaced our former anger and defensiveness. For me, this conversion came to a climax one evening during our 1978 Provincial Chapter. The top six nominees for provincial shared their reflections about our Midwest Province and how they would serve as provincial.

When I had a chance to speak, I spoke about my former anger and the resulting defensiveness of so many. "But I'm not angry anymore and neither are you," I said to the brothers that night. "I've changed and you've changed. We have all grown in care. In the process we have begun working together more effectively. And as we continue to work together, our province will become a dynamic force for good in this country and the world."

Mercy builds up people, groups, and the whole world. Mercy is always part of that covenant sealed in Christ's blood. This blood can never be just for us, but for the many. And the "many," who are all people in need, become part of that blood which must be poured out (26:28) for the life of the world.

CHAPTER EIGHT

Blessed Are the Pure of Heart; They Shall See God

Surface Obstacles to Achieving Purity of Heart

So far, no satisfactory interpretative background for this beatitude has been offered by Scripture scholars. "Purity of heart," as it is described in the beatitude, seems to be more an ethical attitude than an interior disposition; yet the two can never be separated. "Seeing God" does not mean the beatific vision as we would understand it today. Rather, it means to dwell in God's presence. Jesus said that the angels of the just ones "constantly behold my heavenly Father's face" (18:10). "Seeing God's face" depends on a purity of heart that represents total commitment to God's plan. This inner dedication is manifested by sharing with those in need (25:37). For Matthew, seeing God is the reward for purity of heart, for doing good, for showing care.

Perhaps the closest Scriptural foundation for this beatitude can be found in Psalm 24. Here the psalmist links the experience of seeing God's face with purity of heart and righteous deeds:

> Who can ascend the mountain of the Lord?
> or who may stand in his holy place?
> He whose hands are sinless, whose heart is clean.
> who desires not what is vain,
> nor swears deceitfully to his neighbor.
> He shall receive a blessing from the Lord,
> a reward from God his savior.
> Such is the race that seeks for him,
> that seeks the face of the God of Jacob [Ps. 24:3–6].

Jesus fulfilled this psalm and his own beatitude. Because he was faithful to his call (3:15; 11:2ff.), Jesus experienced the blessedness of God's favor on the Mount of Transfiguration. Here his external appearance evidenced the interior transforming light of God's presence-with-him. What happened momentarily at the transfiguration was indicative of Jesus' relationship with God at the depth of his being. The favor of God's presence was constitutive of his experience (17:1–5) because Jesus' works showed he had lived according to God's ethical plan for the world (Isa. 61; 11:4–5, 27).

Matthew consistently stresses that the righteous or the just ones are those who respond to God's word with their works. The just ones are those wholehearted people who are poor in spirit, who listen to God's word and obey God's will (6:33; cf. 5:17–20; 25:31–46). Matthew contrasts the just ones with the unrighteous ones. He uses the word "evil" *(poneros)* to describe those who do not obey God's will by their works. They are double minded in obeying God's will (5:37; 6:23f.; cf. 7:15–20; 12:33–37; 18:23–35; 25:14–30).

For Matthew's Jesus, one's external actions indicate interior preoccupations. To determine where the heart, or inner life is based, one should consider words and behavior: ". . . where your treasure is, there your heart is also," Jesus said. "The eye is the body's lamp. If your eyes are good, your body will be filled with light; if your eyes are bad, your body will be in darkness. And if your light is darkness, how deep will the darkness be!" (6:21–23).

The eye is the body's lamp. It reflects the inner commitment of the heart. If the eye is clear-sighted or undivided, it will reflect the inner dynamic of light that flows from God's blessed presence and favor. If the eye is evil or preoccupied *(poneros)*, it reflects an inner reality of darkness, confusion, or *tohu wabohu*. In the Sermon on the Mount, the lesson is reinforced that if the eye is pure or simple, so is the heart. If one is absorbed in the experience of God's reign and will, the whole personality will be endowed with light's perfection (see 5:48).

Matthew considers the inner attitude of wholeheartedness from the perspective of being ready to sacrifice one perceived good for a better good. "No man can serve two masters. He will either hate one and love the other or be attentive to one and despise the other. You cannot give yourself to God and money" (5:24). Giving one's self to God or wealth indicates the sacrifice of turning over, or submitting one's whole life to someone or something. Giving one's self to God wholeheartedly evidences a new disposition toward those things that formerly were sources of preoccupation. In giving one's self over to the ways of God, one necessarily is given over to the needs of others (see 22:34–40).

To give one's self generously to God's reign by responding to others' needs and to be liberal in this giving, manifests a godly attitude. "The kindly man [one with a 'good eye'] will be blessed, for he gives of his sustenance to the poor" (Prov. 22:9). On the contrary, to be selfish is to manifest an "evil eye" (Prov. 28:22). Those in the community who advocated inequality in resource-sharing reflected an evil eye or divided commitment: ". . . are you envious *(poneros)* because I am generous?" (20:15).

Poneros and *porneia* are closely related. *Porneia* shows itself in various attitudes or "looks" that keep us from an inner commitment. These obstacles hinder us from serving God and implementing God's plan for the world. According to Jesus, these surface expressions originate in internal dispositions in the mind, or heart: "Do you not see that everything that enters the mouth passes into the stomach and is discharged into the latrine, but what comes out of the mouth originates in the mind?" *(kardia)* (15:17–18). *Kardia* is Greek for heart. The heart speaks in the looks.

Surface or external "looks" are expressed in attitudes as actions, words, and works. If these "looks" assume authority over one's life, they are the source of worry, tension, and anxiety instead of rest, reconciliation, and peace. To the degree that the "cares of the world" are part of the surface-self, or the "looks" we manifest, they keep us from experiencing God's word in the ground of our being (13:18–22).

What are the forms of *porneia* that "evil looks" take? How can their control keep us from the contemplative experience of realizing God's presence-with-us? The Cistercian Richard Byrne has written a powerful thesis entitled *Living the Contemplative Dimension of Everyday Life.* [1] In it he describes various "looks" as obstacles to seeing God contemplatively. While "seeing God" in this beatitude cannot be equated exactly with our notion of contemplation, it approximates an experience of the divine. Thus Byrne's insights can apply here for our consideration of this beatitude as it might relate to contemplation.

Byrne's "looks" represent Matthean impurity of heart. If we can be free from these looks we can be open to the divine gaze and vision; we can be seen by God and see God. While we will always have some obstacles to "seeing God," to the degree we remain in the control of these "looks," to that degree we cannot see God.

The first look Byrne describes as an obstacle to the experience of God is the curious look, or the attitude of being full of cares and anxieties. Jesus described a person controlled by this look as "the man who hears the message, but then worldly anxiety and the lure of money choke it off" (13:22).

While there is nothing wrong with normal curiosity, people controlled by the curious look are not only beyond the experience of the word; they are not rooted in *themselves* either. They reflect a kind of chaos, a separation, an alienation within themselves. They have not integrated their surface-selves with their real-selves. Since contemplation means to stand in one's depth with God, and since such people are not grounded in themselves, they are nowhere. They are outside themselves, literally and figuratively. They have no depth.

According to philosopher Martin Heidegger, curiosity is one of the chief characteristics of the inauthentic self. [2] Heidegger viewed curiosity's elements as "not tarrying," "distraction," and "never dwelling anywhere."

According to Heidegger, the person with the curious look does not tarry. The curious look neither slows down nor stops. Rather it is "always running after these things" that supposedly alleviate fear and anxiety (6:32). As a result, a person controlled by this is always distracted and preoccupied with surface concerns and worries. These worries touch our acceptance needs as well as our livelihood needs such as food and clothing (6:31).

Because of the culture's ideology—which plays on people's fears and anxieties—those who are controlled by the curious look never "dwell anywhere." "The avaricious man [the one with an 'evil eye'] is perturbed about his wealth and he knows not when want will come upon him" (Prov. 28:22). People perturbed or worried about their power, possessions, and prestige are not grounded. They can be preyed upon because their values are surface-based instead of God-based.

Jesus was aware of the power of the curious look. He offered a new spirituality that would help us go beyond surface concerns to experience and trust in life's author (6:25):

> Look at the birds of the sky. They do not sow or reap, they gather nothing into barns; yet your heavenly Father feeds them. Are not you more important than they? Which of you by worrying can add a moment to his life-span? As for clothes, why be concerned? Learn a lesson from the way the wild flowers grow. They do not work; they do not spin. Yet I assure you, not even Solomon in all his splendor was arrayed like one of these. If God can clothe in such splendor the grass of the field, which blooms today and is thrown on the fire tomorrow, will he not provide much more for you, O weak in faith! Stop worrying, then, over questions like, "What are we to eat, or what are we to drink, or what are we to wear?" The unbelievers are always running after these things [6:26–32].

When we are controlled by the curious look, our needs remain at the surface level of life. Our "seeing" is controlled by those who control that "look," especially the advertisers who tell us what we need to be accepted. One time, for instance, when the "Annie Hall look" was dominant, I complimented someone who was wearing the style. "I really like it too," she replied. "But I just hope they don't tell us we have to wear hats." Another time, when we were first allowed the use of small amounts of money, a classmate said, "I'm going to go downtown to see what I need." When we are not integrated in our true selves, where God's power should have full authority, other powers like the media have authority over us. The attitude of curiosity found in each of us is manipulated by the media through advertising. It exploits our curiosity and fears. It plays on our identity and security needs. Yet, for Jesus, the greatest are those whose security rests in finding their identity in him (see 11:28; 18:1–4).

The next obstacle to seeing God is the lustful look, or the "eye of pleasure." "From the mind (*kardia*, or heart) stem evil designs—murder, adulterous conduct, fornication, stealing, false witness, blasphemy. These are the things that make a man impure" (15:19–20), Jesus said. Most of us are not engaged in the activities that Jesus elaborated. Yet today these forms of *porneia* are reflected in other ways. These find a home in many of our attitudes and actions. This is especially so in the way the eye of pleasure controls us in our dealings with people, events, and things.

When we are controlled by the lustful look, we seek instant gratification. We instinctively avoid any pain. The Alka-Seltzer ideology plays on the lustful look. Instant relief. To the degree that we remain controlled by this approach to life, we will find it difficult to find our meaning, identity, and pleasure in doing God's will. This may happen when we realize that doing God's will might bring some form of pain or rejection from others in society (see 10:16f.). Where this sixth beatitude says that the pleasure of God's favor results from fidelity to the divine will, the eye of pleasure says that beatitude rests in instant relief from pain, being with "significant" people, having exciting experiences, and accumulating goods.

James and John, along with their mother, were under the influence of the lustful look or the eye of pleasure. They were attracted to Jesus because they sensed he would meet their power needs (20:20–28). We tend to be attracted to those who meet our surface needs—be they our power, prestige, identity, or sex. Honest teachers or counselors will admit that we are attracted to those people, situations, and things that invite us to immediate pleasure and gratification rather than pain and difficulty.

The rich young man was attracted to the person of Jesus. Yet he was kept from conversion by his surface self, by the eye of pleasure. He could not give up his wealth (19:22) to become truly free. He went away depressed.

Reinforced by social norms that keep us at a surface level, our very depressions often indicate our inability to relate to God at the level of our real selves. Therefore, we meet the empty needs of our surface selves by seeking immediate pleasure as we try to avoid pain at all costs. Pornographers know how to appeal to this dynamic better than most.

One time I was giving conferences to a religious order. I saw someone walking toward me in a good-looking outfit. "Gee, those clothes are handsome on you," I said.

"You really like it?" came the response with evident happiness at the fact that I had noticed. "I was depressed one day. So I decided to buy this. It cost me only fifty dollars."

Some people might be concerned about the expenditure of fifty dollars. I was concerned that this person did not seem able to transfer pain to discover ultimate value in a relationship of fidelity to the living God (26:36f). When identity becomes so locked into a commodified self that we can be bought and sold, our victim-status keeps us at the surface level.

What clothes can be to someone in a state of depression, drugs, cigarettes, food, sex, power, possessions, prestige, can be for each of us. We only need to realize how we respond to our depressions to discover how these control us, or who or what else may have power over us.

Many times prayer itself can be controlled by the lustful look or the eye of pleasure. We can seek the face of God to meet our own pleasure. We covet extraordinary religious experiences and gifts rather than submitting all these to God. Because many in the community were controlled by their surface needs, Matthew's Jesus railed against some of the wandering charismatics. Their prophecies, exorcisms, and miracles (7:22) appealed to their own surface needs rather than to God's plan. Such religious experience, which tickled the eye of pleasure, had already brought them their reward (6:5). The same held true for other acts of piety and justice (6:2,16).

Often the lustful look keeps us from experiencing God in our depths because we want immediate returns. We are unwilling to take sufficient time or we flee from the pain of unknowing. Contemplation takes too long; there are no results; it is too much effort. We cannot control what we do not know. So we stop being still to know and admit God is a God who knows what we need. We fail to get "high" at our prayer meetings; we cannot recapture the original experience of the Spirit's release in us; we limit God's presence to one prayer-form that now seems beyond our experience. So we quit praying by ourselves or in our prayer group, or say evil or the devil is present. Yet, "none of those who cry out, 'Lord, Lord' will enter the kingdom of God but only the one who does the will of my Father in heaven" (7:21).

The third form of *porneia,* or evil eye, that can keep us at the surface level is the "ideal look." One of the characteristics of the "ideal self" is that people under its control are preoccupied with comparing themselves and others in terms of power, possessions, or image. Usually this comparison takes the forms of "more or less," "better or worse." One's stimulation, identity, and security come from meeting this "ideal look." Since we never seem to attain that ideal image, depression, a negative self-image, and fear result.

When the rich young man came to Jesus, he asked, " 'Teacher, what good must I do to possess everlasting life?' He answered, 'Why do you question me about what is good? There is One who is good.' " (19:16–17). Many of us are controlled by our very striving to be good, better, and best. We want to be a good leader or teacher, a better parent or religious, the best preacher, healer, or cook. Rather than believing our lives are empowered by the only One who is good (see 19:21) and submitting to God's way of perfection, we climb the ladder of success. We seek not only to be good, but to be better (than others). Like the Zebedees (20:20–21), the more we are controlled by this ideal of being better or having more, the more we will be dominated by should, ought, and must. Our own personal control at this level will be reflected in the way we relate to others. If others are to be "good," they also should, ought, or must do as we say and/or do (see 20:25; 23:2). Since we never reach these ideals, we experience alienation.

Unable to accept our true selves, we cannot accept others. Since we really do not care about or love ourselves, we cannot love or care about others. Frustrated at never meeting our goal of perfection, we often relate to others with anger and judgmentalness. Thus Jesus warned:

If you want to avoid judgment, stop passing judgment. Your verdict on others will be the verdict passed on you. The measure with which you measure will be used to measure you. Why look at the speck in your brother's eye when you miss the plank in your own? How can you say to your brother, "Let me take that speck out of your eye," while all the time the plank remains in your own? You hypocrite! Remove the plank from your own eye first; then you will see clearly to take the speck from your brother's eye [7:1–5].

Matthew's community was being torn apart by rash judgment, competition, sarcasm, resentment, and criticism. Its tensions had become a scandal. Ambition dominated the needs of many members (18:1). Instead of becoming truly integrated as people poor in spirit toward God and each other (see 18:2–5), many community members resorted to actions which perpetuated division. Controlled by their surface needs, these members disrupted community life and peace. To become integrated in their real selves, they needed to do violence to those scandals by abandoning them:

. . . woe to that man through whom scandal comes! If your hand or foot is your undoing, cut it off and throw it from you! Better to enter life maimed or crippled than be thrown with two hands or two feet into endless fire. If your eye is your downfall, gouge it out and cast it from you! Better to enter life with one eye than be thrown with both into fiery Gehenna. See that you never despise one of these little ones [18:7–10]

Truly contemplative people are beyond scandal. Truly contemplative people have become like little children; they have experienced God's power in their lives and want to live in its aura (see 18:4). Truly contemplative people are not controlled by anger, bitterness, or criticism.

Evelyn Underhill, one of the great mystical writers of this century, stated that authentic contemplative experience demands a suspension of critical attitudes so that no surface entity separates us from God. She spoke about the need to have one's attitude correspond perfectly with "the essence of things."[3] This is another phrase for spiritual realism or meekness. Meekness directly opposes the violence that is expressed in judgmentalness and criticism. Meekness does not yoke others. The meek submit their lives and all of life to the yoke of God's plan for the world (11:25–30).

The final look which stands as a surface obstacle to seeing God is resentment or unforgiveness. Murder was viewed by Matthew's Jesus as a form of *porneia*. The surface attitude of murder in its various forms reflected a void within (15:19). However, more often than not, murder takes its expression in anger, criticism, envy, gossip, and, especially, unforgiveness. Always seeking to unmask the inner attitudes that indicated alienation from God, Jesus said:

You have heard the commandment imposed on your forefathers, "You shall not commit murder; every murderer shall be liable to judgment." What I say to you is: everyone who grows angry with his brother shall be liable to judgment; any man who uses abusive language toward his brother shall be answerable to the Sanhedrin, and if he holds him in contempt he risks the fires of Gehenna [5:21–22].

When such forms of anger dominate us, we are not only cut off from ourselves and each other; we are alienated from the divine presence. We cannot see God. Thus, Matthew had Jesus warn the community to examine its total situation in light of resentment and unforgiveness. If these forms of the critical look dominated, reconciliation had to be sought on the surface levels of person and group to achieve union with God:

> If you bring your gift to the altar and there recall that your brother has anything against you, leave your gift at the altar, go first to be reconciled with your brother, and then come and offer your gift. Lose no time; settle with your opponent while on your way to court with him. Otherwise your opponent may hand you over to the judge, who will hand you over to the guard, who will throw you into prison [5:23–25].

As we examine the various "looks" that are obstacles to experiencing the fullness of this beatitude, we discover that these forms of *porneia,* or impurity of heart, are exploited by the infrastructure. Advertisers play on greed. Militarists exploit fears. Racists and sexists run from their enemies. Clerics are threatened by the laity. Producers disparage consumers. As a result, these arrangements within our culture can so dominate our attitudes that we remain addicted by their power. We are kept from entering the circle of God's care.

Controlled by these looks, we cannot see. Because we cannot "see," we remain unconverted. Jesus contrasted the "looks" of the leaders of his time with the "seeing" of the disciples, who were to live the beatitudes, when he said:

> "Sluggish indeed is this people's heart.
> They have scarcely heard with *their* ears,
> they have firmly closed *their* eyes;
> otherwise they might see with their eyes,
> and hear with their ears,
> and understand with their hearts,
> and turn back to me,
> and I should heal them."
> But blest are *your* eyes because they see
> and blest are *your* ears because they hear
> [13:15–16; emphasis added].

The Call to Move beyond the Surface by Entering the Circle of Care

"How can you utter anything good, you brood of vipers," Matthew's Jesus challenged the Pharisees and the church leaders, "when you are so evil *(poneroi)?* The mouth speaks whatever fills the mind *(kardia)*. A good man produces good from his store of goodness; an evil man produces evil from his evil store" (12:34–35). Whatever fills the mind or heart determines if we are on the surface side of alienation or the depth side of care. Whatever good or evil we do reveals the good or evil intentions that parent our actions.

Since it may seem almost impossible to be free of the control of *porneia* (evil looks) and *poneros* (evil itself), we might ask ourselves how can we utter or do any good? What will it take to be free from these inauthentic cares, which the unbelievers are running after (see 6:32)?

The process of coming to purity of heart demands that we move beyond these surface cares to be grounded in authentic cares. This process begins by "looking" in a new way at ourselves, others, and God. However, we can only begin to look at ourselves, others, and God, from insights gained from our own resources, those given by others, or those received from God.

First of all we might be able to move beyond our surface level by a divine intervention. We might become like Isaiah and have a deep religious experience. Then, looking at our lives, we can say, "Woe is me" (Isa. 6:5). We can become converted and begin a process of living in God's presence (Isa. 6:6–8). Or, we might have an experience like Peter's. We can be affected by God's presence in such a powerful way that we are "overcome with fear." As we receive the affirming touch of Jesus' healing power, we might decide to begin living a new way (see 17:6–7).

Another way we can move beyond the surface level may be by our own insight (realizing God's grace is never separated from this). As we grow in union with God we might come to a deeper form of personal wisdom. Wisdom is the gift that helps us understand what is truly important. With wisdom, we can independently see how our surface reactions of defensiveness, curiosity, pleasure-seeking, anger, envy, and resentment seek to control us. Realizing how easily we can be controlled by these attitudes, we might recognize our need to be free of their domination.

While coming to purity of heart can result from divine intervention or our own wisdom, we usually are invited to move beyond our surface selves when other people look at us in a new way. Such people must be quite free of manipulative and exploitative looks. Thus, when they respond to us free of these looks, it can become an invitation to freedom. We now are better able to look at others from the perspective of genuine care.

The leper was controlled by his negative self-image. He was also reinforced in that self-hatred by society's looks. Rather than be controlled by those looks, which were part of his infrastructure, Jesus *saw* the leper in need, *cared* about him for his own sake, and *called* him to experience more deeply God's healing presence in his life (8:1–4). Experiencing himself being freed by someone who looked at him in a new way became an invitation for the leper to begin looking at himself and his world in a new way, the way of care.

The parable of the merciless official also shows how God's power in Jesus (which is now in us) can invite people beyond their surface obstacle and fears. Previously, the king's "looks" meant disaster for the official, his family, and his resources. Yet, the king was able to be freed from the looks that had kept the official in debt and burdened with pain. Care became the new power that dominated the king. He *saw* the official in need, *cared* about him, and *called* for a removal of the debt. However, the official's experience of care from the king should have been the foundation for a new way of showing care for the official's world. Unfortunately it was not. The official did not *respond* in *care* in a way that reflected his own experience of care. As a result, because he was unable to do good as was done to him, he was cut off from God's *sight* (18:33–35). Though his storehouse had been filled with good deeds toward him, he could not bring them forth (see 13:52).

When I began ministry at St. Elizabeth's I had an accident. It was almost totally my fault. All the "looks" coming from passersby, the police, the person whose car I hit pushed me further into a rejection of myself for being so negligent. Instead of facing the present reality, my curious look made me anxious about a lawsuit. Even though the dent was only minor I became preoccupied with what I could have done differently. My lustful look wanted to avoid the embarrassment of failure and getting "points" on my driving record. The fact that I kept telling myself that I should have done this or that showed how the ideal look was dominating me at that point—to say nothing of what I was thinking about the way the person drove whom I had hit! The fact that she drove a Cadillac and came from the suburbs added to my resentful and judgmental look. (At that time, I had antipathy toward white people, especially rich white people).

The brunt of these looks brought me into such an experience of self-negativity that only a person free from those looks could offer me freedom. When I finally returned to my Capuchin fraternity, I figured I would be met by more looks, especially the ideal look that would be saying, "Why weren't you more careful?" or "You should have been more observant." Fully expecting such responses, I walked into the living room saying, "I feel terrible." Instead of laying more guilt on me, Austin Schlaefer, our Capuchin Guardian, simply said, "I think we ought to have a pizza!"

Because of his genuine care, Austin called me to go beyond my surface looks to become grounded in a new way of looking at myself. I would then be able to look at life-in-general in a new way. Because he was a minister of healing to me, Austin invited me to begin looking at myself, others, and God in the way of freedom.

To move beyond surface obstacles and looks, in order to achieve purity of heart, we must first determine the level of our care. A parent foregoes all personal needs to bring care to a sick child. We are called to experience the reality of God's care for us in such a way that we can forego all "these things" and begin to live in care toward others. Because Peter had experienced Jesus as one who cared for him for his own sake and wanted the very best for him (namely, the reign of God), he was able to say, "here we have put everything aside to follow you" (19:27).

Once we experience being called from our surface needs by the experience of genuine care, we can move from our surface cares. At the same time, we can be open to the next step of achieving purity of heart. We can enter Peter's ritual of care by leaving all things.

The Response to the Call: Ritualizing Care in the Ascetical Life

When we consider our own lives and the life of our society, we can easily see how little genuine care they often reflect and we can become quite depressed. It will seem we are so uncaring. Yet at this time of depression, Richard Byrne's reflection might bring us hope:

Is there anything I can do? Yes, I can begin looking at my own life and asking, "Do I really care? Who or what do I care about?" And when I see my lack of care—my lack of humanity—I can begin taking the first faltering steps toward a life of care. I can make my own the words of T. S. Eliot:

Blessed sister, holy mother,
spirit of the fountain, spirit of the garden,
Suffer us not to mock ourselves with falsehood
Teach us to care and not to care
Teach us to sit still.[4]

Jesus would invite his disciples to leave old cares behind; he would teach his disciples not to care. His new way would invite new cares to become matters of concern; he would teach his disciples to care. But first they would have to come to him (11:28) with all their cares, be freed of them, and sit still at his feet to learn the beatitudes as the way of care (5:1–12).

Perhaps more than any liturgical ritual, the needs of our world demand that we develop a new care-ritual in our lives, groups, and institutions. This ritual of care will find us joining Peter as we leave unnecessary cares behind (19:27) to become grounded in that genuine care which arises from the experience of God's revelation in our lives (16:17). This grounding of our surface selves and all our looks into our real selves where light dwells can only be accomplished through an asceticism of the heart (15:10–20).

Asceticism, or purification of heart, is achieved by learning to care and not to care, as well as by taking time and making space to be still. Learning to care and not to care are the forms of mortification and detachment that traditionally have been considered by spiritual writers as "purgation." On the other hand, the process of becoming quiet and still has been termed "recollection." Purgation and recollection are the next steps that must be taken as we climb the mountain to purity of heart. Living under their influence, we become more open to the grace of God's presence; we become more disposed to "see" God.

Purgation has two dimensions: detachment and mortification. Detachment is the process of not caring; mortification is that process of caring in which we choose some things as we leave other things behind.

Detachment is the process of giving up comforts for rest (see 26:42–45). It is the process of seeking and finding, selling and buying (13:44–46). It is the process of surface-self-stripping to discover the true self in whose ground God's presence reigns with us.

I never agreed with my novice director who urged me to "die to yourself." I always thought that phrase reflected some kind of masochistic spirituality. With the negative self-image I had at that time, I certainly was willing to die to my negativity, but not to my real self (which I had not even found as yet!). I told him that I never saw people die to their selves *unless* it was on behalf of something they could live for more fully. Consequently, I would ask: "Why don't we ever hear about experiencing God more fully so we'll want to die to certain things?"

The call to detachment can also catch us off guard as it asks us to part with our power, possessions, and prestige. In this way it becomes an invitation to depth. The invitation to detachment may come in a job change, as we enter junior high school, in having our "name" maligned, in losing some possession. One time, for instance, I lost my winter cap in Stapleton Airport in Denver. The way I hunted for that never-to-be-found cap indicated how attached I had become to this piece of material. However, once I realized it was gone, I could be invited to not care.

While the call to detachment can come from outside us, it is better if detachment is freely cultivated. One of the strongest remembrances of being invited to detachment and to not care came to me when I realized all my art had been destroyed. I considered myself to be a halfway decent artist. Throughout my college and theology years I had built up quite a portfolio of my work. In 1966, I worked at the Franciscan Communications Center in Los Angeles. While there, I became acquainted with Corita Kent, then a nun at Immaculate Heart of Mary College. At that time, she was gaining international renown for her art work. After I left Los Angeles, I would periodically send Corita my latest endeavor and she would send me something of hers. Soon I had many of her seriographs in my art folder. To say the least, I treasured them.

One time I left the folder on a cart in the kitchen instead of bringing it to my room. A few weeks later I noticed that the folder no longer was on the cart. So I asked one of the Capuchins (who happened to be a compulsive cleaner), "I left a blue folder on the cart a while ago. Do you know where it is?"

"You mean that blue thing with some pictures in it?" he responded. "Oh, I threw that out a week ago. Because it was just lying around, it didn't seem important."

Thud! Part of my life on the garbage heap! The reality of the moment offered me an immediate choice. I could be controlled by surface looks, especially the "ideal look" that would have said "You should have . . ." both to my brother, the Capuchin cleaner, and to myself. My "critical look" could have controlled me by an outburst of anger. Or I could respond by moving into the ritual of care. I could leave *all* things behind, including this very deep part of my life.

I recall going through some mental gymnastics: "You knew he was a compulsive cleaner. You should have taken that folder to your room; you walked by it many times. You've got nobody to blame but yourself. Now it's in the dump. And you don't even know where the dump is. By now the folder must be buried under millions of pounds of garbage. What's gone is gone. So what are you going to do about it? You can be controlled by the loss or you can show that God is your all. Have you really left *everything* behind?"

In just about the time it took to go through these reflections, I was able to experience detachment from this important expression of my life. Even though I wished I still had my art, I merely said to him something like, "Oh, I see. . . ." But what that "seeing" implied! Without alluding to the fact, I had entered more deeply into the experience of the sixth beatitude. I could be free from the luggage of life in order to climb the mountain to see God's face.

The next form of purgation, after not caring or detachment, is to begin to care for what truly matters. This is mortification. In many ways, detachment is easier than mortification. Once my art was lost, it was gone. "Out of sight, out of mind." Mortification, however, is the attitude we bring to bear upon the choices we make toward people, possessions, and priorities. It is easier for me to live in a small Capuchin fraternity where we decide not to have certain foods than to live in a large friary where the various kinds of food and drink are always available. In such a situation, I must make a free choice not to take the second salad or go to the liquor cabinet. My choice will be based on my own attitudes toward my self, my God, and my brothers and sisters throughout the world.

Mortification is the discipline we bring to bear upon the choices we make regarding the two central projects of life—the reign of God's will or society's way of running after all things (6:24, 33). It is the process of discovering what is truly important in our lives. Mortification is part of the gift of discernment. It is based on our experience of God's justice in us, which in turn finds our lifestyle reflecting our solidarity with others, especially in their need. We experience solidarity with others in need, because we know God has come to us in our need. In this light, Paul could write to the Philippians:

I am sure of this much: that he who has begun the good work in you will carry it through to completion, right up to the day of Christ Jesus.

My prayer is that your love may more and more abound, both in
understanding and wealth of experience, so that with a clear conscience
and blameless conduct you may learn to value the things that really
matter, up to the very day of Christ. It is my wish that you may be found
rich in the harvest of justice which Jesus Christ has ripened in you, to
the glory and praise of God [Phil. 1:6,9–11].

The more we grow in the wealth of our experience of God, the more we
grow in understanding its treasures. Understanding plus experience, reflection with action, enable us to become beatitudinal in our conduct. With a
clear conscience we become free of *porneia*. We are nearing purity of heart.
We are taking time to sit near the seat of wisdom. We are able to value what
truly matters and begin to desire only what God wants. We are emptying
ourselves in order to listen to our divine teacher. We are expressing recollection.

Through recollection we are better able to simplify our lives. We begin to
"sit still," instead of running after all these things. Whereas our surface self
can be controlled by illusions and ideologies, recollection is the process of
slowing ourselves down, entering into silence and space to experience solitude and the truth of God's revelation to and in us (11:27–28).

Recollection is a way of being free from cares on the level of the surface self
that we might begin to care with God's loving care. The more we enter into
the experience of God's care, the more we remember all the obstacles to the
care that controlled us in the past and that can still separate us from God.
Consequently, recollection helps us develop a deep, abiding sense of sorrow
for these sins and these obstacles to being touched by God.

I never understood how Ignatius of Loyola or Francis of Assisi could spend
extended periods in tears, until my own recollection helped me experience
the reality of my memories. Memory made me more conscious of my own
sinfulness and separation from God. The more Ignatius and Francis integrated their surface selves into their true selves, the more they sensed the
presence of God. The more they understood the presence of God, the more
they came to meekness or spiritual realism as well as care or love. In this
process they realized how far they still were from that fullness of life they
sought. At this point in their spiritual lives they were experiencing purity of
heart in the form of the prayer of quiet, which Eastern spiritual writers call
hesychasm.

Hesychasm is built on purgation. It leads, through the quiet of recollection, to the experience of the indwelling God as universal care. This experience makes us more aware of where un-care still controls us. It leads us to
deep sorrow for this sin in ourselves and in the world.

The process of achieving purity of heart is deepened by our emptying and
listening. The more we listen in our memories and experiences—to God, to
our true selves, to reality—the more we find ourselves approaching wisdom.

We begin to understand with our hearts (Prov. 2:2; Sir. 17:5). We begin to see life in a new way; we hear God's call in silent words; we are open to turn back to God who will heal us (13:15).

Listening begins with becoming quiet. We take time and make space to quiet our surface selves and our inner voices so we can not only hear, but understand. This quieting of our surface selves leads to silence. Next, silence enables us to become still. The more still we become, the more our silence takes us beyond the surface to the stillpoint of solitude. At this place, it is much like being in a quiet room by ourselves only to sense that we are in another's presence. Silence is surface stillness with ourselves; solitude becomes solidarity with God who is present at the heart of the world. We discover ourselves there, in our heart, with God, but there we also discover ourselves in solidarity with the universe itself.

In solitude we sense God in the spaces between the words and prayers that no longer seem important. We begin to discover everything has already been said in one word, Jesus. We simply want to be still, knowing that God is God; and God is with us in Emmanuel. As we grow in our ability to listen to our selves, we discover in this growing solitude that we are filled with a Presence who cares and listens. At the same time we discover that our listening to the way God enters into our lives is in proportion to the way we listen and care about all those voices and all those cares of the universe (see 25:31–46) that are part of God's concern. Because we have brought our solidarity with humanity to our solitude we begin to experience ourselves now as part of the very revelation of God.

Many times, in solitude, we merely sit. And we wait. Unlike people waiting in bread lines and in welfare offices who despairingly rely on human whims, we wait in hope because of the everlasting promise made by our God. In this experience of waiting, however, we cannot escape acknowledging our absolute need for God to see us in need (6:32). This very awareness of our need and our powerlessness, in itself, should inspire us to greater solidarity with all others in their need and powerlessness; in addition, fully expecting to be heard, we ask to receive, seek to find, and knock to have opened to us the experience of God's presence with us (7:7). And then we wait, in need. What has helped me during this time of waiting is an easy-going, slow recitation of a little phrase (*mantra*). A quiet repetition of a little saying gradually merges surface distractions and preoccupations into a deeper part of our being. To aid this process, the Eastern spiritual writers often centered their asking, seeking, and knocking around the repetition of a prayer called the Jesus Prayer: "Lord, Jesus Christ, Son of the Living God, have mercy on me a sinner."

I first learned about the Jesus Prayer in 1963 when I read J. D. Salinger's *Franny and Zooey*. For a while I tried to repeat these words whenever I would be distracted in prayer; yet I never seemed able to make this *mantra* part of my reality. I did recognize, though, that something like the Jesus Prayer could be a great aid to prayer, especially when I realized my prayer was limited to waiting on God. Invariably, God seemed to want me to experience nothing but void, *tohu wabohu!*

How can I have a *mantra*, or something like the Jesus Prayer, suited to the goals of my spirituality? A book I once read said, quite simply, that I could create my own *mantra* be reflecting on my reality. By considering what I wanted my spirituality to become, I could summarize it in six to eight syllables. The more I would give voice to this summary statement of my spirituality, the more disposed I might be to become what I prayed.

So I examined my spirituality. How did I want to live in union with God? What phrase would summarize my goal? I decided my *mantra* would be seven syllables: "Be in the name of Jesus." Jesus is Emmanuel, God-with-us, always empowering me in the depths of my being to take away the sin of the world (28:18–20) with the good news of the gospel. The more I would pray this personalized *mantra* from my heart, the more I might become what I prayed. Now, during the days as I seek the face of God, my process of coming to purity of heart is helped when I pray from my heart, "Be in the name of Jesus."

Despite *mantras* and all the other ways I try to achieve purity of heart, so often it seems I still sit at prayer. And I wait. Still nothing seems to happen. I can call on God all I want, yet I continue to sit there until God decides to grace me with an experience of the divine presence that I know by faith is always in my depths. In faith, I know the Spirit who gave flesh to God's word in the depths of Mary is praying with my spirit, even though I do not experience this fact.

Whether I know it or not, fidelity to the prayer of faith is bound to have some effect on my surface self, my preoccupations and vocal prayers. Even though "nothing" seems to happen when we pray with purity of heart, without realizing it, our hearts are growing in conversion (see 13:15). I discovered this deepening process at work in a member of our Capuchin fraternity when I returned home from Europe in late 1978. While I was away, Perry McDonald, one of our brothers, had made an eight-day directed retreat at our Retreat Center in Marathon, Wisconsin.

One day we were having our fraternity's weekly review of life. Perry had mentioned the fact that he had made a retreat commitment to get up early so he could spend more time in prayer. He was beginning to backslide, he said, "because nothing ever seems to happen."

"That's really a coincidence," I responded. "Because I have noticed since I've been back that your spontaneous prayers at Mass and common prayer seem so much deeper than when I left. Maybe nothing has happened to you that you have experienced, but your externals show that God must be at work in the depths of your life where the Spirit is praying with your spirit."

Realizing that God's action in us is often beyond our experience of it, we all felt a little more free. We rejoiced that we were able to wait in hope, open to God. And it is God who would see us in need, who cared for us, and would call us to union at the appointed time. However, "as for the exact day or hour, no one knows it," Jesus has said of the direct experience of God's presence by the community (24:36). Yet, if we bring to prayer our good deeds of justice and care, we will always be seen by God as having the correct disposition of watchfulness and preparation (24:43–51). If we live in this way of wisdom, we will be open to experience God's reign (25:1–11) that is always at hand (10:7). Without such a disposition, God will not recognize the divine goodness in our deeds (25:12,41). In turn, we will recognize God in the purity of our hearts. Our eyes will have been opened to see God approaching us (25:13) to bring joy to our hearts.

The Blessedness of Seeing God

In the Old Testament, to "see God" meant to experience God's favor, to be in God's presence. At the transfiguration, the surface of Jesus' exterior reflected a deeper reality. Jesus evidenced God's favor because his eye had been sound; he had been faithful to God's plan (17:5). Because his eye was sound, his body was filled with light (6:22; 17:2). Jesus saw God because he had achieved purity of heart.

In urging us to make sure our "looks" are not creating obstacles to the experience of God (6:23), Matthew's Jesus warned: "No man can serve two masters. He will either hate one and love the other or be attentive to one and despise the other. You cannot give yourself (*douleuein*) to God and money" (6:24).

Giving yourself, or *douleuein*, reflects liturgical overtones: we offer our lives to God and thus have access to the sanctuary of God's presence. When we make our lives this kind of sacrifice by submitting our surface selves to our real selves, we are disposed to enter the divine presence. We can have access to the face of God. Having worked to bring about justice and reconciliation, we can enter into the reality of the one to whom we have given our lives. As Paul wrote to the Ephesians:

> But now in Christ Jesus you who once were far off have been brought near through the blood of Christ. It is he who is our peace, and who made the two of us one by breaking down the barrier of hostility that kept us apart. In his own flesh he abolished the law with its commands and precepts, to create in himself one new man from us who had been two and to make peace, reconciling both of us to God in one body through his cross, which put that enmity to death. He came and "announced the good news of peace to you who were far off, and to those who were near"; *through him we both have access in one Spirit to the Father* [Eph. 2:13–18; emphasis added].

Giving ourselves over to union with God enables us to have access in the one Spirit of Jesus to God; it is to become a living sacrifice of praise. We have climbed the mountain through our effort to be free from *porneia* and surface looks. We have struggled up the heights by our purgation and recollection. We are ready to face the divine presence and to experience its blessed light (Ps. 24:3–6).

We have brought our fidelity to the yoke of the divine plan that God placed on our shoulders. In our solitude we have come to rest in the peace of God's presence-with-us.

In this presence we experience that we are part of the revelation, the life of God. In the power of Jesus' care for each of us, we too can say in care to our world that God's revelation has become part of our life:

> Father, Lord of heaven and earth, to you I offer praise; for what you have hidden from the learned and the clever you have revealed to the merest children. Father, it is true. You have graciously willed it so. Everything has been given over to me by my Father. No one knows the Son but the Father, and no one knows the Father but the Son—and anyone to whom the Son wishes to reveal him. Come to me, all you who are weary and find life burdensome, and I will refresh you. Take my yoke upon your shoulders and learn from me, for I am gentle and humble of heart. Your souls will find rest, for my yoke is easy and my burdens light [11:25–30].

In the experience of God-with-us, we discover we are with God. There we dwell in power, *exousia*. Here we discover that all the words of our lives are being summarized in the one word we have received as gift from God in the depths of our hearts: Jesus-Emmanuel. Wanting only to dwell in this presence of Jesus, we can praise God with Jesus' Spirit and ours. In this experience of power we discover we too are being transfigured into the very image of God. We experience our whole bodies becoming light, because we are seeing that God who is recognizing the pattern of Jesus' life in the care of our lives. Now, on us, God's favor rests. We discover ourselves entering into the blessedness of God's reign (25:34).

From this perspective we can best understand Paul's Second Letter to the Corinthians. Here Paul summarizes all that we have said in this chapter. Going beyond surface needs, we are led to the experience of seeing God. We enter that experience of God with our ministry of justice in an alien world of duplicity and *porneia*. Recognizing the image, the pattern, of Jesus' life in us, we are received into the divine presence by God. Because we have tried to live in purity of heart, we can see God. We live in awe-filled hope in God's world and our broken world:

> Our hope being such, we speak with full confidence. We are not like Moses, who used to hide his face with a veil so that the Israelites could not see the final fading of that glory. Their minds, of course, were dulled. To this very day, when the old covenant is read the veil remains

unlifted; it is only in Christ that it is taken away. Even now, when Moses is read a veil covers their understanding. "But whenever he turns to the Lord, the veil will be removed." The Lord is the Spirit, and where the Spirit of the Lord is, there is freedom. All of us, gazing on the Lord's glory with unveiled faces, are being transformed from glory to glory into his very image by the Lord who is the Spirit.

Because we possess this ministry through God's mercy, we do not give in to discouragement. Rather, we repudiate shameful, under-handed practices. We do not resort to trickery or falsify the word of God. We proclaim the truth openly and commend ourselves to every man's conscience before God. If our gospel can be called "veiled" in any sense, it is such only for those who are headed toward destruction. Their unbelieving minds have been blinded by the god of the present age so that they do not see the splendor of the gospel showing forth the glory of Christ, the image of God. It is not ourselves we preach but Christ Jesus as Lord, and ourselves as your servants for Jesus' sake. For God, who said, "Let light shine out of darkness," has shone in our hearts, that we in turn might make known the glory of God shining on the face of Christ [2 Cor. 3:12–4:6].

Truly, how blessed are those whose good deeds show the light of God's glory. These deeds will be coming from those who are pure of heart; they shall see God in light, as light.

CHAPTER NINE

Blessed Are the Peacemakers; They Shall Be Called God's Children

Jesus: Sign of God's Favor and Messianic Peace

To understand how we can work for peace in a way that will find God calling us sons and daughters, we first must examine how Jesus made peace in such a way that he was called God's Son.

Matthew's Jesus twice was called "son" by a voice from the heavens. The first was Jesus' inaugural experience of baptism, when he committed himself to the way of justice (3:15). In his transfiguration, Jesus' experience of God's *dikaiosyne,* or presence within him, was revealed to others (17:1–8). In both these experiences the voice proclaimed of Jesus: "This is my beloved Son. My favor rests on him" (3:17; cf. 17:5).

Matthew's spirituality for the church showed that Jesus' biography was the fulfillment of the theology of Isaiah 61. The prophet's promised "spirit of the Lord God" came upon Jesus at the Jordan (3:16–17), anointing him "to announce a year of favor from the Lord" (Isa. 61: 1,2). Jesus' life proclaimed a year of favor. Because he experienced God's favor in his depths, Jesus was able to be the first to live the beatitudes as concrete expressions of Isaiah's theology. In this way, Matthew showed that his community's restoration and jubilee would occur to the degree it lived the beatitudes.

Throughout his life, Jesus' fidelity showed his commitment to God's will. God's plan called for a reordering of the divine image in the least of the brothers and sisters. This reordering would take place by sharing resources. By Jesus' abandonment to this plan, he would establish order or justice. This justice would become the essential requirement for peace.

In Matthew, God's favor is identified with messianic restoration. This restoration expresses itself in an experience of peace that reflects God's unity of life, or *shalom.* Sharing in this unitive way demands that God's unity and

178

peace be witnessed to others. The gift of God's power and peace, which the disciples received (10:1,7), was to be shared with every community, house, and person. "Look for a worthy person in every town or village you come to and stay with him until you leave. As you enter his home bless it. If the home is deserving, your blessing (*eirene*) will descend on it" (10:11–12). The initial activity of the first evangelizers was to extend the blessing of peace.

God's power is experienced in blessing. The blessing is *eirene*, peace. Just as the disciples were told at the Mount of Transfiguration to listen to Jesus (17:5), so the world that will not listen to the disciples' proclamation of God's way of peace and be evangelized (see 10:40–41) will lose the peace once given it (10:13). The disciples were assured of God's presence of peace with them (10:20). Consequently, Jesus made clear to his first followers:

> If anyone does not receive you or listen to what you have to say, leave that house or town, and once outside it shake its dust from your feet. I assure you, it will go easier for the region of Sodom and Gomorrah on the day of judgment than it will for that town [10:14–15].

When a society rejects the justice and order that leads to peace, that society receives Jesus' reproach (see 11:20–24; 23:33–39).

Because he was obedient to God's plan throughout his life, Jesus was called Son by God. Unwittingly, he was also called Son of God by the representatives of the society that rejected his message of peace. At the very time he appeared least like God's Son to them (27:42), he proved he was God's Son (27:54); he had remained faithful. Even though Jesus' fidelity brought him to his passion and death, he remained abandoned to the will of God (26:36–46). His commitment stood in direct contradiction to the way society envisioned the way messianic peace ought to come into the world:

> People going by kept insulting him, tossing their heads and saying: "So you are the one who was going to destroy the temple and rebuild it in three days! Save yourself, why don't you? Come down off that cross if you are God's Son!" The chief priests, the scribes, and the elders also joined in the jeering: "He saved others but he cannot save himself! So he is the king of Israel! Let's see him come down from that cross and then we will believe in him. He relied on God; let God rescue him now if he wants to. After all, he claimed, 'I am God's Son'" [27:39–43].

The one who said that the Temple would be deserted (23:38) because society refused to convert (23:37) would himself become the Temple of God's presence-in-community. Because he was faithful to God's plan, even when it was difficult and even when it seemed the whole world was against him, Jesus experienced the gift of God's favor and peace. He rose from death's power over him. Experiencing this peace of the resurrection, he was able to share it with his disciples. "Suddenly, without warning, Jesus stood before them and said, 'Peace!' " (28:9).[1]

Matthew shows that the peace of God's favor results from faithful obedience to God's order in our life and in our efforts to establish that order in society.

Ministry, Fidelity to God's Will, and the Experience of Peace

Toward the end of my five years at St. Elizabeth's Parish in Milwaukee, I would have been considered successful in the eyes of many people in the world. I had been instrumental, with other Capuchins from the Midwest Province, in making St. E's a model for central city ministry. We had worked with parish leaders to create Harambee Community School, a parent-controlled education center. We were able to turn the convent into a community-based health center. Because I could write proposals, we were able to get Federal monies for a huge youth program. We tried to integrate the black experience in liturgy. The "Elements of Soul" youth choir enlivened liturgy with liturgical dance and gospel music. I pushed a reorganization plan that enabled the senior citizens of the parish to have their own area, complete with a kitchen and sewing room.

Even though these programs and activities seemed so successful (at least to outsiders) I sensed something was missing. When I heard about the work of the Ecumenical Institute in renewing parish and neighborhood life as part of a wider global effort, I attended one of its Parish Leadership Colloquies.[2] Following that, I recruited forty parishioners to make a PLC. Because we had so many recruits, we became the first group in EI history to have enough people to hold a PLC in our own parish. The 25–30 people who graduated that Easter Sunday, 1972, became the "cadre" of leaders. It would be the "cadre's" role to bring about the hoped-for restoration, the new life of the resurrection at St. Elizabeth's.

Despite these efforts, I sensed something was still missing. St. E's, I was beginning to feel, was quite void of what I thought was authentic religious experience. I made efforts to try to deepen this part of the parish's spirituality by starting a prayer group. Yet it seemed there was little felt-need for this essential element of spirituality. In the main, the people seemed quite happy with what religion was providing for them. Most were basically pleased with what I, as a minister of religion, had contributed to their happiness in the form of education, health care, liturgy, recreation, and leadership sharing. After all, what more was there to being a Catholic?

But there was something more. Something was missing, I realized, not only in the parishioners but particularly in me. I lacked depth in my own experiences of God. I had little or no personal identification with the God of my words. Having little or no depth, I could not expect to know how to communicate about religious experience in a way that would touch others. I discovered I was bankrupt.

I came to the conclusion that I could do no more at St. E's than maintain what was already there. The people did not want more; I could not give more. As this realization deepened within me, I became very depressed.

A real fear developed in me about my future in the church. I began to think, "Here you have been in parish ministry only five years. Already you've come to the conclusion that the way it's being done today is something you want no part of. But what are you going to do? You weren't trained to have any other approach to parishes but this. You don't know any other way. And you've got forty or fifty years ahead of you for more of the same!" To add to my depression, I told myself, "It seems that few others in ministry are asking the same questions. They seem quite pleased with what they are doing."

Not wanting to leave the Capuchins, but feeling alienated from the way so many seemed to be reinforcing their existing ministries, my depression grew. How could it be that so many ministers seemed content to exercise a function and a role or preside over rituals when the hearts of the people seemed so far away? How could we continue divorcing our faith from the primary demand for religious experience and commitment to Jesus as "Son of the living God" (16:16)?

One morning I happened to be sitting by myself in the dining room, again having these thoughts. By now I had announced I would be leaving. The realization that the people did not really seem to care, as long as I would be replaced, only added to the pain. In that experience of pain, I happened to look up at the wall. Seeing the crucifix on the wall, the thought came to me, "What more did you expect?"

What more did I expect? Any more than Jesus received on the cross? Jesus brought his depression to that cross (27:46). But he also brought to that cross a life of fidelity in trying to accomplish God's will. All I had in my depression was the similar realization that, despite my faults (which were many), I *had tried*. I had tried to be faithful too. Now strength could be made perfect in my weakness; I could learn obedience in this suffering.

The realization that came to me with the words, "What more did you expect?", brought comfort to my mourning and the blessed experience of God's favor. In my depression I had descended to a form of death. But this death-in-the-form-of-depression did not need to control me. I could rise again; I had tried to be faithful.

My effort to be faithful now brought me peace, *eirene*. I worked for justice and the tranquility of order at St. Elizabeth. I thought this effort would promote God's plan for that part of the world. Because I had worked for that kind of peacemaking, I experienced God calling me "Son." Like the disciples at the Mount of Transfiguration, Jesus touched me (17:7) with peace.

The cultural addictions we face and the problems before us are huge. At the same time it often seems we are so ineffective in restoring society to God's way of peace. So, it is important that we stop measuring success in the way society views it. I no longer believe we can even console ourselves with the saying we used to hear over and over during retreats: "If I could die realizing I had saved but one soul, I could die in peace." Such a dream is more than Jesus died with. The measure of success cannot be defined in quantitative terms.

The realization dawned on me more fully during an interview I was having with Tom Stevenson of the *The National Catholic Reporter.* He was writing an NCR feature story on the corporate responsibility movement. (Corporate responsibility is the effort of institutions to use their investments in corporations and banks to promote the dignity of all people and a more equitable distribution of wealth.)

"Father," Tom asked, "now that you've seen so many religious groups promoting corporate responsibility, how successful would you say you've been?"

In corporate responsibility work, we consider it a victory if 3 percent of the shareholders vote with us on an issue. The 3 percent margin has been decided by the Securities and Exchange Commission as the percentage needed to return a following year to the corporation with the same resolution. Despite this seemingly insignificant percentage, there are many times we fail to muster even this 3 percent. In the case of large corporations like GM, IBM, and GE, where so much stock (another form of wealth, or "land") is concentrated,[3] we have rarely received 3 percent on any issue.

Realizing this, I returned to Tom's question. "I guess I don't have the same definition of success that used to motivate me," I responded. "I look at Jesus on the cross. He wasn't very successful at what he had been trying to do. But he was faithful. So I guess I'm trying to be faithful to the process. In this sense I think we've been very successful. We've been trying to be faithful to the process of bringing the ethics of the gospel to bear upon this significant part of the world."

Making Peace in a Warful World

Because he tried to make peace through truth and justice, Jesus was constituted God's son. In Jesus' transfiguration the disciples experienced the transformation in peace that can come to anyone who tries to live this beatitude. Experiencing God's power and favor within us, we too can be transfigured before the world's eyes as was Jesus. On the mountain "his face became as dazzling as the sun, his clothes as radiant as light" (17:2).

Our liturgy on the Feast of the Transfiguration recalls the splendor of a moment long ago when the divine favor in all its effulgence glorified Jesus for his fidelity to the process of making peace. On that day we are told to "listen to him" (17:5) that we too might be faithful to God's way of peace and favor in our world. But even as we celebrate, we are forced to recall a recent August 6 and contrast the light emanating from the power within Jesus with the light emanating from another radiant light that flashed with the brilliance of the sun. Whereas the light coming from Jesus brought peace and hope into the world, the light coming from the atom bomb over Hiroshima brought fear and death to at least 65,000 people and unleashed the arms race. Being prepared for war would become the new name for making peace, a direct contradiction to this beatitude.

Instead of leading people to the power and peace that could be found in Jesus, another power was unleashed in the name of "peace." It has since proceeded to break humanity apart. Surviving under this new power has become a way of life. The resource once intended by Einstein to promote peace has become, in military and energy-related technology, a source of heightened fear and mistrust, greed and hate, division and insecurity.

In the name of peace and security, both militarily and materialistically, mighty forces (who often tend to benefit from nuclear power) promote it as the only secure path for our nation's journey into the future. Backed by huge lobbies demanding increased spending on nuclear power for the military as well as for the energy needs of the nation, people are whipped up to be angry with those who may question its continued use.

The attempt to defend the vested interests of the political-military-industrial complex by playing on the people's consumer needs, with their concomitant fears and anxieties, is nothing new. It happens today when people are led to believe that economic conversion cannot work at nuclear armaments plants or that nuclear power is the only energy alternative. It happened in the Acts of the Apostles, which showed that another industry was threatened by the early community, much like workers are threatened today. "At about that time a serious disturbance broke out concerning the new way," which had become a threat both to idols and ideology:

There was a silversmith named Demetrius who made miniature shrines of Artemis and brought in no little work for his craftsmen. He called a meeting of these men and other workers in the same craft. "Men," he said, "you know that our prosperity depends on this work. But as you can see and hear for yourselves, not only at Ephesus but throughout most of the province of Asia, this Paul has persuaded great numbers of people to change their religion. He tells them that man-made gods are no gods at all. The danger grows, not only that our trade will be discredited, but even that the temple of the greatest goddess Artemis will count for nothing. In fact, she whom Asia and all the world revere may soon be stripped of her magnificence" (Acts 19: 23–27).

The story continues with the disciples being dragged before a public gathering: "Various people were shouting all sorts of things, with the whole assembly in chaos and the majority not even knowing why they had come together" (Acts 19:32). Mike Clark notes:

In Demetrius we have an individual who defends his own self-interest by playing upon the fears and anxieties of others—the fear of having one's work called into question, the fear of losing one's job, the fear of having one's world-view displaced by another. He calls together his fellow craft workers to remind them of their vested economic interest in the continued worship of Artemis. He then proceeds to defend that interest by arousing the support of the people. His efforts are a response to Paul's forceful preaching that "gods made with hands are not gods."

The story of Demetrius reflects a disturbing contemporary reality: the influence of U.S. military contractors upon governmental policy and public opinion. But the military-industrial complex and the first-century makers of metal objects serve an unbiblical concept of security. The ease with which large corporations equate "their" economic interest with "our" national interest is as transparent as Demetrius' similar efforts among the people of Ephesus.[4]

What happened in the Acts of the Apostles is significant for us to recall as we try to live this beatitude in our reality. This experience of the early community can shed light on reactions to be expected when we try to bring the authority of God's way of peace to issues related to nuclear armaments and power. Trying to influence the military-congressional-industrial complex with resurrection peace is essential for discipleship.

This complex tries to debunk efforts to convert a war-related economy to one that develops jobs that promote community welfare. Its public relations efforts cost millions of dollars each year. The fact remains that every billion dollars spent on education creates about 30,000 more jobs than the same amount spent on defense. Similar ratios apply to housing, health care, mass transit, and other public needs.

In addition, the truth is also leaking out on both sides of the Atlantic that, instead of creating jobs and maintaining them, the arms business loses jobs. Even though you cannot make a simplistic analysis that money for armaments could be totally used for social needs, there is a connection between guns and butter that cannot be overlooked. Such a thesis was reinforced by Pope John Paul II in his first encyclical, *Redemptor Hominis*. It offers an interesting connection to Matthew's Gospel:

> At the basis of this gigantic sector it is necessary to establish, accept and deepen the sense of moral responsibility which human persons must undertake.
> . . . This responsibility becomes especially evident for us Christians when we recall—and we should always recall it—the scene of the last judgment according to the words of Christ related in Matthew's Gospel (25:31–46).
> This eschatological scene must always be "applied" to human history;

it must always be made the "measure" for human acts as an essential outline for an examination of conscience by each and every one: "I was hungry and you gave me no food . . . naked and you did not clothe me . . . in prison and you did not visit me" (25:42, 43). These words become charged with even stronger warning when we think that, instead of bread and cultural aid, the new states and nations awakening to independent life are being offered, sometimes in abundance, modern weapons and means of destruction placed at the service of armed conflicts and wars that are not so much a requirement for defending their just rights and their sovereignty but rather a form of chauvinism, imperialism and neocolonialism of one kind or another. We all know well that the areas of misery and hunger on our globe could have been made fertile in a short time, if the gigantic investments for armaments at the service of war and destruction had been changed into investments for good at the service of life.[5]

I quoted another colleague, Bill Cunningham, earlier, "If you and I are on an island and you have the loaf of bread, you will never sleep." To protect any form of our power, possessions, or prestige, to insure our continued consumerism and vested interests, we have to defend ourselves from the "other," who must be considered hostile to us. This applies to us on all levels: the individual, the interpersonal, and the infrastructural.

The "need" to defend our land arrangements, even to the degree of going to war, helps us understand those dynamics that lead to war itself. Whenever power, possessions, or prestige are threatened or called into question, the first reaction is always defensiveness. If that attitude controls the members of the particular social arrangement instead of inviting them to conversion, a process will have begun that can lead to actual violence. This violence can be verbal, attitudinal, or even military war itself.

Ralph K. White has shown that every war has underlying and precipitating causes. Without six underlying causes, he discovered, there could be no war. For instance, the First World War would not have occurred when it did simply because of the killing of the Archduke Ferdinand of Austria by a Serbian nationalist. Austria and Serbia needed mutually hostile attitudes that justified going to war over this incident.

All parties in conflict tend to justify their "cause" for going to and remaining at war by an appeal to six attitudes, White discovered. For instance, during the War in Vietnam both sides viewed each other according to the six underlying attitudes listed below. By invoking them unconsciously, an ideology was created that justified their war-making.[6] Controlled by these underlying attitudes, both the "enemy" Vietnamese and "enemy" Americans were viewed by each other as the cause of the conflict.

1. The first step in any conflict is to perceive the opponent in terms of the *diabolical enemy-image*. The other is seen as diametrically opposed to what one represents. The enemy Vietnamese were "the gooks"; they could never be

trusted. Even their eyes showed how slanted and shifty they were! The enemy Americans were "the running-dog imperialists"; their soldiers were the lackeys of the capitalists who were trying to take over the world. To stop such a diabolical enemy, strong steps had to be taken.

2. The *"virile" self-image* provides the weapons. Whether these armaments be words or silence, missiles or guns, each side believes it has the physical resources to win. The Vietnamese were guerrillas; just as they outlasted the Japanese and French with guerrilla warfare, they would also beat the United States. The United States was the strongest nation on earth; it had never lost a war. It could bomb the Vietnamese into submission. Furthermore, if it lost Vietnam, all the other nations would fall like dominoes. To capitulate would be humiliation. Commitments had to be honored.

3. Buttressed by the *moral self-image*, both sides view themselves as peace-loving, rational, orderly, and just. For U.S. citizens, God was the protector of democratic values. The nation was challenged to protect its values for future generations. The Vietnamese saw themselves protecting their own interests; their struggle was an internal matter. The foreign aggressor should be taught not to interfere. U.S. citizens saw themselves safeguarding democracy and freedom. With Cardinal Spellman blessing the troops and Billy Graham blessing the Commander-in-Chief, God had to be on the American side!

4. *Selective inattention* focuses only on the extremes; mitigating circumstances and significant historical background are glossed over. The Vietnamese refused to consider that their internal problems had created a situation that resulted in many people calling for outside aid. U.S. patriots refused to remember the fact that, like Vietnam, the United States was a nation conceived in a revolutionary war. The founders did not like it when the Prussians helped the British colonizers in their effort to squelch the nation's independence movement.

5. The *lack of empathy* means that both sides are unable to see matters from the other's view. Bluntly, neither side cares. The Vietnamese were so controlled by their fear of the "Americans," seeing them as the personification of evil, that they could not understand their belief in democracy. The Americans, controlled by an ideology reflecting the white experience, never understood the Asian mind. What resulted from this insensitivity, combined with the previous attitudes, was the final step.

6. Each side developed an overconfidence reflecting an overall *irrational interpretation of reality*. Both sides were so controlled by their ideologies and subjective interpretations that it was simply impossible for them to think otherwise. Each side viewed itself as correct and justified in its position. Anyone within those nations who questioned that "party line" would be considered disloyal. Thus Catholics in North Vietnam who wanted some of their rights were considered subversive. Those in the United States who questioned the morality of the war were probably pink, if not out-and-out communists.

Chaos and violence exist in fact or possibility not only among nations. They can be found within many "isms": among sexes and races, among producers and consumers, gays and straights, doctors and nurses, clerics and lay, and on and on. All parties to these social arrangements can be helped to peace by understanding how easily they can be controlled by the six underlying attitudes. Understanding how such attitudes can lead the way to tension and war can also help both parties reduce potential conflicts. Understanding what leads to war can make it easier to structure peace by avoiding these forms of underlying, potential violence. The chinks in the ideological armor will have helped structure this peace.

Three Steps for Making Peace in Community Life

If an understanding of these background attitudes can be applied to the "isms," or the social arrangements of the infrastructure, how much more, I discovered, can an understanding of their influence help bring this seventh beatitude to bear upon potential conflicts within our families, between wives and husbands, parents and children, as well as within organizations and communities. Failing to understand how subtly these attitudes can infect perceptions among members of these groups can leave the members open to the too-many forms of war that rule many households. The case of the Third Street Capuchin Community going to "war" is a case at point. After the war had begun, I realized I was one of the combatants.

It all started in spring 1978. Four of us Capuchins were living in a rented house in Milwaukee. I was the only solemnly professed member of the community. The simply professed Capuchins were Mark Ramion, Larry Webber, and Bill Erickson.

Larry and I were too much alike. We both had a deep desire to discipline ourselves into a form of gospel living; we both had a kind of obsession with perfection. Our problem resulted from the different ways we expressed these goals and how we perceived each other in the process.

I had come to accept my spirituality, including my weaknesses. To the best of my knowledge, I was not letting these sins control me. While I thought I was dealing with them, Larry thought otherwise, especially about two weaknesses—my intolerance manifested in judgmentalness and my response to affirmation coming from my "successes." In his mind, I was very intolerant of the brethren. He also wanted me to be more concerned about what I would do when the affirmation I was receiving in my ministry would not be forthcoming. I thought I was trying to face these difficult areas. But it did not seem that I was trying hard enough from Larry's perspective.

For his part, Larry had come to accept his spirituality, including his weaknesses. To the best of his knowledge, he was not letting these limitations control him. While he thought he was dealing with them, I thought otherwise, especially regarding two areas. His notion of God seemed to be that of someone divine making so many demands on him that spirituality became a struggle. Secondly, even though he was very successful in jail ministry, he never shared these successes. His silence, I thought, reflected a sense of false humility. In Larry's mind, no matter what he did, Michael was always questioning his spirituality. It was outdated and not appropriate to the needs of our time.

At various times and with various degrees of emotion, we tried to discuss our differences and thoughts about each other. As each of us justified our positions, we gradually came to a standoff. Larry did not think he could do much of anything right in my eyes. And the feeling was mutual. Unconsciously each of us was starting to build up our defenses. We were legitimizing our defensive positions around the six steps that lead to war. This hostility was aggravated by a situation which started developing around Bill.

Bill had just come to Milwaukee. He was trying to be a full-time senior in college while exercising a full-time ministry as a Country and Western disc jockey. To complicate matters, his deejay hours were eleven p.m. to six a.m. The community agreed he should go to bed in the morning, rather than waiting until 7:30 for Mark, Larry, and myself to pray.

I was growing concerned that Bill not only was unable to pray with us; he seemed to have little time for prayer at all. Although I had discussed this with him, I also brought it up with Mark and Larry. Once when I did this, Larry countered, "Why don't you give Bill a chance; you really seem hard on him!" Realizing he was probably correct, I said to Larry, "Well, maybe you're right; I should lay off." So I made a real effort to become more sensitive and caring in my subsequent thoughts and discussions about Bill. Certainly I should have, because Bill is a sincere and dedicated person.

A short time after this we discovered that Bill had gone to St. Benedict's to discuss the possibility of moving there. It seems he realized his evaluation for vow renewal would raise questions about his over-extendedness. We were told Bill did not consider our house as good a community as St. Benedict's for various reasons, including the fact that we had no direct ministry connected to our fraternity.

One night Mark, Larry, and I were washing dishes and discussing Bill's desire to get a transfer. "We are going to have to do something about Bill," I said with my usual passion, "so that this kind of stuff he's been doing will stop."

At that, Larry shot back, "Mike, why are you always on Bill's case?"

Immediately I countered, "I am not ALWAYS on Bill's case!" (After all, I reasoned to myself, I had kept my mouth shut three whole weeks, hadn't I?)

Just as quickly, the subject was changed. The verbal barrage may have stopped, but the war was on. Salvos had been fired from both sides. The subject was changed, but the Third Street Community had gone to war. Mike and Larry were combatants. Just one sentence coming from each of us had been the precipitating cause. Bill was no longer the issue, any more than the Archduke Ferdinand was the real issue between Serbia and Austria.

Larry and I had never dealt with our growing alienation. Now, these underlying attitudes came to legitimize what we had done with our verbal barrage. Furthermore, each of us justified why, at this time, we should not lay down our arms.

How did each of us regard the other from the six underlying causes that lead to war? How did our attitude toward each other parallel the way the United States and Vietnam justified their hostilities?

1. Both of us needed to view the other from the perspective of the *diabolical enemy-image*. Each of us saw the other as diametrically opposed to the truth we each tried to represent. The enemy Larry was so self-righteous; his piety turned me off. The enemy Michael was so conceited; his so-called "spirituality" was really dangerous. To stop each other, a stand would have to be taken. This brought us to the next step.

2. We both thought of ourselves as having the weapons necessary to conquer the other. This was our *"virile" self-image*. The enemy Larry was in simple vows; in no way would I support such a spirituality for final vows. Larry had to change. It was my responsibility to use my role as a solemnly professed to make him change if he wanted to stay around. If I did not do it, who would? The enemy Michael was so transparent in his failings. Anyone could see through him to uncover what made him tick. Only Larry would have the guts to stand up and not be cowed by him. Whether he was on the Provincial Council or not, Larry could cut through Mike's defenses. After all, if Larry did not do it, who would?

3. With our common obsession for perfection, both of us would justify our stance with a *moral self-image*. The enemy Larry really could become a problem in the future. How could God want him to have such a warped notion of perfection? It was in Larry's best interest that I keep pressing and not give in. On the other side, the enemy Michael was really a phony. With his judgmentalness and pride, how could God be blessing him? If Larry would not expose such an approach, who would? After all, if his housemates keep quiet, who in the province would have the guts to stand up to Michael Crosby?

4. To legitimize our positions we both needed to focus on each other's extremes by *selective inattention*. Larry could not consider that I really was concerned about Bill. Furthermore, Larry could not admit that I was honestly trying to be faithful, despite my faults. On the other side of the battlefield, I could not consider that Larry was also concerned about Bill. I would have to "forget" that Larry was one of the most serious and dedicated Capuchins in the province, despite his failings. If either of us would have attended to those and other factors, we would have found less reason to remain at war.

5. Since we both expressed our desire for perfection in differing ways, neither of us could regard matters from the other's viewpoint. In addition, despite our words to the contrary, we really did not care about each other. We both *lacked empathy*. The enemy Larry, so controlled by his understanding of God and the way spirituality should respond to God, simply could not accept Michael's style. The enemy Michael, so controlled by his very desire to manipulate, could not consider this a form of domination. Even though I was

like Larry when I was his age, I could show no weakness and give in. Larry had to learn; so did Mike, from Larry's viewpoint.

6. Reinforced with such attitudes both of us could be confident that we were justified in attacking each other. We would have cause not to lay down our arms because of our *irrational interpretation of reality*. Even though meekness means a rational interpretation of reality, or spiritual realism,[7] our pride had to defend our positions, irrational as they might be. We were without mercy.

The morning after the dishes episode, Larry, Mark, and I came together for the liturgy. We could have applied the steps of community-conscientization-conversion (see Crosby, *Thy Will Be Done,* pp. 186–211) in a eucharistic setting.[8] But we—like so many others—celebrated the ritual without the reality of mercy and reconciliation.

After beginning in the name of the God who promised to be with us in *community* if we two or three gathered with our gifts in the name of Jesus, we came to the reconciliation rite, which initiates the *conscientization* process. Reading our reality would have definitely shown how we were enslaving each other by our anger and resentment. We could have also known that God's power could have healed us. But, despite the reconciliation service, our anger justified continuing in our warlike positions. We had no problem mouthing, "Lord, have mercy. Christ, have mercy. Lord, have mercy."

The next part of the Eucharist brings us, with our enslavements and empowerments, to hear the Word of God that we might be *converted*. Into that battlefield, which had moved from the kitchen the night before to the living room that morning, the day's first reading began with a selection from First Corinthians. "Now I will show you the way which surpasses all the others," it began. "If I speak," it continued, and, at that point I realized what passage was to follow. Panic hit me as I said to myself, "Oh, hell!"

[If I speak] speak with human tongues and angelic as well, but do not have love, I am a noisy gong, a clanging cymbal. If I have the gift of prophecy and, with full knowledge, comprehend all mysteries, if I have faith great enough to move mountains, but have not love, I am nothing. If I give everything I have to feed the poor and hand over my body to be burned, but have not love, I gain nothing [1 Cor. 12:31–13:3].

At this point of the reading I thought, "If it ends here, I think I can get by."

But the Word of God addressing the world of Michael Crosby with a call to conversion continued: "Love is patient. . . ."

At that point I remembered what a retreat director had once suggested: we should insert our name instead of the word "Love." God's Word judging my life-reality was saying:

Michael is patient; he is kind. Michael is not jealous, he does not put on airs, he is not snobbish. Michael is never rude, he is not self-seeking, he is not prone to anger; neither does he brood over injuries. Michael does not rejoice in what is wrong but rejoices with the truth. There is no limit to Michael's forbearance, to his trust, his hope, his power to endure. Michael never fails [1 Cor. 13:4–8].

Now, thirteen hours after the battle had begun between Larry and Michael, what were we going to do about our World-at-War, having heard God's Word? Would we respond "Thanks be to God" and make it a sign of conversion? Or would "Thanks be to God" be another empty cliché? Would the idolatrous worship continue in face of the reality of irreconciliation? Although not another round had been fired, both of us definitely knew we were at war. With that realization of our sin, I looked at Larry as he was looking at me and said, "I'm sorry, Larry." And he simply replied in kind, "I'm sorry, too, Mike."

How could this have happened to two people both honestly seeking God's will? We discovered we had not *structured* a way to insure we would not be controlled by underlying attitudes that could easily lead to various forms of rejection. Never dealing with such attitudes as they built up, it was only a matter of time before war would be declared.

Once we came to share the one bread in the eucharistic service, we discovered each other's brokenness in a whole new way. We could now say, "Amen," to this bread of life. Because we had finally opened our eyes to recognize the real presence in the bread we found each other there as its members. Now we could say, "Amen" to each other. Since "Amen" means "Let it be," I was now saying, "Let Larry be, Mike." Larry was saying to himself about me: "Just let him be, Larry." No longer could we continue trying to remake each other into our own images.

Making peace does not end at the point of avoiding attitudes that may lead to war. Awareness and avoidance of these underlying causes leading to war is just the first step in making peace. Larry and I would come to understand the next step when we found ourselves living together again in another house a few months later.

Our move from Third Street was precipitated by various facts. Bill had decided to leave the Order; Mark would be away for his diaconate experience; Larry had to move because formation policy dictated that simply professed friars change communities every two years. Since no friars wanted to move from their local fraternities to Third Street, we decided to close it down. In looking around for the best possible fraternity (given various considerations), I decided on the Capuchin Prenovitiate. This fraternity was composed of Perry McDonald, Steve Wettstein, Mike Merkt, and Larry Webber.

At our first monthly day of reflection, Perry asked us to consider four questions: (1) What gifts was I bringing to the fraternity? (2) What were my personal goals for this year? (3) What did I envision for the fraternity this year? (4) How did I see this vision being realized?

Returning from our private reflection, we breezed through the first two questions quite rapidly. Then we addressed the third and fourth questions. After hearing what the others envisioned for the community, I said: "You know, we tried something at Third Street to help us make peace and it didn't work. But I think the reason why it failed was that we didn't structure a form of accountability. This would have made sure we did what we had promised to do.

"I still dream of the time in our fraternities when all the members will be able to just live according to one ground rule," I continued. "It would go something like this: Say, for instance, the five of us would be able to affirm each other. I could affirm you and you could support me. But, building on this affirmation, we'd also let each other know what was bugging us. So I could correct you and you could confront me. Do you think," I concluded, "that we could do something like this during the year?"

While I do not have the exact words of their responses, Perry said something like, "I've been in the Capuchins nineteen years. This sounds to me like it could be the greatest year of my life if we lived this way."

Steve said, "It sure makes all the sense in the world. We would not have to do another thing as a community if we would live according to this one rule. Everything else would fall into place. If we would affirm each other and confront each other, we'd really be trying not to let anything divide us."

Then Larry looked at me and the rest and said, "Well, you know we tried something like this at Third Street and it didn't work. But I still believe it's the way communities should be living. I realize it may be rough at times and we have to work off some of our tensions, but I want it. I want it badly."

Mike Merkt was the last to speak: "Well, I don't know much about it; it sounds all right to me. I'll be happy to go along with it."

We started calling the way we could make peace in our house the "ground rule." Then I said, "You know, I think the word of God is telling us that what we're about to do in community is just what Jesus wants." We went to the eighteenth chapter of Matthew. There, in his advice to a community-in-transition that experienced alienation and division, we discovered the way the brothers and sisters could structure their coming-together to create peace.[9]

Building on a prior awareness of those attitudes of negativity that can engender mistrust, we can now consider the second step in peacemaking offered by Matthew.

Community, for Matthew, begins with the realization of the dignity of each member. Each person is considered by the others as precious in the eyes of God. Thus, in response to the disciples' question regarding greatness (18:1), Matthew's Jesus "called a little child over and stood him in their midst and said: 'I assure you, unless you change and become like little children, you will not enter the kingdom of God' " (18:2–3).

At the time of Jesus, children were denied, by their age as well as by law, the rights of persons or access to needed resources. Now whoever would be greatest would reflect a childlike abandonment, wanting to fulfill the ideal of God's reign. Such people would orient their rights and resources to God's rule: "Whoever makes himself lowly, becoming like this child, is of greatest importance in that heavenly reign" (18:4). In any community where everyone defers to the other out of reverence for each other's rights and need for resources, the image of Jesus is recognized in the one who is in need. Furthermore, the image of Jesus is reflected in the one who may be responding to the one most in need (see 10:40–42; 25:31–46) as well:

> Whoever welcomes one such child for my sake welcomes me. On the other hand, it would be better for anyone who leads astray one of these little ones who believe in me, to be drowned by a millstone around his neck, in the depths of the sea. What terrible things will come on the world through scandal! It is inevitable that scandal should occur. Nonetheless, woe to that man through whom scandal comes! [18:5–7].

Since Jesus always let the little ones come to him, the disciples would mirror Jesus if they did the same (19:13–15).

In this part of his outline for church discipline, Matthew addressed those in the community who had power, possessions, and prestige. They seem to have created situations that were stumbling blocks to the dignity of those who needed their basic rights met. If we would apply this ethic to the contemporary universal church, it seems quite reasonable to speak about the scandal of being a Christian in the richest country on earth. Christian churches in the United States are a part of a global infrastructure. If the church remains silent regarding its members' responsibility to reflect the sharing of the early churches (see 2 Cor. 8), this silence shouts "scandal," from the viewpoint of biblical spirituality. As Pope John Paul II said to Catholic citizens of the United States:

> Within the framework of your national institutions and in cooperation with all your compatriots, you will also want to seek out the structural reasons which foster or cause the different forms of poverty in the world and in your own country, so that you can apply the proper remedies. . . . You will [not] recoil before the reforms—even profound ones—of attitudes and structures that may prove necessary in order to recreate over and over again the conditions needed by the disadvantaged if they are to have a fresh chance in the hard struggle of life. The poor of the United States and of the world are your brothers and sisters in Christ.[10]

Pope John Paul II was very conscious of the connection between the group of Catholics to whom he addressed these words in Yankee Stadium and the poor. He was quite aware of their lifestyle as a predominantly white, middle and upper middle class group of people who were the beneficiaries of unjust social arrangements. He was quite aware, having previously visited Harlem and the South Bronx, as well as the Dominican Republic and Mexico, that the group in Yankee Stadium needed to be told of its responsibility to be aware of the total community that was part of that eucharistic body that was being celebrated at the stadium. Thus he said to them:

> The poor of the United States and of the world are your brothers and sisters in Christ. You must never be content to leave them just the crumbs from the feast. You must take of your substance, and not just of your abundance, in order to help them. And you must treat them like guests at your family table.[11]

The church should listen seriously to such words of Pope John Paul II, as well as to the gospel of the eighteenth chapter of Matthew. It needs to recognize that it must become a true reflection of the beatitudes in society. Such a spirituality will bring with it a blessing. It will take the place of the *scandalon,* or stumbling block, that is assured when we continue a style of life that shows we do not care about the brother or sister in need. In commenting on the absolute need to convert from such ways, John Meier notes,

> Such scandals, caused by man's unbridled will to power, are, to be sure, the unavoidable destiny of a sinful world. It is especially disastrous, though, when the world's standards are introduced into the church. The disciple who causes such scandals will suffer the severest punishment imaginable (v.7). When we realize that these words would apply particularly, though not exclusively, to church leaders, we can appreciate the seriousness and sharpness of Matthew's admonition. However, adds Matthew, scandal is not just a danger for church leaders or even for members of the church in their interpersonal relations. Each Christian can be the source of his own fall. Any of our faculties, any of our drives, can lead us into sin and so into eschatological loss. A true disciple will judge it preferable to suffer any temporal, physical loss here and now rather than risk the loss of oneself for all eternity. Matthew does not hesitate to threaten any Christian, however secure or exalted may be his position in the church, with the fires of hell.[12]

Having established the need for all people in community to make sure they are not leading a life that hinders the faith of any brother or sister, Matthew's Jesus goes on to outline the next three steps. In a particular way, these would become the Scriptural basis for our ground rule in the Capuchin Fraternity House.

The first understanding we were to share related to the dignity of Perry, Steve, Mike, Larry, and myself. In no way should we reject each other or do anything negative toward each other. Why? Because each of us was a unique and precious image of God. As images of God, we were to be like God's angels revealing God's plan for each other (see 18:10). Thus the primary need for affirmation. Furthermore, the structure of the whole community itself would have to be seen existing to affirm the dignity of each of us. It could not be the other way around, that we existed for the community. As Jesus showed clearly, community exists for each of its members:

> What is your thought on this: A man owns a hundred sheep and one of them wanders away; will he not leave the ninety-nine out on the hills and go in search of the stray? If he succeeds in finding it, believe me he is happier about this one than about the ninety-nine that did not wander away [18:12–13].

If we lived within an environment of affirmation (affirming and being affirmed) we would be much better able to sense if something was hurting any of the brothers. We could more easily stop business as usual, go to that friar, and try to meet his needs. We could see the brother in need, care for him, and call him to wholeness. In this care and affirmation he could respond to others in need by caring more for them than for his own problems. "Just so, it is not part of your heavenly Father's plan that a single one of these little ones shall ever come to grief" (18:14). This whole process would find our fraternity in the circle of care.

Many times in families and religious communities members get the feeling that they are being taken for granted. An affirming stroke coming out of the blue can be a tremendous way to deepen the bonds of community.

After we had made the ground rule, I returned home after being on the road just a few days. "Am I glad to see you," Perry said, giving me a big bear hug. "Welcome home again!" I looked quite stunned at his spontaneous sign of affirmation and affection. Then I realized I had come to expect nothing from anyone in the way of recognition. But Perry saw me as precious, as extraordinary, as one of the greatest in God's reign. He wanted me to know how he felt. It was a little gesture, but it meant a lot. Sharing this sign of affection and care, he would be for me an angel of God's care. He would also be inviting me to become more sensitive by affirming others. I could say more positive things to these others—from the way they looked, to the prayer they led, to their insights, to the simple joy of having them around.

If members of a community experience each other's support and affirmation, they are more open to each other's correction and confrontation. We soon discovered that the other half of our ground rule flowed from the affirming touch of care for each other. If we could build each other up, that would enable us to correct each other: "If your brother should commit some wrong against you, go and point out his fault, but keep it between the two of you. If he listens to you, you have won your brother over" (18:15).

In confrontation, the initial step should be a private sharing of what might bother us, even the petty things. A week after we made the ground rule I was packing for a trip. Larry came to my room. "I feel a little funny coming like this, Mike, but 'Remember the ground rule'?" (We had agreed that "remember the ground rule" would become the symbolic phrase that would get our "care system" in gear.)

I said, "Sure, I remember. What's the matter?"

At that, Larry recalled our social after the Saturday's Day of Reflection. He thought I had said I did not believe people when they said something like, "The Lord said to me. . . ." He was concerned that, since he used this terminology quite regularly, I was again questioning his spirituality.

"Oh, no, Larry," I said. "I didn't say that. I just said that I couldn't use those words. And even though I can't I have no reason to question many of the friars who honestly believe God does speak to them like that."

"Wow, isn't the ground rule great," Larry said. "It sure becomes better when you don't let a little thing like that start to build. This way you can head it off at the pass."

Some might say you can get too petty about correcting and confronting each other. Immature people will get petty. So the ground rule is not practicable with immature people. But, assuming a family, group, or community is composed of basically healthy people, it can also be said that the petty things are usually those little things that can build up and lead to war. You can't get much more petty among mature people than, "Why are you always on Bill's case," or "I am not always on Bill's case!"

Larry had been faithful to the initial step of correction. He had come to me (18:15). If he hadn't gotten anywhere with me that night, he could have moved to Matthew's next step: "If he does not listen, summon another, so that every case may stand on the word of two or three witnesses" (18:16). If Larry and I had not been able to work out our problem, Larry could have discussed it with Perry, Steve, or Mike. They could have offered another perspective, because I might be blinded by anger or my inability to be as objective with Larry as I ought.

Sometimes people use this second step instead of the first step—going to the person himself or herself. While it may be done for Matthean reasons, often this process takes the form of talking behind the other's back. If each of us in the fraternity is conscious of when this happens, then we can ask, "Did you share your problem with Mike?" This, in turn, might be a reminder to meet with the one who has inflicted the perceived hurt.

If the first two steps in the correction process prove unworkable in making peace (making peace is work!), Jesus said that the matter should be taken to the community itself (18:17–18). We decided that our weekly Review of Life and monthly Day of Reflection would serve this purpose. As part of the ritual of each subsequent meeting, the leader would ask, "Does anyone have anything they want to bring up about the ground rule?" Soon we had disciplined ourselves to such a point in practicing the first two steps that we rarely had to invoke that ritual. Yet it was always good to recall the phrase about the ground rule as part of structuring peace.

The Friday after we initiated the ground rule was the first and only time

Larry saw fit to invoke it with me. We both tried to respect each other and build up our relationship in care. As a result, within a few months, we were able to come to full reconciliation not only in our heads but in our hearts as well.

On one occasion I came back earlier than expected from some speaking engagements. When he saw me, Larry wrapped his arms around me exclaiming, "Mike, we didn't expect you until next week!" That hug meant an awful lot. As we both realized a few days later, at that moment we both *felt* like we meant we were happy to be with each other again.

"Again I tell you," Michael and Larry, "if two of you join your voices on earth to pray for anything whatever, it shall be granted you by my Father in heaven. Where two or three are gathered in my name, there am I in their midst" (18:19–20). When we reflected on this third positive step for a reconciled community, following affirmation and correction, we realized how powerful all other dimensions of our community life could be. This would bring new meaning to prayer itself as well as all other forms of communication. With such a ground rule, someone mentioned, we could finally understand what Francis meant in our Rule when he wrote, "Wherever the friars meet one another, they should show they are members of the same family. And they should have *no hesitation* in making known their needs to one another."[13] Without such a ground rule, soundly articulated, the fear of possible rejection always remains. With the structure for making peace, we can approach each other in confidence, without hesitation. We can *confidently* make known our needs so the circle of care can begin.

We ended up making Matthew 18 our Word Service that Saturday afternoon. Then we articulated the ground rule in specific words as our way of realizing this new vision as a covenant between each other. We signed our names to it and made this covenant of fidelity our sacrifice of offertory praise to God.

Trying to avoid any tensions and working to affirm and confront each other in care, a community that senses itself gathered in the name of Jesus would do well to try to make various Scripture passages more evident in its lifestyle and relationship. As part of that community's faith-experience, each person could ask the other in equal care how a specific statement was fulfilled in her or his individual life. The community could ask the same of its corporate expression.

I have a hobby of visiting Christian and non-Christian, Protestant and Catholic, groups of a religious nature whose founders are still alive. From the viewpoint of the sociology of religion, they are more movemental than institutionalized. Pursuing my hobby, I once visited a Focolare community in Brooklyn.[14] From the moment I arrived I sensed I was with a community seriously trying to structure certain Scripture texts within its relationships and lifestyle. At the end of the meal, I said, "I think I am able to tell you what Scripture passages mean a lot to you." To their surprise, not having really read any of their literature, I said, "Where two or three are gathered in my name, there am I in their midst" (18:20) and "I have given them the glory you gave me that they may be one, as we are one—I living in them, you living in me—that their unity may be complete. So shall the world know that you sent me and that you loved them as you loved me" (John 17:22–23). Indeed, they told me, these were very much part of their "story." To keep the story being told each month, every community would receive a text, which would be displayed in a prominent place to help it structure God's word of peace in its local setting.

In applying this new insight to making peace in community, it seems family, group, and religious life could become a renewed source of hope to a broken world. By working to avoid obstacles and stumbling blocks to peace, by structuring affirmation and correction, and finally, by symbolizing Scripture passages to remind us how we can relate as we gather in the name of Jesus, we can more easily hear a voice from heaven say to us in our depths, "This is my beloved. Here, in my beloved, my favor rests."

As we become beloved, we gradually hear the voice from heaven calling us God's children. Not only that, we are blessed with God's life. Blessed are those who work to make peace. They will be called God's children. We cannot experience more favor than this way of sharing in God's own life!

CHAPTER TEN

Blessed Are Those Persecuted for Justice' Sake; the Reign of God Is Theirs

Persecution from the World and Fidelity to the Beatitudes

The eighth beatitude reflects the unique experience of Matthew's community-in-transition. Because his church not only preached the beatitudes but actually implemented them in its lifestyle, Christians were experiencing persecution. Thus Matthew added this last beatitude. He wanted to reassure his community's members about two things. First, if their lives incarnated the previous beatitudes, they would become a scandal to the world's authorities (as well as to some of the church leaders); consequently, they could expect rejection and persecution. Second, if they were persecuted, it would be a concrete sign that they had been faithful. Thus, the final beatitude (which is a combination of two "blessed" passages) became Matthew's redaction to bring hope to his community as it experienced both rejection *(scandalon)* and blessing *(makarios)* (10:11–42):

> Blest are those persecuted for holiness' sake; the reign of God is theirs.
> Blest are you when they insult you and persecute you and utter every kind of slander against you because of me. Be glad and rejoice, for your reward is great in heaven; they persecuted the prophets before you in the very same way [5:10–12].

For Matthew, the very act of being persecuted for justice' sake is a sign of eschatological fulfillment for all those who concretize the living of the beatitudes in their society and world. As Robert Guelich notes:

Indeed, in light of Isa. 61:1–3, those who are "persecuted for the sake of righteousness" (5:10) are none other than the "poor in spirit" (5:3), the *anawim*. The subjects as well as the promises of the first and eighth Beatitudes form an *inclusio* by means of synonymous parallelism. Consequently, the eighth Beatitude bears every mark of being a redactional product of the evangelist.[1]

Matthew's very terminology for the last beatitude reflects an environment of persecution. The lines were being drawn. An "outgroup" and an "ingroup" were starting to define their identities. If one examines, from a sociological perspective, a community that is experiencing alienation from a more powerful group, words referring to the division between "us" and "them" become noticeable. W. D. Davies, one of the best authorities on Matthew's Sermon on the Mount and the beatitudes, has noted that the frequent use of words referring to "you" and "they" manifests the attitude of a persecuted and alienated group within a wider, alien culture.[2] Perceiving itself to be at odds with the majority culture, the early church viewed itself as a persecuted subgroup.

The experience of persecution, misunderstandings, and tensions has reinforcements throughout Matthew's Gospel. The ideology of "us" and "them" is particularly evident, for instance, when Matthew speaks of Jesus as teaching "in *their* synagogues" (4:23; 9:35). Since his christology reflects ecclesiology, such terminology reflects the existential condition being experienced by Matthew's community; already, it seems, it had been evicted from the synagogue.

As a minority group, the Christians were beginning to differentiate between "their" synagogal sacrifice (which had been replaced by law) and "our" synagogal sacrifice (which has appeared in the living presence of the risen Jesus in community). Again in 11:1, Matthew's christology reflects the lived experience of his community. Jesus, having "finished instructing his twelve disciples . . . left that locality to teach and preach in *their* towns."

Evidence such as this suggests that the church was already outside "their" towns." Quite possibly it was settled in such non-Jewish areas as Antioch, in Syria. John Meier goes so far as to say a break with the Jews had already been clearly established: "The church's celebration of its own Christian rituals (baptism for all nations in 28:19, Eucharist in 26:26–29), its rejection of both food laws (15:11, 17–18) and Pharisaic teaching in general (15:12–14; 16:5–12) all indicate that it has broken with Judaism."[3] Whatever its relationship with the Jewish synagogue, the experience of rejection is central to the community's experience at the time of Matthew's final redaction.

Matthew tells the community that its experience of persecution results from its fidelity in promoting *dikaiosyne,* or God's justice. The community's fidelity to its call is equally a sacrament. It signifies the disciples' experience of another reality, namely that "the reign of God is theirs" (5:10).

The last beatitude contains the only other expression outside the first beatitude where, as the result of a specific activity or attitude, the reward of God's reign can be immediately expected. Since God's reign is constitutively linked with justice, the disciples' ministry for justice automatically deepens within each disciple the experience of God's reign, which is justice. The inevitable sign that the disciples are being faithful to this ministry of justice is evidenced in the experience of misunderstanding and persecution from various elements within their world.

Matthew's community was suffering from persecution within and without. This beatitude told the community that rejection from within the community was to be expected. Even members of the disciples' own families might not be willing to convert to a gospel message that called into question some of those gods that, like the unbelievers, they too were running after (6:32):

> Do not suppose that my mission is to spread peace. My mission on earth is to spread, not peace, but division. I have come to set a man at odds with his father, a daughter with her mother, a daughter-in-law with her mother-in-law; in short, to make a man's enemies those of his own household. Whoever loves father or mother, son or daughter, more than me is not worthy of me. He who will not take up his cross and come after me is not worthy of me. He who seeks only himself brings himself to ruin, whereas he who brings himself to nought for me discovers who he is [10:34–39].

Christians today have been used to a religion that often *carte blanche* endorses the infrastructure. As a result, some will not easily understand when the word of God starts being addressed to the institutional powers and principalities that promote and reinforce unjust aspects of that society. Some will not easily hear the scriptural call for the promotion of those dynamics that advance the dignity of every person and that help all people share more fully in the earth's resources. As a result, many Christians will not be readily open to the questioning of an ideology that heretofore had reinforced their share in society's power, possessions, and prestige.

Persecution and misunderstanding are not to be expected only from members of one's own family and former friends. It can be anticipated from society itself:

> What I am doing is sending you out like sheep among wolves. You must be clever as snakes and innocent as doves. Be on your guard with respect to others. They will hale you into court, they will flog you in *their* synagogues. You will be brought to trial before rulers and kings, to give witness before them and before the Gentiles on my account [10:16–18; emphasis added].

Assured that this very persecution will be the inevitable sign of God's presence and reign with them, the disciples have no need to worry how they should respond to such powers and principalities. They will be under another *exousia*: "When *they* hand you over, do not worry about what you will say or how you will say it. When the hour comes, you will be given what you are to say. You yourselves will not be the speakers; the Spirit of your Father will be speaking in you" (10:19–20; emphasis added).

Those representatives of the Jews' and Romans' infrastructures did not kill Jesus because he went up a mountain, sat down, gathered his disciples around him, and taught the beatitudes (5:1ff.). Because Jesus came down that mountain and concretized in *exousia* his teachings of wisdom, many of those leaders became upset. Jesus was put to death because he put his preaching into practice. In this light, Matthew's Gospel was letting his community members know that they were suffering the same fate as Jesus. They too had not been content with just mouthing the beatitudes. They too had tried to concretize them in their hearts, shared faith, celebrations, and ministry. Now they were experiencing how scandalous an unjust world considers them to be.

Nineteen hundred years later, it is not enough for individuals, communities, families, and institutions—dioceses and local churches, congregations and institutes, provinces and orders—to talk about the beatitudes or celebrate them on the Feast of All Saints, saying, "Lord, Lord." Only when the beatitudes are put into practice will Christians be able to experience this last beatitude's assurance of being within God's reign.

Those who hunger and thirst to experience justice and to manifest it in a just lifestyle within a seriously unjust society[4] must be open to the very real possibility of rejection and persecution. Controlled by the rationalizations and ideology of the infrastructure, society will not understand what is being stated by such a witness. Much less will society be open to the conversion that is being requested by this witness. It is little wonder then that suffering at the hands of "them" is the only earthly promise made for fidelity and commitment to God's plan. The world's reaction to Jesus, for faithfully committing himself to live the beatitudes, will be the same response his disciples can expect for their fidelity (10:24–27, 32–33).

What society considers normative is reversed by the lifestyle of Jesus and his faithful community. What Jesus calls a blessing stands as a scandal to what society considers blessed (11:6). Only the poor in spirit, who experience the authority of this new reign of God in their depths, can be equipped to withstand the persecution from a society. The disciples' persecution stands as a sign of society's refusal to be converted from those ideological reinforcements and structural patterns that deny the dignity of every person and perpetuate inequity in the way the earth's goods are distributed.

Fidelity to a life of the beatitudes means continual resistance and readiness to reverse those norms in society that do not reinforce God's plan.

Persecution from the World and Prophetic Witness

Over and over Jesus declared that fidelity to God's plan needs to go far beyond pietism and angelism, as well as authoritarianism and legalism, and even beyond separatism and nationalism. Realizing the implications of this spirituality for their vested interests, the leaders rejected not only Jesus' message, but Jesus as messenger: "When the chief priests and the Pharisees heard these parables, they realized he was speaking about them. Although they sought to arrest him, they had reason to fear the crowds who regarded him as a prophet" (21:45–46).

Matthew presents Jesus in the role of a prophet rejected because of his prophetic lifestyle. The same form of societal rejection could be expected by all those in the church who would also manifest a similar prophetic charism and mission. Commissioned by Jesus to preach the beatitudes to the world, they too would suffer a prophet's rejection from that world:

> For this reason I shall send you prophets and wise men and scribes. Some you will kill and crucify, others you will flog in your synagogues and hunt down from city to city; until retribution overtakes you for all the blood of the just ones shed on earth, from the blood of holy Abel to the blood of Zechariah son of Barachiah, whom you murdered between the temple building and the altar. All this, I assure you, will be the fate of the present generation [23:34–36].

Society's rejection of Jesus is every generation's rejection of those disciples who, at any point of history, lead the prophetic lifestyles of the beatitudes. Rejection can be expected by anyone preaching Jesus' word to a world that refuses to change its ideology and be converted. As Matthew showed in the thirteenth chapter, a society that has legitimated its accumulation of "more," even at the expense of "what little" others have (13:12), will refuse to convert to a new ethic that promotes "just enough" in order to be more. The reaction of the infrastructure of Jesus' day and Matthew's day would be the same as in Isaiah's day:

> I use parables when I speak to them because they look but do not see, they listen but do not hear or understand. Isaiah's prophecy is fulfilled in them which says:
>> "Listen as you will, you shall not understand,
>> look intently as you will, you shall not see.
>> Sluggish indeed is this people's heart.
>> They have scarcely heard with their ears,
>> they have firmly closed their eyes;
>> otherwise they might see with their eyes,
>> and hear with their ears,
>> and understand with their hearts,
>> and turn back to me,
>> and I should heal them".
>
> But blest are your eyes because they see and blest are your ears because they hear. I assure you, many a prophet and many a saint longed to see what you see but did not see it, to hear what you hear but did not hear it [13:13–17; cf. Isa. 6:9–10].

It is significant that, in explaining the hardness of society's heart to conversion's call, Matthew here has Jesus quoting another "fulfillment" text (Isa. 6:9–10). Paradoxically, this text was written by the Isaian community in the context of its sense of persecution, during the exile. However, as Matthew applied it, persecution represented the reaction of a hardened society to the spirituality of the beatitudes (5:10–12).

As we have seen in our reflections on this specific beatitude, Jesus' self-understanding of his spirituality and vocation, as well as that of his disciples, included definite prophetic characteristics (13:57). In a special way, this prophetic spirituality reflected the theology of Isaiah. The Isaian text that describes the consequences of prophetic ministry is Isaiah 6:9–13. Matthew incorporated this text to show that Jesus' prophetic words would be rejected by his society (13:13–17).

Society's hardened reaction to the prophet's call for conversion (Isa. 6:9–13) is a consequence of fidelity to the prophetic call itself (Isa. 6:1–8). Isaiah's prophetic theology would be, for Matthew, Jesus' spirituality. In turn, Matthew's christology would be ecclesiology. Finally, Matthew's ecclesiology should be our spirituality.

Prophecy was central to Matthean spirituality. Given the environment his church-in-transition faced, we can better understand the implications of the prophetic vocation for our changing era. As our church-in-transition experiences similar religious, legalistic, and cultural problems within our wider environment of injustice, a reflection on the steps involved in Isaiah's call to prophecy (Isa. 6:1–8) can help us understand what the prophetic vocation implies for our generation. Such an examination will reinforce our thesis that spirituality must be lived concretely in society in a way that integrates deepening religious experience and hope-filled prophetic activity.[5]

1. The prophetic call occurs within concrete historical exigencies. "In the year King Uzziah died" (Isa. 6:1), Isaiah had the mystical experience that led to the formation of his prophetic consciousness and to a commitment to change his society. Faithful to the historical setting for all vocations, Matthew placed his whole Gospel not just in that part of history which took place "during the reign of King Herod" (2:1), but in all history (1:1–17) "until the end of the world" (28:20). The prophetic vocation of Jesus and the disciples is to be lived within the struggles of human history, not apart from them. The call to be faithful to God's plan in a world marked by the grave sin of social injustice must include a social analysis of the infrastructures of which we are a part.

2. The prophetic call is first experienced in being touched by the transcendent (Isa. 6:1–4). The transcendent is that which takes one beyond the controls of given reality. Isaiah had a mystical experience or vision of "the Lord seated on a high and lofty throne" (Isa. 6:1), surrounded by the Seraphim (Isa. 6:2) proclaiming God's holiness (Isa. 6:3) in a way that filled the environment with power (Isa. 6:4).

While direct experience of God similar to Isaiah's religious experience can happen, more often the transcendence that transports us beyond our surface-selves occurs less dramatically. More likely, the deepening of God's word in us and our commitment to live under its power happens as a result of going through our hermeneutic circle in which something jars our traditional frame of reference. Waking up to reality, one can consider its contradictions in light of God's order for the world experienced in transcendence.

Research done at the Justice and Peace Center by Dale Olen has shown that people become committed to a spirituality that evidences societal concern in two ways. They either have a shattering experience of poverty and injustice, or they do studies that deepen their understanding of poverty and injustice. Whether it be in religious experience or prophetic concern, we must first be taken beyond our given reality.

3. The reaction to this transcendent experience is a concrete awareness of sin, both personal and societal (Isa. 6:5). After his mystical experience, Isaiah was immediately aware of those areas of his life that contradicted the divine manifestation that had touched him. He now accepted them as obstacles to a deeper experience of God. "Then I said, 'Woe is me, I am doomed! For I am a man of unclean lips. . . .' " (Isa. 6:5).

Peter immediately sensed his own sinfulness in face of a transcendent experience (14:30; 17:6). Similarly, great saints like Ignatius and Francis of Assisi spent very long periods mourning over their sins the closer they came to God. They discovered how far they were from the divine experience the more they were touched by it. The closer we come to the divine throne, the more we adore in awareness of our poverty.

Isaiah not only admitted his own sin; he recognized he was part of a world that contradicted the divine experience that should be normative in society as well as in individuals. "For I am a man of unclean lips, living among a people of unclean lips; yet my eyes have seen the King, the Lord of hosts!" (Isa. 6:5). Moving beyond the initial jarring experience, more reflection brings one to the second part of the hermeneutic circle: the realization that one's whole way of life and ideology can no longer be supported. This is where a realization of the infrastructure's power and our powerlessness comes to play. At this point, one can despair and be controlled by the power of personal and social sin that contradicts the experience of prayer and God; or one can submit to God's power. In submitting to God's power, one joins with others in community who share the same experience.

4. The awareness of sin makes one realize the absolute need for a power beyond sin's control. "Then one of the seraphim flew to me, holding an ember which he had taken with tongs from the altar. He touched my mouth with it. 'See,' he said, 'now that this has touched your lips, your wickedness is removed, your sin purged' " (Isa. 6:6–7). In Isaiah's vocation, it was his ever-deepening reflection on that word that had touched him in transcendence that brought him to a new realization. This word now became incarnated within him as a new source of power greater than his sin, freeing him from its control.

In the case of each of us being touched by God's word, it is the growing faith experience of God's word saying, "I am with you" (28:20; cf. 10:19–20) that incarnates an equally powerful sense of call to be faithful to God's plan despite the consequences.

5. Experiencing a share in the *exousia* of the word within, the prophet has been seen in need and cared for by God. Now the prophet hears the voice of the Lord as an empowering call saying: "Whom shall I send? Who will go for us?" (Isa. 6:8). The response to this call from the Trinity experienced as divine presence can only be: " 'Here I am,' I said; 'send me' " (Isa. 6:8).

The response to the call must be free. Unlike the ideology of society which persuades through mass media and other forms of control and manipulation, the response to the experience of God must always be free. By stressing freedom in our answer to the call, fidelity to the mission is placed on more solid grounding when difficulties arise.

6. Remaining faithful to the call by living and promoting a life of care involves the possibility of being rejected by one's world, both familial and structural. The world's ideology cannot understand or support this new way. People have too much at stake in that old world and cannot be converted to God's ever-new word (Isa. 6:9–10).

Where society's heart has grown cold, commitment to a person or to a cause can stir one's depths to a fidelity that is willing to give up one's life for the sake of a greater good. Thus, every faithful disciple should be able to say, "Here [in your presence] I am; send me" (Isa. 6:8), and be willing to face the consequences:

> Do not fear those who deprive the body of life but cannot destroy the soul. Rather, fear him who can destroy both body and soul in Gehenna. Are not two sparrows sold for next to nothing? Yet not a single sparrow falls to the ground without your Father's consent. As for you, every hair of your head has been counted; so do not be afraid of anything. You are worth more than an entire flock of sparrows. Whoever acknowledges me before men I will acknowledge before my father in heaven. Whoever disowns me before men I will disown before my Father in heaven (10:28–33).

Prophetic Spirituality and the Life of Discipleship

The disciple willing to be committed to go into the whole world witnessing to this faith-stance can expect persecution (Isa. 6:9–13). Reinforced with the *exousia* of Jesus' Spirit, the disciple's faith will not be in vain (8:18–27). This faith will be buttressed by the realization that such a stance places one directly in the prophetic line that Matthew has applied to Jesus' life as a model for all spirituality in the church. According to Reginald Fuller,

It is the unexpressed, implicit figure of the eschatological prophet which gives a unity to all of Jesus' historical activity, his proclamation, his teaching with *exousia* (authority), his healings and exorcisms, his conduct in eating with the outcast, and finally his death in the fulfillment of his prophetic mission. Take the implied self-understanding of his role in terms of the eschatological prophet away, and the whole ministry falls into a series of unrelated, if not meaningless fragments.[6]

Jesus' biography is to become the spirituality of the community in a way that his theology becomes the very biography of each of its members. The wisdom teaching and the compassionate expression of Jesus' *exousia* is to be continued in the words and works of the disciples for all time.

Faithfulness to his teachings through ethical obedience and to the expression of his power through charismatic ministry (especially the gifts of prophecy and healing) is essential to discipleship. With the same *exousia* in the church (10:1, 8; 28:20), the community of faithful disciples becomes empowered to live a vocation that combines the expression of charismatic activity with deeds of justice.

The deeds of *dikaiosyne* (or ethical obedience/righteousness) are to be normative for all those who witness to its experience of being constituted in the *exousia* of God's justice. Since the other pole or dynamic of spirituality that is equally essential to Matthean discipleship is the manifestation of charismatic experiences, it is essential that we examine their role and necessity in the church. Speaking to this need, James P. Martin has written:

Matthew's redaction of his tradition reveals that he wishes to affirm charismatic discipleship in a positive way. A charismatic healer must follow Jesus, and to follow Jesus is to be called to a ministry of healing. Jesus' declaration to his disciples that nothing will be impossible for them (17:20) shows, in this context, that the authority of genuine faith is proved in charismatic healing.

The importance of charismatic ministry for Matthew's understanding of discipleship and church is reinforced when we relate the term "disciple" to other terms used to describe them, especially "little ones," "prophets," and "righteous men." Eduard Schweizer concludes that prophet refers to the charismatic activity of a disciple, whereas righteous man describes the disciples' obedience toward God's law as interpreted by Jesus, and little ones is a general description of the Matthean church as "ascetic," "charismatic," and "anti-official."

For Matthew, the life of the church is above all else discipleship. Thus its post-Easter mission is to disciple the nations. This must mean, on the basis of the evidence, that the true church (as Matthew understands it) is characterized by charismatic ministries of healing, exorcism, and prophecy. The ministries are not restricted to the time of Jesus' earthly ministry alone, but through the authority and power of the risen Lord are valid and constitutive for the church until the end of the age (28:19f.).[7]

In recent years, spiritual writers have been trying to integrate the charismatic ministry dimension of Matthew's discipleship with ethical obedience and *dikaiosyne*. Unfortunately, many who stress one pole tend to emphasize it at the expense of the other. Pointing to deviations or inconsistencies in the "other" expression of spirituality they often say, "If that's what it means . . . then I want no part of it." As the Scriptures are advanced to justify each position, selective inattention legitimizes misunderstanding or rejecting the other perspective. Such rejection takes place at the expense of solid biblical basis.

As our study of Matthew has shown, the tension we experience between the "charismatics" and the "justice-and-peace folk" existed in the early community as well. Integrated spirituality resolves the tension by demanding that both are co-equal poles of discipleship. To offer a way to experience and promote this integration was one of the goals of Matthew's spirituality. It is no less a reason why Matthew remains so relevant to our church today.

I began to become keenly aware of this need for integration in my own life in the mid-1970s. Even though I was very involved at the Justice and Peace Center, I was becoming increasingly aware of a definite lack in my spirituality. I was not experiencing the charisms or gifts of the Holy Spirit.

These gifts, which are becoming more manifest in the church today, once were considered normative to its very life. Not wanting to place obstacles to any expression of the Spirit's *exousia* in my life, I sensed a need to go to the annual National Catholic Charismatic Conference for Priests and Deacons at Steubenville in 1977. I realized that Jesus enabled people to experience power within their lives by touching them (8:15; 9:25; 9:29; 20:34) and by extending his hands toward them (8:3; 14:31; 17:7; 19:15). He shared that energy with his disciples in the church. In this light I wondered, "Could not Jesus empower his disciples today to lay their hands on me? Couldn't they help free me of an obstacle to God's power in me?"

Not long after I arrived at Steubenville, I had an experience that made me very aware of the mighty deed that God is accomplishing in our province.

I was outside the large assembly tent with Kieran Hickey, then our vicar provincial. "I'm really glad you came, Mike," he said, "because you are the prophet for our province."

"Oh, Kieran, I'm not a prophet," I answered. "I do know I'm working to bring about the things that I sense God wants for our province and the world. But I know from the Scriptures that prophecy isn't just a matter of working for justice. Prophecy has another empowering dimension. That's why I'm here. I don't want to place any obstacle if any inner power can become more externalized in my life too."

I was going to the corporations, calling for some of the things the prophets preached about. I was also very involved in renewal in the province. I felt that these efforts were linked too closely to my own reading *about* God's word and the world. Yet, I did not sense that this normative dimension of the circle of care was as deeply rooted as it should have been in the experience of *exousia*, in the constitutive dimension of Gods' power, or justice, in me.

To be a true prophet I could not just speak about God's will; I had to speak from a personal experience of it. In "The Nature of the Prophetic Role," Sonya A. Quitslund has noted:

> That their words reveal a deeper knowledge *of* God rather than new knowledge *about* God distinguishes them from the other religious teachers of Israel. Their encounter with the Word of God meant a totally new way of life, total dependence on the Lord, the loss of all normal social and economic securities. . . .
>
> Of the 241 times the expression "the word of the Lord" occurs in the Bible, 221 or 92% relate to a prophetic oracle. When "the word of the Lord" came to a person, it was truly a mystical experience, setting that person in a new historical situation, in a new relationship to God. It was always *the* Word that came, never *a* word, indicating the completeness of the Word addressed to a particular situation. This word made the recipient an authoritative teacher of Israel. However, what happened as the prophet faced his contemporaries and was faced by God, or what was actually experienced when "the hand of the Lord came upon" him, defies the imagination.[8]

At Steubenville, I wanted Capuchins from our Midwest Province to be the instruments of "the hand of the Lord" touching me. I wanted them to invoke the Spirit to be as fully operative in my life as possible. So, when we gathered together that first night of the meeting, I asked the brothers to pray over me.

"What gifts do you want," one of them asked as they laid their hands on me.

"Well, I don't really want to place any obstacle to God's gifts. That's why I'm here. I just want you to pray over me so that the Spirit can be as fully part of my life as possible."

"Okay, so what gifts do you want from the Spirit?" someone else asked again.

"Well," I said, "from reading the Scriptures, I'd really like to ask for the gifts of healing and prophecy since they were so much a part of Jesus' life and that of the early church."

"Okay, what about asking for tongues?" another brother asked.

"No, I've really got no interest in asking for tongues," I responded.

"Well," someone asked, "what if you get the gift of tongues?"

"I'll take whatever gifts I can get!" I could only reply.

The experience of these fine men praying over me was beautiful and moving. However, I had already experienced a deep sense of God's healing and consolation that freed me from the control of any known sin. This had happened in New York a couple of weeks before.[9] Maybe this is why, in the room at Steubenville, I experienced no great emotion. In fact, I felt nothing at all. My only experience was a sense of honor and joy knowing that we Capuchins could share our faith this way. We could pray over and for each other as our ancestors did in the early church.

As the days went on, I entered as fully as I could into the tent sessions as well as the small group afternoon prayer meetings. But I began to realize that my inability to speak in tongues put me in the minority among the hundreds of priests and deacons and brothers. As the humming, singing, and praying in tongues increased, so my ability to be part of it decreased. In the group it was just expected that everyone had the gift of tongues. I had been passed by.

At our Thursday afternoon prayer group, one of the priests asked to be prayed over. He was one of the last of our group to ask for prayers. As usual, after he shared his fears and concerns, we all gathered around him. While some touched him and others laid hands on him, I thought I would like to offer a prayer. After a few others had prayed, I started to express prayerfully some of the thoughts I had been mulling over in my mind. Almost immediately, I sensed the words I had begun to say were being redirected under another power. This power was not totally from my own resources. While I was freely giving voice to the words, what I was saying was originating from another energy. These words were encouraging this priest with words of hope. They were almost *verbatim* the words Second Isaiah used to encourage his community in the exile! "I, the Lord, have called you for the victory of justice, I have grasped you by the hand; I formed you, and set you as a covenant of the people, a light for the nations" (Isa. 42:6). When I finished praying, the "Amens" from the others confirmed the words I had offered as from God. Their response was a sign of the community's affirmation of God speaking to us through the words I expressed.

That night, since I was quite in awe about what had happened. I said to a good friend of mine: "You know, when I prayed over that priest this afternoon, something seemed to happen to me. I'm wondering what you thought about it?"

"Well, Mike," he said: "Something really did happen. That was a prophecy you expressed."

"I thought so," was all I could say.

More than ever, I was in awe at what God can do in us when we truly try to be open. That divine presence and reign is always available to be experienced in our midst.

Prophecy, such as I experienced functioning in me that afternoon, is always initiated by God's action. It helps people better open themselves to hear God's word as it is proclaimed publicly. In this way, individuals, groups, and institutions can experience the *exousia* of the Spirit being extended more fully in the world through them. The word of God acts always to evangelize the one who makes the address. In turn, as others hear the address, they too are invited to be evangelized.

Prophecy, as a charismatic ministry, can take many forms. In my case, it affirmed, encouraged, and built up another to be more faithful to his role in the church as priest. At other times it can function as corrector, persuader, consoler, inspirer, and guide. Like any manifestation of the Spirit's power, it comes best when we recognize it as a needed power that is beyond our control. Our faith assures us that God, who wants us to lack nothing (7:11) and who cares about us when we are in need of the Spirit's gifts, also wants us to ask for these gifts. We are to seek them and knock for them in prayer (7:8).

Given our membership in that part of the world that contributes significantly to the grave disorder of injustice, the possibility of many having this needed gift latently within them might have to be seriously faced. As Moses said: "Would that all of the people of the Lord were prophets. Would that the Lord might bestow his spirit on them all" (Numb. 11:29).

Today, as they face the power, possessions, and prestige of the twentieth-century kings, priests, and false prophets, people inside and outside the church are demoralized and perish for want of prophecy (Prov. 29:18). Consequently, there is more reason than ever (especially for religious, whose life is to sacramentalize the prophetic dimension of discipleship) to ask seriously if one might not have this gift. Since the Spirit's gifts are already given in baptism, one might have to submit to the community, prayerfully asking its members for help in discerning and releasing this gift.

We should not only desire to place no obstacle to the expression of prophecy, we should also exercise the gift, if it has been expressed in our lives, by using the gift on behalf of others. In any case, we should simply ask and pray for it, as Paul urged the community at Corinth. While he insisted that love is the greatest gift to be desired, he went on to say:

> Set your hearts on spiritual gifts—above all, the gift of prophecy. A man who speaks in a tongue is talking not to men but to God. No one understands him, because he utters mysteries in the Spirit. The prophet, on the other hand, speaks to men for their upbuilding, their encouragement, their consolation. He who speaks in a tongue builds up himself, but he who prophesies builds up the church. I should like it if all of you spoke in tongues, but I much prefer that you prophesy [1 Cor. 14:1–5].

If we are not willing to set our hearts on spiritual gifts, especially the gift of prophecy (1 Cor. 14:1), it may be good to investigate our motivation. I have found in my own life that a reason why I might not be willing to ask for a gift of the Spirit is often my unwillingness or fear of giving up something. As a result, it may be an idea, an attitude, or action that becomes the very obstacle to the exercise of the gift I refuse to pray for. I remain controlled by my own sin. We may be calling for the normative order that reflects a prophetic ethic. Yet if we are unwilling to be more fully constituted as prophets, anointed in the spirit of God, it may well be we are unwilling to truly convert. We may be refusing to become abandoned and poor in spirit to such a degree that we will live under the power of God's word and reign.

Praying for the gift of prophecy—to experience the word of God making us just in a way that empowers us to call for justice—seems to be the only viable way to address the cultural addictions of our era. Facing their immense power, it would seem that anyone with an ounce of meekness, or spiritual realism, would sense the need, as all prophets did, to gather with likeminded "little ones" or "children" to create a support group of disciples. This was the first thing prophets like Isaiah, Jeremiah, and Jesus did. Upon experiencing God's power in them, they gathered the *nabiim,* the "little ones" around them to form a prophetic community.

In response to society's cultural addictions, those who radically commit themselves to God become a remnant community. They begin a new process of hope in a world unwilling to admit its addictions lest it be converted from them.

Gradually such disciples desire to be free from that infrastructure. They no longer want to be caught in its network of domination, oppression, and abuses, which stifles people's freedom and keeps the greater part of humanity from sharing more equitably in the resources.[10] As a result, likeminded disciples discover each other in a common bond. They come together, with their cultural addictions, to form *community.* Regularly gathering together with their gifts in the name of Jesus (18:19–20), they commit themselves in a common Spirit to Jesus and one another. Reflecting on their cultural addictions in light of the twelve steps, these disciples *conscientize* themselves. They look at the reality of their world, in light of the history that has been formed by God's word. Such disciples recognize their enslavements and powerlessness. They seek empowerment; they seek to be freed. Seeking to discover a power stronger than their addictions, the community comes to experience *exousia* at work among its members. The Spirit of God comes with anointing. With this power at work in the continually-conscientized community, a sign of *conversion* is given. This sign states, more by faith-practices than professions of faith, that there are still some in the world who seek to be freed from society's domination and need to control. Experiencing this new awakening, the members of this community hunger and thirst to share their good news of freedom with other cultural addicts. They will not be satisfied until they share with everyone this new way, this lifestyle, that has restored them to sanity, integrity, and peace.

Even within the institutional church such support groups are especially needed in our transitional times. In many ways, it seems we have come to stress a form of ethical obedience at this period of the church's history to the exclusion of charismatic ministry. We have come to stress loyalty to the institutional church's magisterium more than obedience to God's justice, which demands that we promote God's image in all by more equality in resource sharing. While Matthew seemed to try to stress a spirituality that would honor both dimensions, while attempting to correct overstresses and abuses of the one in favor of the other, he never questioned that both were vital to the church.

Unfortunately in contemporary spirituality, it seems we have suffered from too much stress on one part of one pole of discipleship. Limiting ethical obedience to its interpretation from the position, power, and prestige of bishops and priests has muffled the voice of prophecy within the church or the world. The case of Cardinal Spellman using his position of power to silence Daniel Berrigan's speaking against the Vietnam War can be cited as a blatant example. In many ways, clerical domination has effectively redefined spirituality in terms of prayer and ministry from the perspective of clerical leadership. Prophecy, once considered essential to the upbuilding of the church, is effectively killed. Sonya A. Quitslund has noted:

> Unfortunately, because of abuses of or difficulty in recognizing true prophetic words in the early Church, attempts to control teaching apparently stifled or silenced the prophetic voice. For centuries prophetic figures have been rare, acceptance and recognition in their own lifetimes even rarer. A certain ecclesiastical skepticism has greeted any departure from the established norm, having decided the prophetic or teaching office to be embodied in the office of bishop. Perhaps greater familiarity with the prophets will enable us to be more attentive to and receptive of their voices in our world today.[11]

As a Capuchin Franciscan, I am the inheritor of the charism of a prophetic figure whose original inspiration for the Order was based on the image of the institutional church (signified by St. John Lateran) falling into ruins. The church of that day was clerically controlled. It used that social arrangement to link the religious, economic, and political institutions into an infrastructure that also controlled the ideology. Deviations could be met with excommunication. Yet into that world, God's word was spoken in the words of St. Francis of Assisi. This prophetic figure called for a renewed Gospel spirituality to the very leaders who no longer thought it could be accomplished.

Paradoxically today, even the mention that the institutional church may have problems, much less be falling into ruins, is often considered disloyal.

The Hebrew Scriptures showed the need for a healthy tension between priest, prophet, and king. Franciscan literature speaks of the prophet Francis inviting both pope and emperor to conversion. Yet many modern Franciscans are repelled at the thought of contemporizing the expression of Francis' charism. They reject the fact that one can, in care, question the pope or lobby the president, Congress, or file a shareholder resolution! Such an attitude indicates how we have come to live in a church dominated by a clerical ideology that no longer reinforces the traditional tension among roles in the community. Rather it shows we have come so far as to equate obedience to church leaders with loyalty to the reign of God itself. In this light, there is more reason than ever to return to Matthew's spirituality. For, Matthew was also responding to this false use of authority in church leadership 1900 years ago!

This realization makes it all the more imperative to follow Paul's advice. We must seek after the gift of prophecy (1 Cor. 14:1) lest we be led astray. In our eagerness to bring the normative dimension of God's justice into our world, and particularly into our own church, we can easily be guided by motives of anger, guilt, resentment, retaliation, and manipulation instead of genuine, Spirit-filled care. Thus we have a special need to be constituted under the authority of God's word of justice. This will help us discern correctly what kind of prophecy is needed within and without the church.

We can no longer be controlled by our fear or unwillingness to ask for prophecy either because of what it may demand of us in the form of personal conversion or persecution from others. The realization that the sinful dimension of our world's infrastructure (including the religious sector), calls for a return to a beatitudinal lifestyle will make this need for prophecy more evident. It demands that fear give way to faith in God's promise. As he promised to be with Matthew's community in its societal difficulties (10:16–42), so Jesus promises to be with us (28:20).

The Commission to Be Prophets in an Unjust World

Because his community was experiencing societal rejection for practicing a beatitudinal spirituality, Matthew added this last beatitude. He wanted to provide a perspective in face of internal and external scandals of tension and persecution the church was experiencing. However, it seems there is also a strong possibility that Matthew placed this beatitude last, and at this precise position, to indicate something much more powerful.

According to M. Jack Suggs, it might well be that this special redaction of Matthew's serves as more than a conclusion to the beatitudes.[12] It may also be the initial empowerment and commissioning of the disciples to enter the world of that day. Isaiah's call outlines what it means to be a prophet (Isa. 6:1–8). But since the world's rejection of the prophetic word (Isa. 6:9–10) was to be expected by the disciples (13:13–15), we can find in this final beatitude the way Jesus wanted to extend the authority given him to his disciples for all time.

Showing that Jesus desired to bring God's care into the world (9:35–37), Matthew employs a unique triad. First he shows Jesus gathering his disciples to give them the blessing of his *authority* (10:1). Then they are *named* (10:2–4). Finally they are *commissioned* (10:5) to go to a select group of people (10:6) to preach (10:7) and heal (10:8).

In Matthew 28:18–20, this triptych of being gathered for *authority* (28:16–18), by sharing "in the *name* of the Father, and of the Son, and of the Holy Spirit" (28:19), makes an addition to the preaching and healing *commission* of 10:7–8. Now the power of teaching is no longer to be limited to a select group; it is to be extended throughout the world (28:19–20).

Nowhere is the threefold connection among the blessing or authority, the bestowal of a name, and the commission to minister in the world clearer than in Matthew 16:17–19. This section, which established Peter's role in the church, has many parallels to the wise and foolish ways of building a house, which Matthew describes at the conclusion of the Sermon on the Mount (7:24–27). Peter's call and commission in the new house of Israel (which is being battered through internal and external persecution) consists of three parts. The first begins with the pronouncement of an empowering blessing for the faithful Peter: "Blest are you, Simon son of Jonah! No mere man has revealed this to you, but my heavenly Father." (16:17); secondly, a new name is bestowed on him: "I for my part declare to you, you are 'Rock,' and on this rock I will build my church, and the jaws of death shall not prevail against it" (16:18). Finally, the commission to manifest this power concretely in society is given: "I will entrust to you the keys of the kingdom of heaven. Whatever you declare bound on earth shall be bound in heaven; whatever you declare loosed on earth shall be loosed in heaven" (16:19).

M. Jack Suggs links the loosing and binding of 16:19 with the functions of the scribe (23:13). He also shows that the passage, "Every scribe who is learned in the reign of God is like the head of a household who can bring from his storeroom both the new and the old" (13:52), serves as a conclusion to that part of Matthew's Gospel that has often been called the Book of Wisdom (11:2–13:53). Noting these passages, as well as the interrelatedness of scribe, wise men, and prophets (23:34) Suggs goes even further. He links the last *beatitude* (which empowers us with God's own reign) with the *naming* of the disciples who are *commissioned* to be faithful to their call:

> In the light of this evidence, I want to suggest that 5:11–16 has been constructed by Matthew so as to form the first commissioning saying in the Gospel. The well known problem of the shift from the third person in the beatitudes of 5:3–10 to the second person in that of 5:11–12 is to be explained as due to the fact that Matthew here moves from the beatitudes proper (which announce in a general way the conditions of entrance into the Kingdom) to a commissioning of the disciples (who are the primary audience, although the subject matter of the Sermon is of universal validity). This commission is made up of three independent sayings which Matthew has arranged to conform to the pattern of Peter's commission in chapter 16. It consists of the three elements previously identified in that passage.[13]

Matthew begins that last beatitude by assuring the community that it will receive the blessing of the reign of God for its fidelity to the ministry of justice, even as it experiences persecution from a world that calls this blessing a scandal. Then he presents Jesus giving another *blessing*: "Blest are you when they insult you and persecute you and utter every kind of slander against you because of me. Be glad and rejoice, for your reward is great in heaven; they persecuted the prophets before you in the very same way" (5:11–12). If we honestly live the beatitudes we both experience the blessing of God's justice and call for this blessing of justice concretely in society. This blessing thus gives us a new name:

> You are the salt of the earth. But what if salt goes flat? How can you restore its flavor? Then it is good for nothing but to be thrown out and trampled underfoot.
> You are the light of the world. A city set on a hill cannot be hidden. Men do not light a lamp and then put it under a bushel basket. They set it on a stand where it gives light to all in the house. [5:13–15].

The disciples, blessed with God's power, are given a *name* in whom the world can again find hope (12:21). The first name given to those who witness in society to the spirituality of the beatitudes is "salt of the earth" (5:13). The Greek word for salt is related to the verb for foolish. It also refers to endurance. Thus by using this word, Matthew seems to be saying that it is quite foolish to give in to tensions and persecution rather than to endure them wisely, knowing these forms of rejection are inevitable signs that we have been faithful. In explicitly associating his disciples with salt, Jesus is linking their spirituality to the way of wisdom, which the world will always view as a stumbling block.

In his reflections on salt as a metaphor for discipleship, Wolfgang Nauck has shown that Matthew's salt metaphor has its roots in Rabbinic instructions to disciples. Herein "to be salted" means "to be wise." This becomes more convincing for our purposes when we realize that the passive, *moranthe,* can be used both to mean "go flat" and "to become foolish."[14]

If what should be salt that wisely endures in the face of the world's rejection becomes part of that world, it goes flat. "How," Jesus asked, "can you restore its flavor? Then it is good for nothing but to be thrown out and trampled underfoot" (5:13). If an alternative foolishly becomes part of the earth's infrastructure, it will be good for nothing but to be rejected, along with the world.

The second name given to those who witness in society to the spirituality of the beatitudes is "light of the world" (5:14). Experiencing light comes from purity of heart. In the depth of such a heart, experiencing the touch of care from the God of Light, the disciple comes to the source of life (see Eccles. 11:7). Being touched by this light (17:2), the disciple gains wisdom in such a way that it can be said, "There is a man in your kingdom in whom is the spirit of the holy God; . . . he was seen to have brilliant knowledge and god-like wisdom" (Dan. 5:11). Empowered by the Light of the Wisdom Teacher, the prayerful disciple can walk in light so that others can be illuminated within the community (5:15).

This light, however, cannot be limited to the community alone. Whoever is blessed by God's Spirit and is called in light is *commissioned* to illuminate the whole world as well: "In the same way, your light must shine before men so that they may see goodness in your acts and give praise to your heavenly Father" (5:16). "At this point," Suggs writes about the third dimension of commissioning:

> it becomes apparent that Matthew has in view some group of opponents. Whether it is the Pharisaic scribes who "preach but do not practice" (23:3) or Christian false prophets who cry "Lord, Lord," but are evildoers (7:15–23), or both, is not for the moment of importance. In any case, the Christian scribe is told that unless he performs "good works" . . . he has put his light under a bushel, made his salt insipid. The commission is, not merely to teach the law but to do it to the glory of God.[15]

The world had seen goodness in the acts of Jesus, the disciples, and the church of Matthew's time. The world was witnessing a spirituality that not only proclaimed the beatitudes but practiced them (see 11:2–5). Because this way of wisdom was being manifested, Jesus could thank God that the world was indeed witnessing a people faithful to their commission to implement God's plan for the world. No longer did people have to submit to the yoke of falsehood or self-seeking interpretations of the law promoted to advance the prestige of the lawmakers. Now Jesus could thank God for extending that revelation, that plan, to everyone through him:

> Father, Lord of heaven and earth, to you I offer praise; for what you have hidden from the learned and the clever you have revealed to the merest children. Father, it is true. You have graciously willed it so. Everything has been given over to me by my Father. No one knows the Son but the Father, and no one knows the Father but the Son—and anyone to whom the Son wishes to reveal him.
> Come to me, all you who are weary and find life burdensome, and I will refresh you. Take my yoke upon your shoulders and learn from me, for I am gentle and humble of heart. Your souls will find rest, for my yoke is easy and my burden light [11:25–30].

The yoke fitted for each disciple is the commission to walk in wisdom's way and to proclaim this way prophetically to a society that will reject it. The commission to go into the whole world (28:19–20) demands that we become its salt and light. But even more, as a blessing for the world, we are to show every age and every nation, for all time, that the beatitudes are at the heart of Gospel spirituality.

Living the beatitudes may bring down society's yoke of oppression and rejection. Yet, submitting to this way of wisdom, deepens in everyone going through transition a sense of peace and rest. Living the beatitudinal life on this limited planet will ultimately bring us wisdom's reward: "Come. You have my Father's blessing! Inherit the kingdom prepared for you from the creation of the world" (25:34).

Notes

Chapter One

1. Russell Pregeant, *Christology beyond Dogma: Matthew's Christ in Process Hermeneutics* (Philadelphia: Fortress Press, 1978), p. 15.

2. Ibid., p. 27. Another way of describing how Matthew's Gospel can be applied to contemporary realities is by "paradigms" that inform, influence, and inspire our thinking (theology) and lifestyle (spirituality) in the church today. Since the paradigms arise from past existential circumstances they can inform, influence, and inspire contemporary circumstances that touch the present, lived experience of the community and its members. According to James M. Gustafson, "Paradigms are basic models of a vision of life, and of the practice of life, from which flow certain consistent attitudes, outlooks (or "onlooks"), rules or norms of behavior, and specific actions. ... (T)he paradigm *in*-forms and *in*-fluences the life of the community and its members as they become what they are under their own circumstances. By *in*-form I wish to suggest more than giving data or information. I wish to suggest a flowing into the life of the community and its members. A paradigm allows for the community and its members to make it their own, to bring it into the texture and fabric of life that exists, conditioned as that is by its historical circumstances, by the sorts of limitations and extensions of particular capacities and powers that exist in persons and communities." James F. Gustafson, "The Relation of the Gospels to the Moral Life," in D. G. Miller and D. Y. Hadidian, eds., *Jesus and Man's Hope* (Pittsburgh, 1971), p. 111. See also W. Wink, *The Bible in Human Transformation: Toward a New Paradigm for Biblical Study* (Philadelphia: Fortress Press, 1973).

3. Eduard Schweizer, *The Good News According to Matthew,* trans. David E. Green (Atlanta: John Knox Press, 1975), pp. 24–25. For other resources on the times of Matthew, see William G. Thompson, S. J., "An Historical Perspective in the Gospel of Matthew," *Journal of Biblical Literature* 93 (1974).

4. I have not changed quotations from *The New American Bible* or other quotations to correct sexist terminology.

5. James M. Reese, O.S.F.S., "How Matthew Portrays the Communication of Christ's Authority," *Biblical Theology Bulletin* 7, 3 (July 1977), pp. 140–41.

6. John P. Meier, *Law and History in Matthew's Gospel* (Rome: Biblical Institute Press, 1976), p. 22.

7. The Antioch-origin of Matthew's Gospel is by no means a settled question. See, for instance, Dr. H. Dixon Slingerland, "The Transjordanian Origin of St. Matthew's Gospel," *Journal for the Study of the New Testament* 3 (April 1979), pp. 18–28.

8. G. D. Kilpatrick, *The Origins of the Gospel according to St. Matthew* (Oxford: Clarendon, 1946), pp. 132–33.

9. Jack Dean Kingsbury, "The Verb *Akolouthein* ('To Follow') as an Index of Matthew's View of His Community," *Journal of Biblical Literature* 97, 1 (March 1978), p. 67.

10. Ibid., p. 68.

11. Pregeant, *Christology*, p. 15.

12. Walter Brueggemann, "The Kerygma of the Priestly Writers," *Zeitschrift für die Alttestamentliche Wissenschaft* 84, 4 (1972), pp. 397–413.

13. Juan Luis Segundo, *The Liberation of Theology* (Maryknoll, N.Y.: Orbis, 1976), p. 9.

14. Schweizer, *Good News*, pp. 69–70.

15. For a more detailed explanation of society and its infrastructures see my *Thy Will Be Done: Praying the Our Father as Subversive Activity* (Maryknoll, N.Y.: Orbis, 1977), especially pp. 163–85.

16. "Justice in the World," Introduction, *The Pope Speaks* 16 (1972), p. 377.

17. Ibid.

18. Richard Byrne, O.C.S.O., "Living the Contemplative Dimension of Everyday Life," unpublished dissertation (Pittsburgh: Duquesne University, 1973), p. 198.

19. Donald P. Senior, "The Gospel of Matthew and the Ministry of Social Justice," *Spirituality Today* 31, 1 (March 1979), pp. 20–21.

20. Gerhard von Rad, *Wisdom in Israel,* trans. James D. Martin (Nashville: Abingdon, 1973), p. 173.

21. Ibid., p. 128.

22. Friedrich Hauck, "Makarios," *Theological Dictionary of the New Testament,* ed. Gerhard Kittel, trans. G. W. Bromily (Grand Rapids: William B. Eerdmans, 1967), 4:369.

23. "Justice in the World," II, p. 381.

Chapter Two

1. Anne Gaylor, "Dialog," *The Milwaukee Journal,* May 6, 1979.

2. In an address to 900,000 people, Pope John Paul I said that God "is a father, but even more mother." However, no mention of this was included in the "official" paper of the Roman Catholic Church, *L' Osservatore Romano* (38, 547), which did print the speech on September 21, 1978. Ideology serves the purposes of those who control the media inside and outside the church.

3. Walter Brueggemann, *In Man We Trust* (Atlanta: John Knox Press, 1972), p. 120.

4. Charles E. Lindblom, *Politics and Markets: The World's Political-Economic Systems* (New York: Basic Books, 1977), p. 18.

5. Ibid., p. 13.

6. For more background on oligopoly and its influence via advertising, see my *Thy Will Be Done: Praying the Our Father as Subversive Activity* (Maryknoll, N.Y.: Orbis, 1977), pp. 80ff.; 150–54.

7. Barry Newman, "Do Multinationals Really Create Jobs in the Third World?" *The Wall Street Journal,* September 25, 1979.

8. Barry Newman, "Profits in Indonesia Enrich Military Men—and Their Branches," *The Wall Street Journal,* June 27, 1980.

9. Gregory Baum, "Values and Society," *The Ecumenist,* January-February 1979, pp. 26–27.

10. Lindblom, *Politics and Markets,* p. 356.

11. James P. Gannon, "Getting Off the Treadmill," *The Wall Street Journal,* April 12, 1974.

12. Dominic Crossan, *In Parables: The Challenge of the Historical Jesus* (New York: Harper and Row, 1973).

13. This series ran regularly on the inside of the back cover of *Advertising Age,* e.g., November 13, 1978.

14. "Statement on the Family Viewing Policy of the Television Networks," Administrative Board, United States Catholic Conference (Washington: United States Catholic Conference, 1975), p. 10.

15. In late 1979, many energy companies were accused by the Energy Department of overcharging for oil and oil products. The Capuchin Province of St. Joseph had filed a shareholder resolution with Mobil for the Spring 1979 annual meeting asking the company to establish a Review Committee to investigate "all allegations and/or convictions for price-fixing related activities by any subsidiary and/or officer of our Company between 1972 and 1979."

We raised the issue because of published allegations in late 1978 that Mobil was one of the energy companies that was overcharging. The Company urged shareholders to vote against our resolution, so over 98 percent of them did; thus we lost the chance to return with the same issue in 1980.

At the annual meeting May 3, 1979, Raleigh Warner, Chairperson, said to me regarding our resolution: "And let's remember one thing, here: everything you've referred to, every comment you've made, is an accusation by the Department of Energy in the newspapers, and has yet to come before any court or any trial. We're confident that any court proceedings will show we followed the regulations in good faith. In the suit filed in Washington, January 4th, and announced at a press conference, the Government contends that nine major oil companies overcharged customers a total of at least $1 billion. The Government, however, had no figures to offer as to what portion of the total involved Mobil. So, we've been accused, but they haven't put one dollar on our side."

Besides such protestations of innocence, Mobil also gave the definite impression of its clean hands in another of its Op-Ed pieces shortly after the announcement of price-fixing was made.

Yet, less than a year later, according to Mobil's own press release (9/18/79), "Mobil Oil Corporation confirmed it has entered into a consent order with the Department of Energy (DOE) concerning crude oil overpricing. Although Mobil is agreeing to $13.8 million settlement, a Mobil spokesman made clear this settlement reflects no willful wrongdoing on Mobil's part, nor does it constitute an admission by Mobil of a finding by the Department of Energy that Mobil has violated any DOE rules or regulations." See also *The New York Times,* September 19, 1979.

16. Herbert Schmertz, quoted in Michael J. Connor, *The Wall Street Journal,* May 14, 1975. For more background, see Crosby, *Thy Will Be Done,* pp. 80–82.

17. Karol Cardinal Wojtyla, September, 1976, quoted in *The Wall Street Journal,* November 9, 1978.

18. Donald P. Senior, "The Gospel of Matthew and the Ministry of Social Justice," *Spirituality Today* 31, 1 (March 1979), p. 122.

19. Pope John Paul II, Homily at Mass at Yankee Stadium, *Origins* 9, 19 (October 25, 1979), p. 311.

Chapter Three

1. Eduard Schweizer, *The Good News According to Matthew,* trans. David E. Green (Atlanta: John Knox Press, 1975), pp. 84, 88.

2. Many Matthean scholars say the Final Judgment refers to the Gentiles who do or do not minister to the disciples (little ones) in need. The thesis still remains: The criterion of spirituality by which *all* nations will be judged is how we minister to those in need. See Eugene A. La Verdiere, S.S.S., and William G. Thompson, S.J., "New Testament Communities in Transition," *Theological Studies* 37 (December 1976), p. 581.

3. "US Hints at Military Role in Mideast," "Blumenthal Warns China on Invasion," *Milwaukee Sentinel,* February 26, 1979.

4. Denis Goulet, *The Cruel Choice* (New York: Atheneum, 1973), pp. 123–52.

5. "Justice in the World," Introduction, *The Pope Speaks* 16 (1972), p. 377.

6. Ibid., II, p. 381.

7. Ibid.

8. Ibid., Introduction, p. 377.

9. It seems God has created community by means of conscientization and conversion. For more on this, see my *Thy Will Be Done: Praying the Our Father as Subversive Activity* (Maryknoll, N.Y.: Orbis, 1977), pp. 186ff.

10. Pope John Paul II continually linked spirituality, ecclesiology, christology, and anthropology. In this sense, the whole person is the most spiritual or the fullest image of Christ. This interconnectedness underlies the therapeutic approach of Josef Goldbrunner and Bernard Tyrrell in their works on psychology.

11. Pope John Paul II, Homily at Mass at Yankee Stadium, *Origins* 9,19 (October 25, 1979), p. 311.

12. Pope Paul VI, "On the Renewal of the Religious Life," 17, *The Pope Speaks* 16 (1971), p. 115.

Chapter Four

1. Donald P. Senior, "The Gospel of Matthew and the Ministry of Social Justice," *Spirituality Today* 31, 1 (March 1979), p. 17.

2. Jack Dean Kingsbury, "The Miracle of the Cleansing of the Leper as an Approach to the Theology of Matthew," *Currents in Theology and Mission* 4, 6 (December 1977), p. 345.

3. Ibid., p. 347.

4. Saul Alinsky was a community organizer who achieved fame in Chicago during the 1960s. He insisted that the only way to get people to work for a common goal was on the basis of their self-interest. Consequently, the self-interest that drew the poor to Jesus was not primarily his preaching or teaching but that Jesus was seen as able to meet their needs with his gift of healing. For more on Saul Alinsky, see his *Rules for Radicals* (New York: Random House, 1971).

5. Barbara Leahy Schlemon, *Healing Prayer* (Notre Dame: Ave Maria Press, 1976), pp. 25ff.

6. I have applied this process of spiritual direction used for individuals by John English to the way the Holy Spirit directs communities. John English, S.J., *Choosing Life* (New York: Paulist Press, 1978).

7. Francis "wished finally that the order should be for the poor and unlearned, not

only for the rich and wise. 'With God,' he said, 'there is no respect of persons, and the minister general of the order, the Holy Spirit, rests equally upon the poor and simple.' He wanted this thought inserted into his rule, but since it was already approved by papal bull, this could not be done." Thomas of Celano, *The Second Life of St. Francis* 193, in Marion A. Habig (ed.), *St. Francis of Assisi: Writings and Early Biographies* (Chicago: Franciscan Herald Press, 1973), p. 517.

8. Rupert Dorn, O.F.M. Cap., "Jubilee Homily," *Messenger: Chapter, 1978,* 8 (Detroit: Province of St. Joseph of the Capuchin Order, 1978), p. 22.

Chapter Five

1. For a good discussion of the relationship of God-Land-Israel, see Walter Brueggemann, *The Land: Overtures to Biblical Theology* (Philadelphia: Fortress Press, 1977).

2. Darryl Hunt, M.M., "Nicaragua's Reign of Terror," *Maryknoll* 71 (November 1977), pp. 51–52.

3. Michael H. Crosby, *Thy Will Be Done: Praying the Our Father as Subversive Activity* (Maryknoll, N.Y.: Orbis, 1977), pp. 62ff.

4. "Justice in the World," III, *The Pope Speaks* 16 (1972), p. 385.

5. Nicholas von Hoffman, "Parochial Funds Plea Unheeded," *Buffalo Courier Express,* August 14, 1977.

6. John Kenneth Galbraith, *The Affluent Society* (Boston: Houghton-Mifflin, 1958), p. 88.

7. *The Spiritual Exercises of St. Ignatius: A New Translation,* nos. 136, 142, Louis J. Puhl, ed. (Westminster: Newman Press, 1951).

8. John P. Meier, *The Vision of Matthew: Christ, Church and Morality in the First Gospel* (New York: Paulist Press, 1979), p. 81.

9. Crosby, *Thy Will Be Done*, pp. 93–94; 151ff.; 223–24.

10. Walter Hilton, quoted in Evelyn Underhill, *The Mystics of the Church* (New York: Schocken Books, 1971), p. 126.

Chapter Six

1. Denis Goulet, *The Cruel Choice* (New York: Atheneum, 1973), pp. 123–52.

2. John P. Meier, *The Vision of Matthew: Christ, Church and Morality in the First Gospel* (New York: Paulist Press, 1979), pp. 160–61.

3. Michael H. Crosby, *Thy Will Be Done: Praying the Our Father as Subversive Activity* (Maryknoll, N.Y.: Orbis, 1977), pp. 79–86.

4. Jim Montgomery, "In Public Relations, Ethical Conflicts Pose Continuing Problems," *The Wall Street Journal,*, August 1, 1978.

5. William M. Bulkeley, "To Some at Harvard, Telling Lies Becomes a Matter of Course," *The Wall Street Journal*, January 16, 1979.

6. Episcopal Conference of Nicaragua, "Message to the People of Nicaragua," June 2, 1979 (Detroit: Capuchin Mission Office).

7. T. Howland Sanks, S.J., and Brian H. Smith, S.J., "Liberation Ecclesiology: Praxis, Theory, Praxis," *Theological Studies* 38, 1 (March 1977), p. 22.

8. Ibid., p. 25.

9. Ibid., pp. 25–26.

10. Ibid., p. 33.

11. Edward Korry, "The Sell-Out of Chile and the American Taxpayer," *Penthouse*, March 1978, p. 72.

12. Rev. Kenneth Jadoff, quoted in "A Report of the 1978 Annual Shareholders Meeting" (New York: International Telephone and Telegraph Corporation, 1978), p. 11.

13. Theodore L. Humes, "Letter" to Michael Crosby quoted *in toto* in Michael H. Crosby, O.F.M. Cap., "Stonewalling at I.T.T.," *Catholic Church Investments for Corporate Social Responsibility* 4, 4–5 (1977), p. 8. Mr. Humes' contention that the corporate responsibility movement is trying to overthrow the "free enterprise system" was echoed in comments made by the Nestlé representative at Senator Kennedy's 1977 hearings on infant formula. Similarly, reacting to corporate responsibility shareholder resolutions filed with Castle & Cooke, Inc., by the Eastern Province of the Passionists and the United Church of Christ, D. J. Kirchhoff, President and Chief Executive, told the New York Financial Writers in late 1979: "I am convinced," he said, "that the majority of church members neither supports nor agrees with the political excesses of some in the clergy. I am still concerned, however, with the persistency and activity of a highly vocal and political minority within these groups. With the support of various pro-Marxists, this activist minority has created tax-exempt institutions to develop strategy, to select target companies, and to coordinate the overall effort of church radicals.

"These groups are engaged in a constant search for divisive and abrasive issues that will destabilize free societies, and are using corporate annual meetings as a primary battleground.

"The anti-corporate movement blames capitalism for the evils in contemporary society. The solution in the eyes of the critics of our system is to replace capitalism with a 'justice and peace' egalitarian economic system—an easily recognized euphemism for a centrally-controlled economy" (D. J. Kirchhoff, quoted in official press release, "Castle & Cooke President Tells Financial Writers of Company's Experiences with Church Group Stockholders," September 12, 1979, p. 3).

14. Crosby, "Stonewalling at I.T.T.," especially, pp. 1–6.

15. Humes, ibid., p. 8.

16. Frank A. Aukofer, "Hunger Pains: Many in World Still Feel Them," *The Milwaukee Journal Sunday Forum,* September 2, 1979.

17. Donald P. Senior, "The Gospel of Matthew and the Ministry of Social Justice," *Spirituality Today* 31, 1 (March 1979), p. 45.

Chapter Seven

1. John P. Meier, *The Vision of Matthew: Christology, Church and Morality in the First Gospel* (New York: Paulist Press, 1979), p. 134.

2. Ibid., p. 135.

3. Abraham Heschel, *The Prophets* (New York: Harper & Row, 1962), p. 11.

4. David Hill, "On the Use and Meaning of Hosea VI: 6 in Matthew's Gospel," *New Testament Studies* 24, 1 (October 1977), pp. 112–13.

5. Meier, *Vision of Matthew,* p. 184.

6. Donald P. Senior, *Invitation to Matthew* (Garden City, N.Y.: Doubleday Image Books, 1977), p. 250.

7. Meier, *Vision of Matthew*, p. 185.

8. R. ten Kate, "Geef ons heden ons 'dagelijks' brood," *Nederlands Theologisch Tijdschrift* 32, 2 (1978), pp. 125–39.

9. Hill, "Hosea," p. 110.

Chapter Eight

1. Richard Byrne, O.C.S.O., "Living the Contemplative Dimension of Everyday Life," unpublished dissertation (Pittsburgh: Duquesne University, 1973). I am indebted to Richard Byrne for his approach to contemplation, which is the base for this chapter.

2. Martin Heidegger, *Being and Time*, trans. John Macquarrie and Edward Robinson (New York: Harper & Row, 1962), pp. 216–17.

3. Evelyn Underhill, *Practical Mysticism* (New York: Dutton, 1943), pp. 21–22.

4. Byrne, "Contemplative Dimension," p. 63. Quote from T. S. Eliot, "Ash Wednesday," *The Wasteland and Other Poems* (New York: A Harvest Book, 1962), p. 66.

Chapter Nine

1. The New American Bible, which is used throughout this book, translates the Greek rendition of Jesus' resurrection greeting as "Peace." The Greek formula word for greeting, *chairete*, was a common expression.

2. The Ecumenical Institute operated under different titles and programs from its base in Chicago. Its purpose was to offer a multi-disciplinary approach to church renewal for the benefit of the wider community and world.

3. For a further discussion on stock concentration, see my *Thy Will Be Done: Praying the Our Father as Subversive Activity* (Maryknoll, N.Y.: Orbis, 1977), pp. 80–81.

4. Michael Clark, "The Great American Blindfold," *The Other Side*, July 1977, pp. 14–15.

5. Pope John Paul II, *Redemptor Hominis* (non-sexist version), 16, *National Catholic Reporter*, April 13, 1979, p. 13.

6. Ralph K. White, *Nobody Wanted War: Misperception in Vietnam and Other Wars* (Garden City, N.Y.: Doubleday Anchor Books, 1970).

7. See the discussion on meekness as spiritual realism in Chapter Seven.

8. The Eucharist is always involved in liberating people. Thus, in the *community*, people gather in the name of the Trinity with their gifts. The *conscientization* begins with a reflection on the people's reality. The reconciliation service deals with enslavements and the absolution offers empowerment, along with the gathering prayer. God's word always shows how God views each person and promotes a better sharing of the earth's goods. The Eucharistic Service stands as a sign to all of the equality of each member able to share in the resources of bread and wine. With the Spirit of Jesus in each member, *conversion* from sin can enable people to enter society to call for the conversion of the world. I am indebted to Dale Olen of Milwaukee for the original idea I have adapted.

9. William Thompson, *Matthew's Advice to a Divided Community* (Rome: Biblical Institute Press, 1970). Thompson begins his discussion about the division of the Matthean community and Matthew's way of dealing with the tension with the second

prophecy of the Passion, 17:22. For our purposes, we begin with 18:1 and, more specifically, with 18:10–35.

10. Pope John Paul II, Homily at Mass at Yankee Stadium, *Origins* 9, 19 (October 25, 1979), p. 311.

11. Ibid.

12. John P. Meier, *The Vision of Matthew: Christ, Church and Morality in the First Gospel* (New York: Paulist Press, 1979), p. 130.

13. St. Francis of Assisi, *The Rule of 1223*, 6, in Marion A. Habig, ed., *St. Francis of Assisi: Writings and Early Biographies* (Chicago: Franciscan Herald Press, 1973), p. 61.

14. The Focolare Movement was founded in Italy during the Second World War. It has a few bases in the United States in the larger metropolitan centers. It has groupings that involve almost every vocation within the church.

Chapter Ten

1. Robert A. Guelich, "The Matthean Beatitudes: 'Entrance Requirements' or Eschatological Blessings?" *Journal of Biblical Literature* 95, 3 (September 1976), pp. 430–31.

2. W. D. Davies, *The Setting of the Sermon on the Mount* (Cambridge: Cambridge University Press, 1964), passim, esp. 289–290.

3. John P. Meier, *The Vision of Matthew: Christ, Church and Morality in the First Gospel* (New York: Paulist Press, 1979), p. 16.

4. See "Justice in the World," Introduction, *The Pope Speaks* 16 (1972), p. 377.

5. The call to the prophetic vocation is the same as the call to mystical experience. For this reason I have adapted the steps of mystical experience outlined by Evelyn Underhill to the prophetic vocation. See Evelyn Underhill, *Mystics in the Church* (New York: Schocken Books, 1971), pp. 32–33.

6. Reginald Fuller, *The Foundations of New Testament Christology* (New York: Charles Scribner's Sons, 1965), p. 130.

7. James P. Martin, "The Church in Matthew," *Interpretation* 29, 1 (January 1975), pp. 48–49.

8. Sonya A. Quitslund, "The Nature of the Prophetic Role," *The Bible Today* 92 November 1977), pp. 1330, 1331.

9. See Chapter Six, p. 83f.

10. "Justice in the World," II, p. 381.

11. Quitslund, "Prophetic Role," p. 1331.

12. M. Jack Suggs, *Wisdom, Christology, and Law in Matthew's Gospel* (Cambridge: Harvard University Press, 1970), esp. pp. 120ff.

13. Ibid., p. 122.

14. Wolfgang Nauck, "Salt as a Metaphor in Instruction for Discipleship," *Studia Theologia* 6 (1952), pp. 165–78.

15. Suggs, *Wisdom*, p. 126.

Scriptural Index

General Index

Abandonment, 46, 56, 62f, 112, 114f, 143, 159, 179, 193, 212
Abbott Laboratories, 42
Abyss, 13, 20
Acid Rain, 94
Action-Reflection, 60, 72, 172, 205; *see also* Conscientization
Activism, 103-104, 134
Adaptation, 87f
Addiction, Individual, 53, 64, 71, 73; *see also* Cultural Addictions
Administration, 91
Adultery, 5, 162
Advertising, 35-36, 40, 44, 81, 104, 162, 166
Advertising Age, 41, 43
Advertising Agencies, 42f
Affirmation, 21-23, 31-32, 41, 53, 61, 81, 85, 162, 187, 192f, 210
Affliction, 67-68, 77, 85, 137; *see also* Need
Affluence, 10-11, 45, 46, 50, 60, 72, 119, 120, 194; *see also* Blessing, Wealth
Ageism, 18-19, 64, 65, 71
Alcoholics Anonymous, 65
Alienation, 18, 20, 59, 65-66, 71, 74f, 147f, 164, 165, 188f
    Environmental, 200f
    as Expression of Sin, 17-18, 81-82, 109, 118, 122f, 136
Aliens, 99, 107
Alinsky, Saul, 86, 221
Alka Seltzer, 163
Allende, Salvador, 127f
Alms(giving), 45, 131, 132-134
Ambition, *see* Wealth
Amen, 31, 191, 210
America, *see* United States of America
American Home Products, 42
American Marketing Association, 42-44
American Telephone and Telegraph, 150
Analysis, *see* Social Analysis
Anawim, 56f, 114, 200
Angelism, 100, 111, 202
Angels, 80f, 111, 195
Anger, 12, 79, 81, 83, 98, 112, 116, 134, 135, 143, 155, 156-157, 165, 166, 167, 171, 190, 191, 214
Anna Christie, 83-84
Anointing, 84, 211, 212

Anthropology, 67, 221
Anti-Semitism, 71
Antioch, 10, 200
Antithesis Statements, 7, 46, 124, 130
Anxiety, 4, 30, 38, 39, 61, 68, 72, 79, 85, 112, 161, 162, 184
Apathy, 143, 144, 157
Apocalyptic, 3, 4, 5, 16, 25, 30, 45, 114
Archetypes, 67
Architect(s), 18
Armaments, 63, 184f
Asceticism, 169f
Atom Bomb, 182
Aukhofer, Frank, 138
Austria, 185, 188
Authority, 1, 2, 6, 7, 27, 33, 34f, 60, 64, 66, 76, 82f, 95, 97f, 118, 143, 161, 162, 199, 214f; *see also* Contemplation, *Exousia*, Power
Avarice, 81, 116, 162; *see also* Consumerism
Awe, 108, 146, 176-177

Babylon, 134-135
Balance of Payments, 12
Bank Street, 109
Bankers Trust, 103
Banks, 12, 100, 102-103, 182
Baptism, 6, 8, 10, 25, 26, 64, 78, 79, 138, 178, 200, 211
    as Mission, 20, 28, 90
    in the Spirit, 209f
Baptists, 105
Basic Communities, 59, 68f, 88, 102-103, 187f; *see also* Community, Gathering
Bathsheba, 5
Baum, Gregory, 37
Beatific Vision, 159
Behavior, 15; *see also* Orthodoxy
Berkeley, California, 13
Berrigan, Daniel, 213
Bertrand, Evarist, 88
Bethany, 55-56
Bethsaida, 70
Betrayal, 30, 148f
Better Business Bureau, 129
Biblical Spirituality, *see* Spirituality
Biography as Theology, 2, 11-18, 74, 93, 139, 178, 207; *see also* Spirituality

Real Self, 136, 163, 169, 172
Recollection, 170, 172-175
Reconciliation, 22, 70, 79, 80, 85, 91-92, 93,
      116, 135-136, 149, 161, 166, 175, 190
Redaction, 1-2, 10-11, 52, 199-200
Redlining, 12, 100
Reese, James, 8
Reflection, 91-92, 156, 191f
Regulation, 36
Reign of God, 5, 11, 25-48, 49, 54, 71, 72, 73,
      75, 89, 90, 95, 97f, 113, 122, 129, 136,
      138, 141, 175, 176, 193, 200f, 215
   see also Plan of God, Presence of God,
      Will of God
Religion, 112, 126, 134, 180, 183
   as Instrument of Oppression, 50, 201, 213
   as Ideological, 14, 149
   see also Church, Domestication, Institu-
      tion
Religious Acts, 131f; *see also* Piety, Justice,
      Works
Religious Experience, 1, 4, 8, 16, 21, 30-31,
      32, 51f, 56, 60, 67f, 72f, 77, 100f, 108,
      119f, 131-132, 140, 159f, 180, 204f;
      see also Faith, Grace
Religious Life, 106, 108, 110, 134-135, 187f,
      202, 211; *see also* Basic Communities
Re-member(ing), 88, 91-92, 106f
Reparation, 71, 103; *see also* Reconciliation
Resentment, 92, 165-166, 167, 190, 214
Resistance, 53, 63f, 138, 177, 202f; *see also*
      Lifestyle
Resources, 20, 28, 36, 39, 62f, 69, 104, 109f,
      119f, 138, 192f
   as Basis of Spirituality, 13, 21-24, 45, 58,
      99f
   Described, 18-19, 42, 51, 57f, 64, 65, 107
   Eucharist and, 147f
   Sharing of, 11, 46, 71
Responsibility, 31, 56, 64, 99, 100, 132, 184
Rest, 99, 144, 161, 170; *see also* Security
Restoration, 7, 17, 74f, 80f, 96, 97, 137, 155,
      178, 180, 212
Resurrection, 2, 9, 85, 92, 153, 179f; *see also*
      Cross
Retreat, 82, 174, 182
Revelation 17, 21
Reversal, 5, 26, 45, 60
Review of Life, 66, 174, 196
Rich, the, 36, 38, 66, 102, 115, 168
Rich(es), 49f, 110f, 132, 193; *see also* Wealth
Rich Young Man, 46f, 49, 110, 163, 164
Righteous(ness), *see* Justice
Rights, as Related to Needs, 57, 63, 106f,
      192f
Ritual, 144f, 169f, 190, 196, 200
Robison, Richard, 37
Rockford, Diocese of, 87
Roman Catholic Church, 12, 72, 93-94, 105,
      133, 186, 193, 197

Rome, 19, 96
Rosary, 135
Ross, Margaret, 134
Rothleuber, Francis Borgia, 29
Rules and Regulations, 26-30; *see also* Law
Rural Life, 11
Russia, 133, 134
Ruth, 5

Sabbath, 99, 144; *see also* Jubilee, Rest
Sacrament, 200
Sacrifice, 7, 143f, 160, 175, 197, 200
Saint Anthony, 27, 174
Saint Augustine Parish, 134
Saint Benedict the Moor Parish, 53-54, 150,
      188
Saint Elizabeth Parish, 12, 14-15, 16, 109,
      157, 168, 180-181
Saint John Lateran, 213
Saint Louis Jesuits, 152
Saint Patrick Parish, 108
Salinger, J. D., 173
Salt, 216, 217
Salvation, 25, 32, 75
Samaritans, 9
San Francisco, California, 13, 41
San Jose Mercury/News, 41
Sanity, 64f, 212
Sanks, T. Howland, 127f
Santa Claus, 109
Sarah, 5
Satan, *see* Powers and Principalities
Scandal, 9, 17, 24, 56, 165, 193-194, 199f
Scanlon, Michael, 135
Schlaefer, Austin, 168
Schlemon, Barbara, 87, 135
Schools, 72, 104-105, 108; *see also* Educa-
      tion, Ideology
Schweizer, Eduard, 4-5, 16, 52, 207
Scribes, 7, 27, 90, 98, 114, 122, 123, 124, 129,
      131, 156, 179, 203, 215, 217
Secrecy, *see* Truth
Sects, 2, 197
Secular Franciscans, 144-145
Securities and Exchange Commission, 129,
      133, 182
Security, 29, 31, 34, 37, 38, 56, 57, 72, 80,
      112f, 162, 164, 183
Sedek, 132; *see also* Justice
Seeing God, 21-24, 30-31, 131-132, 136, 141,
      159f; *see also* Knowledge
Seeking, 36f, 60, 89, 113, 114, 120, 121, 123,
      159, 211
Segundo, Juan Luis, 12, 14-15
Self, 40, 136
   Real, 161, 163, 169, 170, 172, 175-177
   Surface, 161-175, 176
Selfishness, *see* Porneia
Selling, 36f, 49, 56, 170
Seneca, 51